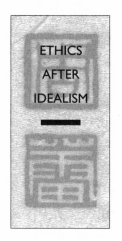

ETHICS

AFTER

IDEALISM

Ethics after Idealism
Theory—Culture—Ethnicity—Reading
is Volume 20 in the series

THEORIES OF CONTEMPORARY CULTURE
Center for Twentieth Century Studies
University of Wisconsin–Milwaukee

KATHLEEN WOODWARD
GENERAL EDITOR

ETHICS
AFTER
IDEALISM

THEORY—CULTURE—ETHNICITY—READING

Rey Chow

INDIANA UNIVERSITY PRESS / BLOOMINGTON AND INDIANAPOLIS

The paper used in this publication meets the minimum requirements of American
National Standard for Information Sciences—Permanence of Paper for Printed
Library Materials, ANSI Z39.48–1984.
Manufactured in the United States of America

Library of Congress Cataloging-in-Publication Data

Chow, Rey.
Ethics after idealism : theory, culture, ethnicity, reading / Rey Chow.
p.   cm. — (Theories of contemporary culture ; v. 20)
Includes bibliographical references (p.   ) and index.
ISBN 0-253-33363-6 (cl : alk. paper). —
ISBN 0-253-21155-7 (pa : alk. paper)
1. Arts and society—History—20th century.
2. Multiculturalism.   I. Title.   II. Series.
NX180.S6C48   1998
700'.1'03—dc21   97-21576

1   2   3   4   5   03   02   01   00   99   98

For Austin

CONTENTS

ACKNOWLEDGMENTS

I OWE THE SUCCESSFUL publication of this book primarily to several people: Kathleen Woodward, who has been giving my work magnanimous support ever since I was a junior assistant professor submitting it to her unsolicited; Iain Chambers, who reviewed the manuscript with generous comments and constructive suggestions; Joan Catapano and Grace Profatilov, who provided indispensable assistance at different stages throughout the production process. My thanks go also to the staff of the Center for Twentieth Century Studies at the University of Wisconsin, Milwaukee, in particular Nigel Rothfels, and the staff of Indiana University Press, for handling the technical aspects of the book's preparation.

The conception and writing of the book were facilitated by two professional honors, both of which provided relief from teaching. The first was a University of California Humanities Research Institute resident fellowship in the winter and spring quarters of 1995, when I participated in the research group "Feminisms and Discourses of Power," organized by Wendy Brown and Judith Butler. In the spring semester of 1996, I was the William Allan Neilson Visiting Professor in Comparative Literature at Smith College, and I remain sincerely grateful to the Neilson Professor Selection Committee. It was during my time at Smith that I completed the draft of the entire manuscript. For the leaves of absence I took in both years from my normal responsibilities, I am indebted to the Department of English and Comparative Literature and the School of Humanities at the University of California, Irvine.

Between 1992 and 1996, different versions of some of these chapters were presented in the form of lectures, seminars, and workshops at various institutions within the United States and abroad. These include the Woodrow Wilson International Center for Scholars, Scripps College, Harvard University, Smith College, Tulane University, Occidental College, the University of Hawaii at Manoa, the University of Technology in Sydney, the MLA Annual Convention in San Diego, the University of Victoria, Rutgers University, Bucknell University, the State University of New York at Buffalo, the University of California at Los Angeles, the University of California at Santa Cruz, the University of Oregon at Eugene, New York University, Duke University, Tufts University, the University of Utah, Rochester University, and the University of California at Davis. Once again, I thank the organizers who allowed me the opportunity to speak and the audiences who came to listen to me.

Even though they were not directly involved in the production of this book, many people must be acknowledged for the eminently enabling impact they have left on my life in the past few years. During my brief visit at Smith, I was the recipient of the courteous hospitality of Hongchu Fu, Marina Kaplan, Christopher Lupke, Thalia Pandiri, Marilyn Schuster, Ruth Simmons, Elizabeth V. Spelman, Taitetsu Unno, and Susan Van Dyne. My special thanks go to Leyla Ezdinli and Elizabeth Harries, who, their own busy schedules notwithstanding, lavished me with attention throughout my stay. In the warmest collegial spirit, Homer Brown, Harry Harootunian, Ping-kwan Leung, Steve Mailloux, Masao Miyoshi, Jane Newman, Brook Thomas, William M. Todd III, David Der-wei Wang, Linda Williams, and Michelle Yeh selflessly offered their time, advice, and assistance when I needed them. Over long distance and often across continents, I continue to be blessed with trust and affection by Sarah Wei-ming Chen, Christopher Connery, Chris Cullens, Lidia Curti, Sally Taylor Lieberman, Kwai-cheung Lo, Tonglin Lu, Livia Monnet, Panivong Norindr, Marina Pérez de Mendiola, Dorothea von Mücke, and Alan Wolfe. The loyalty of these friends touches me in profound ways. I have also been honored by the newer friendships of Sneja Gunew, Smaro Kamboureli, Meaghan Morris, Fazal Rizvi, and Leslie Roman, all of whose kindness toward me far exceeds anything I have ever done for them. In my daily life in Irvine, I feel extremely fortunate to be in the proximity of Jim Fujii and Ellen Radović, friends of exemplary integrity, whose care and camaraderie are vital in an otherwise alienating environment. To Nancy Armstrong and Leonard Tennenhouse, I owe, among many other things, the sustained privileged illusion that the work I do is somehow not without significance. The considerable inflation of my ego over the years is very much a result of their unfailingly good-humored indulgence.

As usual, Austin Meredith assisted with every stage of the writing, editing, revising, and indexing of the manuscript. Many ideas that found their way into the various chapters were the results of intense discussions with him, often into the wee small hours of the morning. His companionship is a gift for which I will never have the means to adequately express my gratitude. This book is for him, with all my love.

Acknowledgments

Previously Published Versions

Early versions of various chapters were published in the following places; I remain grateful to the editors who first included my work in their publications:

Chapter 1 was published in *A Question of Discipline: Pedagogy, Power, and the Teaching of Cultural Studies*, ed. Debbie Epstein and Joyce Canaan (Boulder: Westview P, 1997), pp. 11–26; chapter 2 was published in *Ariel: A Review of International English Literature* 26.1 (January 1995) (guest ed. Pamela McCallum, Stephen Slemon, Aruna Srivastava): 23–50; chapter 3 was published in *diacritics* 23.1 (Spring 1993): 3–22; chapter 4 was published in *The UTS Review: Cultural Studies and New Writing* 1.1 (1995): 5–29; chapter 5 was published in *Human, All Too Human* (Papers from the English Institute), ed. Diana Fuss (New York: Routledge, 1996), pp. 61–92; chapter 6 was published in *Feminisms and Pedagogies of Everyday Life*, ed. Carmen Luke (Albany: State University of New York P, 1996), pp. 204–21; chapter 7 was published in *The South Atlantic Quarterly* 95.4 (Fall 1996) (guest ed. Vassilis Lambropoulos): 1039–64; chapter 8 was published in *Modern Chinese Literature* 7.2 (Fall 1993) (guest ed. William S. Tay): 59–78; chapter 9 was published in *Diaspora: A Journal of Transnational Studies* 2.2 (Fall 1992): 151–70; chapter 10 was published in *differences: A Journal of Feminist Cultural Studies* 5.3 (Fall 1993): 179–204.

All of these chapters have been modified or revised, and freshly copyedited for this book.

INTRODUCTION

THE ADVANTAGE of being situated, since I was a graduate student, in programs and departments where there is a great deal of openness toward critical theory is that it forces me to come to terms with the larger historical implications of "theory" on a day-to-day level, without losing sight of the "resistance to theory"[1] that still persists in many circles. By "theory," I do not mean the comprehensive sweep of philosophy, hermeneutics, and traditions of literary criticism and interpretation that run from Plato to the present day and that continue to be taught in many graduate programs. Rather, I mean what is generally referred to as "poststructuralism" and "deconstruction," terms that stand for ways of reading that have radicalized Anglo-American academic worlds since the 1960s. Needless to say, I am using these terms not in any nuanced, exact sense but instead as a type of widely circulated shorthand, in order to describe the general impact "theory" has had on intellectual work in the past few decades.

The one unmistakable accomplishment of "theory" understood in this restricted sense is what one might call the fundamental problematization of referentiality—a problematization that began, for many, with Ferdinand de Saussure's relativizing of the relationship between the linguistic signified and signifier in his *Course on General Linguistics* (1916). In part through the works of theorists such as Roland Barthes, Jacques Lacan, Jacques Derrida, and Michel Foucault, the general tendency to suspend and destabilize fixed origins that follows from Saussure's structural linguistics has since traveled through the many postmodernist implosions of "the real" (whether the real is defined as language, text, story, author, self, identity, or community) and is currently receiving many echoes in various modes of universalism-critique (through inquiries of gender, race, class, sexual preference, and so forth). And yet, if referentiality—which may be further defined as a presumed transparency between signification and meaning, or better still, as a persistent reflectionism in representation—has indeed been thoroughly problematized and suspended, it has not exactly disappeared. As a theoretical reject loaded with the drudgery of the positivistic, referentiality has instead been displaced onto the area called "cultural studies."

The two conceptions of "culture" that are prevalent in current intellectual debates may be briefly described as follows. One conception, derived from anthropology, refers generally to "lifeworlds" or "ways of life"; the other, more closely defined as the sum of refined achievements of "civilized" life, is usually associated with literary, artistic, and musical classics, which together make up what some call "high culture."[2] The first of these conceptions of "culture" is a foundational one: it sees culture as inclusive of common beliefs, attitudes, and behaviors, and as basic to every group of human beings.[3] The second conception, as pointed out frequently, is ideological and exclusionary, based as it is on the hegemony of particular class interests. At the same time, the two conceptions could also shift their emphases to generate cultural politics of a different kind. For instance, the potentially democratic idea that everyone possesses a "culture" could lead to the conservative culturalist view that every culture must be understood strictly and only in its own "specificity." Conversely, the notion that culture is "high culture," though elitist, may nonetheless allow for "achievements of refinement" to exist in every country, so that "culture" becomes viewed paradoxically with equality, as a cross-cultural, rather than local, phenomenon.

Neither of these conceptions of culture, however, seems to me a satisfactory description of the momentum of cultural studies as it is being practiced today. This momentum stems from the sense that "culture" is an unfinished process, a constellation—never in pristine form—of social relations that are to be continually unworked and reworked. The charge from some critics that cultural studies seems habitually preoccupied with objects of study that are modern and contemporary, and that moreover are unworthy of serious intellectual attention, has precisely to do with this unfinished quality of culture itself. For what moment in time is more emblematic of the open-endedness of history than "now," and what objects are more suggestive of the open-endedness of evaluation than those consigned to the dustbin of history? The unfinished quality of culture is not the result of some metaphysical or ontological "ambivalence" of signification in general, but is rather the lingering effect of massive inequalities inherent in the international divisions of labor; in the access to social representation and political power; and in the possession, exchange, and consolidation of cultural capital. It is such massive inequalities, which have not dissipated but multiplied over the decades in the postcolonial, post–Cold War world, that make the questioning of universal values—a questioning that may in part be attributed to the legacy of poststructuralism—such a necessary political act for all those who want to cling to a semblance of socialist values.

Introduction

Is cultural studies then simply a continuation and extension of cultural relativism—of the understanding that culture is relative rather than absolute—that was set off by the deconstruction of the sign? What is the relationship between cultural studies and critical theory?

If, following the "high culture" versus "lifeworld" formulations of "culture," academic practices in earlier decades took the form of a disciplinary divide between, let us say, "literature" (as the paradigm of the humanities, with man as the subject of language) versus "anthropology" (as the paradigm of the social sciences, with man as the object, the product of his cultural environment),[4] there is, currently, a similar divide between "critical theory" and "cultural studies" in academic politics. This divide, to put it bluntly, signifies an implicit *racialization* of the study of culture in terms I will attempt to elaborate as follows.

As a way into this elaboration, let us ask: What are the reasons for the dismissal of cultural studies coming from those who champion "critical theory"? Apart from the criticism that cultural studies lacks "theoretical rigor," a powerful reason that is often heard is that practitioners of cultural studies reify "culture," assume that it is an organic whole, and repeat the historicism, empiricism, and positivism inherent to a long tradition of continuist thinking. Is it a matter, then, of an incommensurability between two different "regimes of value"[5]—with one regime signifying theoretical vigilance and the other signifying cultural reification? If no articulation of culture is theory-less, is any articulation of theory culture-less? I would argue that *very definite feelings of what "culture" should be are always at work in the "theoretical" rejection of cultural studies.* Borrowing from the clever response that theorists make when their work is being criticized for being "too theoretical"—and I include myself here—namely, that even the most hostile critic of "theory" is always already speaking from a theoretical position, let us say that even the most hostile critic of "culture" and "cultural studies" is speaking from a cultural position, from a definite perspective on culture.

In other words, culture is *not* not at work in "critical theory," but is rather at work in specifically invested forms, which are most readily apparent in some investigations of texts of the Anglo-American, French, and German canons. (I will specify what such invested forms are in a moment.) For those who have prided themselves on an exclusive engagement with critical theory, cultural studies is often perceived as the opposite of theoretical abstraction—as the dumpsite of vulgarities and simplicities, of phenomena that are readily transparent, comprehensible, and accessible. Moreover, as the objects of cultural studies often pertain to the peoples of color, cultural studies also becomes identified with "them" rather than "us." In many cases, even when "critical theory" is used, simply because it is used in relation to the non-West or by non-Western critics, it automatically "descends" into the debased realm of "cultural studies."[6] Because poststructuralist academe is conditioned by this kind of hierarchical divide, the problematization of "referentiality" does not mean that referentiality has disappeared *tout court;* it rather means that "referentiality" has been banished to the study of "culture" with its presumed significatory transparency and thus intellectual inferiority.

What this implies, even though it is seldom articulated as such, is that a *class distinction* is at work in differentiating the labor that goes into "critical theory" and the labor that goes into "cultural studies." Class here is not the orthodox economic marker of social stratification but what John Frow has described in terms of the possession and use of knowledge. Intellectuals, according to Frow, are thus the "knowledge class."[7] With the acquisition of knowledge come certain processes of socialization: writing in a certain style, noticing certain details in texts, finding certain types of literary tropes appealing, for instance, can become part of the *cultivation* of habits that give one certification to live among certain sectors of the professional community. However, I would also add to Frow's notion of the "knowledge class" by saying that *there are class distinctions within the knowledge class itself,* and that such class distinctions are what have given rise to the disputes over the relations between "critical theory" and "cultural studies." This is why, although cultural studies practitioners may be working as hard and reading as carefully, they are nonetheless perceived as generating a kind of knowledge that puts them in a lower class stratum in the academy, in which "cultural capital" still remains not only the possession but also the practices, habits, and sensitivies of the upper classes fluent in "critical theory."[8] When we superimpose upon this division between the different kinds of labor the division between white and non-white cultures, the formation of class distinctions within the "knowledge class" must be recognized as being thoroughly imbricated with racial significance. The division between critical theory and cultural studies is, in a word, also an institutional racialization of intellectual labor, a racialization resulting in an aristocracy and a subordinate class in terms of the production and dissemination of "knowledge."

But what precisely is upper class in this scenario? What is the "cultural capital," the specifically invested forms in question here? As I argue in chapter 1, "Theory, Area Studies, Cultural Studies: Issues of Pedagogy in Multiculturalism," the essence of privilege here is paradoxically a certain *claim to otherness,* which is often defined not in terms of attributes belonging to individuated "other" human beings, nor in terms of anything reducible to the subject-object relation, but in terms of a radical heterogeneity, an infinity, that reveals itself in language, in the discursive passage from the individual to the general.[9] In the hands of poststructuralist theorists, who tend to dismiss positions of otherness defined in positive, phenomenological terms, the claim to otherness becomes a claim to the capacity for *subverting* established signs of social power by putting such signs "under erasure." Otherness in this instance is conventionally accomplished through what Gayatri Spivak calls "the work of the negative,"[10] which may be used to describe the ethical critiques of Western culture from Hegel to Nietzsche, Heidegger, Freud, Lacan, Derrida, Bataille, Nancy, and others. The variety of "subversive" operations involved here are typically performed in a deconstructionist mode, as a revolution based on the differencing—the differentiation and displacement—*internal to* the fundamental forms of logocentric signification—be it language, the text, the psyche, the subject, or consciousness. Even in Marx, Spivak reminds us, the critique of capitalism begins with a labor of negation, a de-fetishization of the commodity form. And "woman," as Derrida's work on Nietzsche shows, has always been theorized as the other, the unsaid, the negative truth of man.[11] Hence class and gender, the two key players that have partaken of the dismantling of Western thought from within, both work negatively, as bearers or markers of differences that underpin Western language, metaphysics, work, and sexuality.

The "upper class" status of critical theory is thus the result of a specific procedure of socialization, a *culture* in which marks of distinction—in the sense of difference and of *superiority*—are achieved, paradoxically, by attempts to be negative and subversive, attempts to blast open the generality of the Western logos with the force of an exotic species/specialization from within. Such attempts have left on Western thought the indelible imprints of an *internal otherness*, imprints which, until the eruption of a different kind of otherness—in the form of other, non-Western cultures—are taken as definitive signs of alterity per se.

The threat presented by cultural studies, then, is the challenge it poses to *this* status of critical theory—*not* critical theory's elitism *tout court* but critical theory's claim to alterity, a claim which was radical in its origins and which became, in the course of time, the mark of a special kind of aristocracy within the "knowledge class." This threat to critical theory's ontological dependence on otherness is perhaps the reason we have been hearing, among theorists that were once the radicals of a previous era, a strong sense of nostalgia for the days when things were much simpler. As cultural studies looms, the "improper" practices of complicating signification through rigorous deconstruction (with its emphasis on the instability and unpredictability of rhetoric) suddenly assume the proprietariness of a firmly established tradition, and the solemn defense of "critical theory" against the onslaught of cultural studies' "barbaric" modes of inquiry is undertaken with something of a religious fervor. Alternatively, Western feminism, also at one time a champion in the fight against Western thought, becomes melancholic, mourning the days when only "woman" was liberating herself from the fetters of patriarchy—when, we might say in parody, "the world was white and we were the genuine and only other."[12] In effect, the kinds of otherness unleashed by cultural studies means the unsettling not only of Western thought per se but also of the very coupling of "otherness" with the work of the negative that has been effective for so long. In the light of cultural studies, it becomes possible to realize that "critical theory" is, after all, a process of cultivation, a process which, despite its claim to radical alterity and heterogeneity, operates by demanding of its adherents a certain *conformity* with its unspoken rules, rules that have gone without saying until they are revealed for what they are: "deconstruct the best you can—but continue to center on the West!"

On the other side, the clamor for "culture" itself is far from innocent or innocuous. Something of an unintended union between what appear to be opponents but are in fact kindred spirits is manifest when those who support "culture," especially non-Western culture, typically do so in the name of debunking theory (as "Western," imperialist, universalist, and so forth). Such debunking of theory usually relies on a valorization of the local, since, one may surmise, localization is revered as the basis for a pluralism with all its "diversities" and ultimately for a stable, respectable liberalism. The localist and pluralist defenders of "culture" are not, however, unlike their enemies, the critical theorists, in that they, too, have been laying claim to a certain otherness through their recourse to cultural or ethnic "specificities," through their specialized, cultivated knowledge of particular non-Western canons, traditions, and histories. Among Asianists, for instance, many of those who promote "culture" against "theory" are no strangers to the cultural capital that informs the construction and perpetuation of canonical practices in reading, teaching, and the handling of their own professionalism. Those who think that we should be teaching Confucius and Mencius instead of Plato and Aristotle are often as hostile to the "vulgar" trends of cultural studies as their Europeanist and Americanist counterparts. Their criticism of "theory" is simply that the West has monopolized the claim to high culture and that they, specialists of non-Western cultures, should enjoy such a privilege also. High culture should now take the form of the spread of non-Western classics! Meanwhile, the progressivist, entrepreneurial ones among such culturalists, correctly sensing the professional opportunities that lie in the discourses made possible by "theory," are quick to adopt various fashionable "positions" in the putative study of the non-West, even if such positions entail theoretically unviable implications. These progressives tend to treat theory as a lucrative business enterprise and, instead of using theory to challenge the conceptual premises, institutional habits, or established authorities of their fields, use it rather as a way to rejuvenate and embellish the old parameters of Orientalism and its related area studies, which they continue to defend with the rhetoric of cultural exceptionalism. The more ambitious ones among such progressives venture even further: with the technical innovativeness of transnational corporate managers and the spiritual dedication of Christian missionaries, they boldly seek to export "cultural studies" to remote corners of the earth such as China and Asia, offering promises of salvation even as they preach against "Western hegemony," "Eurocentrism," and the like.[13]

Whether conservative or progressivist, the argumentative move to distance oneself from theory in the name of cultural "specificity" and "complexity" could easily become a refusal to consider the general relations of *all* cultural work and a determination, despite overt claims of the need for change, to reproduce existing conditions. As Raymond Williams puts it:

> there is a kind of attachment to specificity and complexity which is the condition of any adequate intellectual work, and another kind which is really a defense of a particular kind of consciousness, within very specific cultural conditions: a defense, really, against recognition of the necessarily general relations within which all cultural work, including analysis, is done. Such defenses are easily and even habitually sustained within certain kinds of privileged institution, where privilege is not so much, or not primarily, a matter of income or life style, but rather a condition of relatively distanced, relatively unchallenged relations with the practical and continuing social process.
>
> Thus we have always to distinguish between two kinds of consciousness: that alert, open and usually troubled recognition of specificity and complexity, which is always, in a thousand instances, putting working generalizations and hypotheses under strain; and *that other, often banal, satisfaction with specificity and complexity, as reasons for the endless postponement of all (even local) general judgements or decisions.*[14]

Extrapolating from Williams, we may say that the "privilege," the "condition of relatively distanced, relatively unchallenged relations with the practical and continuing social process" that the cultural localists (or local culturalists) seek to reproduce is precisely, in a manner reminding us of the critical theorists hostile to cultural studies, *their own otherness*—this time an otherness derived from their positions as academic representatives of non-Western "cultures." Whether the claim to otherness is through the route of theory or through the route of culture, therefore, the fundamental fact of the accruing of privilege, capital, and class superiority through otherness has not been adequately challenged. If no criticism of "culture" can suffice simply by reiterating the insights deduced from the *cultural instance* that is Western critical theory, then no criticism of "theory" can suffice simply by assuming the *theoretical stance* of advocating the aesthetic and literary traditions of another nation and culture.[15]

The difficulty of seeing the mutual implications of a disdain for "cultural studies" and a disdain for "critical theory" means that many of those who work in either area tend to remain caught in a prevalent idealism in relation to otherness. As I explain in the chapter that shares this book's title, idealism operates in two major senses. First, it operates in the sense of idealist philosophy,[16] the critique of which we have learned, among others, from Marx and Engels. Essentially, idealism in this instance refers to what might be called mentalism, the tendency that treats the world as the result of ideas, which in turn are construed as the products of the human mind. Second, idealism operates as the tendency to idealize—to relate to alterity through mythification; to imagine "the other," no matter how prosaic or impoverished, as essentially different, good, kind, enveloped in a halo, and beyond the contradictions that constitute our own historical place.[17]

The two senses of idealism are inextricably related, but it is the second, banal sense of the term which concerns me in the intersection between critical theory and cultural studies, and I believe that the chapters in this book all suggest attempts to disengage from predominant forms of idealism in relation to otherness, even as I acknowledge such idealism as, often, an inescapable predicament. To give my readers some hints about what is to come in the pages ahead without excessively repeating my own arguments, my disengagement from idealism involves taking certain decisions in the process of reading. Such decisions include, for instance, refusing to polarize "critical theory" and "cultural studies" or to subscribe to the racializing of knowledge that pertains to the facile dismissal of both; tracing the affinities and divergences between two very different contemporary thinkers, Gayatri Spivak and Slavoj Žižek, through their arguments about ideology, deconstruction, naming, history, and politics; reading a seminal "third world" intellectual figure such as Frantz Fanon through the lenses of gender politics and the attitudes toward community implied in his writings; unraveling the strands of intercultural and sexual exchanges in the film *M. Butterfly* so as to move beyond the essentialism that often accompanies prevalent readings of Orientalism and of homosexual erotics; juxtaposing the film *The Joy Luck Club* with an unlikely though coeval project, *Jurassic Park,* in order to challenge the assumptions behind the quest for "ethnicity"; and analyzing the politically repressive functions of the noble sentiment of "endurance" as it is dramatized in the film *To Live.* As well, I ask what it means for cultural studies and postcolonial studies to encounter a situation such as that of Hong Kong, which in 1997 sees the official end of a century and a half of British colonial rule and the "restoration" to the rightful proprietor, China. For me, as for many who reside permanently in Hong Kong, the espousal of a nationalist idealism derived from the reinstatement of mainland

Chinese sovereignty is impossible; the idea that China, simply because it is a communist, "third world" nation, should be exempt from the charges of colonialism, imperialism, and racism is impossible. My preoccupation with Hong Kong has to do with Hong Kong as what has been continually left out of "proper" discourses of power—"Britain," "China," or "postcolonial studies"—rather than with any simple desire to affirm Hong Kong's "identity" as such.

The guideline I follow in all of these readings is a simple one.[18] I feel strongly that, until and unless we grant non-Western authors and texts—be these texts fiction, theory, film, popular music, or criticism—the same kind of verbal, psychical, theoretical density and complexity that we have copiously endowed upon Western authors and texts, we will never be able to extricate our readings from the kind of idealism in which the East-West divide—which, I'd propose, is also the assailable divide between "cultural studies" and "critical theory"—is currently mired. Granting such density and complexity would mean refusing to idealize the non-West—be it in the form of a culture, a class, or a gender group; a text, an author, or a character—and instead reading the non-West in such a manner as to draw out its unconscious, irrational, and violent nuances, so that, as an "other," it can no longer simply be left in a blank, frozen, and mythologized condition known perfunctorily as an "alternative" to the West. My implied object of criticism is, accordingly, also the controversial identity politics that has unavoidably shaped our readings of "other" cultures. Rather than attacking identity politics per se, however, my point is that we need to be more precise in our attack: we need to point more accurately at the idealism that is at the heart of identity politics.[19]

In the problematic of cultural otherness, the two senses of idealism come together: idealism in the sense of idealization, of valorization; but also in the sense of turning-into-an-idea. Often, in the valorization of non-Western "others," we witness a kind of tendency to see all such "others" as equivalent, as a mere positive, positivist idea devoid of material embeddedness and contradiction. If the long-standing hegemony of Western thought has in part been the result of the successful welding together of otherness and negativity—of the othering, the making-heterogeneous of Western thought from within—why should we refrain from performing the work of negativity on the "other" that is the non-West as well? To be sure, this would be an arduous task, implying as it does the need to work negatively on those who are already bearers of various types of negation—of poverty, deprivation, abuse, distortion, discrimination, extermination. But this is also the reason their encounter with the *well-established* negativity of Western thought would prove poignant and provocative, providing as they will instructive antidotes to facile idealist and idealistic projections.

What is crucial, it seems to me, is not to be able to make a clean break with idealism but rather to *follow* idealism's alluring traces and remnants with a reading practice that is always tactical, that seeks to uncover the theoretical part of even the most specific "cultural" study, on the one hand, and the implicit cultural presumptuousness, aggressivity, and violence in even the most pristinely "theoretical" pronouncement, on the other. Because the anxiety about being accused of conservatism and political incorrectness can cause us to hold back observations of what is equally exploitative, coercive, or manipulative in so-called "oppositional" discourses—because, in other words, idealism is the kind of collective sentiment that often demands the sacrifice of intelligence— such a reading practice must carry with it a willingness to take risks, a willingness to destroy the submission to widely accepted, predictable, and safe conclusions. This risk-taking, destructive process is what I associate with *ethics*, a term I use in contrast to *mores* and its cognates *morality* and *moralism*.[20] The prevalent idealism in contemporary cultural studies belongs in the realm of mores. And yet, to resist such mores is also to be deeply entangled with them. To propose a kind of ethics *after* idealism is thus not to confirm the attainment of an entirely independent critical direction, but rather to put into practice a supplementing imperative—to follow, to supplement idealism doggedly with non-benevolent readings, in all the dangers that supplementarity entails.

Perhaps the most revealing instance of such dangers is the reaction I received from some quarters to one of the chapters, "The Fascist Longings in Our Midst." In an attempt to read against the liberalist celebrations of racial and ethnic "otherness" in the North American academy, I committed the unpardonable crime, at the end of the chapter, of coupling multiculturalism with fascism. When this chapter was reviewed by various avant-garde journals, it provoked two main types of responses, which were, ironically, symptomatic of the very problem that was my topic.

The first type of response was that I could not use fascism in a manner which "dehistoricized" it. Strangely enough, such a response came from readers who were not normally defenders of historicism themselves. But it was the second type of response which I found the more disturbing: "Only she could write something like this," some readers charged, meaning, I suppose, that only a "woman of color" and therefore a double minority, could possibly mount a criticism of multiculturalism as such without getting into trouble, without being labeled "racist." If the first type of response was a pedantic reprimand that I should know my modern European history better than to take "fascism" out of its "historical specificity" and misappropriate it for a critique of other instances of idealist violence, the second type of response put me squarely back into the kind of "referentiality" to which

I was alluding a while ago as the mode in which all non-Western "others" using critical theory to do cultural studies are cast. This response assumed and concluded at once that a "woman of color" could get away with saying anything, even the most outrageous, without being penalized.

But what indeed is so outrageous? That the multiculturalism of the 1990s carries with it precisely the kinds of idealizing tendencies that were at the foundation of the fascism of the 1920s, 1930s, and 1940s? If this is, at the very least, a debatable point, then why is making it outrageous? And why should my making it be immediately interpreted in the light of my *otherness,* onto which is attributed a blank privilege to speak the unspeakable? "The 'other' can say or do anything in the current climate without being considered wrong"—is this not, once again, the imposition of a representational transparency and predictability on the other, which is in fact the point of my criticism in that chapter? As history shows, idealism is always anchored in violence. The readers who decided that "only she could write something like this" were also the ones who denied me my speech. Because, as an "other," I had made statements that were not acceptable to them, that were, in other words, truly other, they did not hesitate to resort to the violent side of fascist strategies—to censorship and suppression.

I refer to this personal incident because it is a pertinent illustration of the crises of idealism—of idealizing otherness—that have accompanied the poststructuralist invalidation of universalist/ethnocentric values of our time. Similar episodes, I am sure, occur every day to many people, and their recurrence is such that they cannot always be documented with full, objective, scholarly evidence and analysis, but can be presented only fragmentarily, in the form of anecdotes. (Etymologically, "anecdotes" are items that have been left out of published historical accounts.) Rather than fulminate against such episodes in private, I believe it is worthwhile to examine, as I try to in some of the pages that follow, the kinds of theories and cultures that make them possible in the first place. My point of narrating the personal as such, I should emphasize, is not to show myself as an oppressed victim of white liberalist discourse—my institutional positionings dispute that—but rather to show the personal as a precarious kind of place in which, sometimes, crises of idealism come unexpectedly into sharp focus. If the judgment "only she could write something like this" was a way of censoring and suppressing my reading of multiculturalism, it nonetheless also serves as a piece of instruction, which I must follow exactly in the manner it was bestowed on me—as a privilege, as an obligation to read and write ethically, against the fascist longings in our midst.

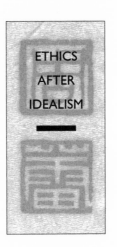

ETHICS
AFTER
IDEALISM

ONE

Theory, Area Studies, Cultural Studies: Issues of Pedagogy in Multiculturalism[1]

I would say that there is no future for literary studies as such in the United States. Increasingly, those students are being taken over by the astonishing garbage called "cultural criticism."

—*Harold Bloom*[2]

UNFORTUNATELY, the negative view toward cultural studies expressed by Harold Bloom is not unique to him. It is shared by many teachers of the humanities in North America, in particular the United States. What is perhaps peculiar about such openly negative sentiments toward cultural studies is that they often come from those who, during the 1960s and 1970s, were staunch promoters and defenders of what is called "theory," when theory itself was derogated and attacked by reactionary humanists as some metaphysical garbage that found its way from continental Europe to the higher education sectors of North American society.[3] Arguments against theory then sounded similar to the arguments against cultural studies today, not in the least by way of the charge that theory, by paying attention to the ideological assumptions that lie behind language, text, and discourse, was introducing issues that were, properly speaking, not about (the intrinsic qualities of) literature itself but instead about philosophy, sociology, and so forth. Twenty some years later, many of those who took pride in the race for theory are precisely the ones who back away from cultural studies. Why?

Genealogical Affinities between Theory and Cultural Studies

The brief history of cultural studies—its origins in the class-conscious analyses of popular culture in England, in particular the work undertaken at the Centre for Contemporary Cultural Studies at Birmingham; its subsequent migration to the United States and elsewhere, a migration that is accompanied by the concomitant forces of "French theory" and "Anglo-American" feminism; and its many recurrent elements—has already been well elaborated by many of its practitioners.[4] As a literary and cultural theorist whose work straddles cultural studies and theory, what I would like to offer in the first part of this chapter is hence not a recapitulation of that history, but rather a highlighting of some of the prominent types of analyses that have been developed in cultural studies in North America in the past fifteen years or so. Four of these are especially worth mentioning because of the tremendous impact they have in shaping discussions from multiple disciplines.

The first prominent type of analysis is the critique of Orientalism—of Western representations of non-Western cultures—that follows from Edward Said's groundbreaking book of 1978. Even though Said's book has been under attack from all kinds of directions since its first publication and even though many refuse to acknowledge their indebtedness to it, the conceptual model of Orientalism-critique has proven to be the kind of critical intervention with which one cannot not come to terms. But if *Orientalism* alerts us to the pernicious effects of an ongoing ideological domination of the West by way of *culture and representation*, it does not exactly offer viable alternatives. Said's work leaves us with an impasse in which the issue of a subordinated otherness, and with it, the other's right to participate in the representation of itself, has irrevocably been raised, without being followed by any practicable notion of how such representation could go beyond the parameters of Orientalism. Instead, because the issue of otherness is delineated by Said on the premise of a racial dyad—namely, the white West as opposed to the non-white non-West—his logic seems to foreclose the possibility of the non-white non-West ever having its own "culture." Said's work begs the question as to how otherness—the voices, languages, and cultures of those who have been and continue to be marginalized and silenced—could become a genuine oppositional force and a useable value.

In the context of an irreversibly demystified West and the uncertainties of representation that follow from such demystification, the racial dyad of Said's conceptual model requires a kind of supplementation that would juxtapose other types of hierarchical discriminations with issues of racial injustice. It is in such a context that Gayatri Chakravorty Spivak's essay "Can the Subaltern Speak?"[5] emerges as the second prominent type of analysis in cultural studies. While the issue of otherness remains for Said an issue of race, Spivak's essay astutely displaces the essentialism of purely racial considerations onto the equally crucial considerations of class and gender. In Spivak's analysis, the female subaltern from an underprivileged "third world" nation—the composite of gendered, class, and racial subordination—becomes the ultimate silent/silenced bearer of the burdens of centuries of Western imperialist history. Because for Spivak "speech" and self-representation signify, by definition, access to the symbolic and to political power, her conclusion is a pessimistic one: the subaltern cannot speak. If the subaltern can speak, Spivak adds later in an interview, then she is not a subaltern anymore.[6]

Between Spivak's radically unsentimental pronouncement, which devolves from the deconstruction of language as Law (whose function is to prohibit rather than to enable), and the more humanistic idealism of those cultural critics who continue to assert that the subalterns have spoken, an enormous discursive dimension unfolds. This discursive dimension, which constitutes the third prominent type of analysis in cultural studies, is that of "minority discourse." As elaborated by critics such as Gilles Deleuze, Félix Guattari, David Lloyd, Abdul JanMohamed, and others,[7] theories of minority discourse share Spivak's criticism of Western ideological domination but not her conclusion. Because this difference amounts to the significant opening up of possibilities, whereby coming to terms with otherness means making attempts to seek and listen for the voices of the subordinated others, minority discourse has become arguably the most prevalent and most productive conceptual model in U.S. cultural studies. Unlike the absolute certainty of a negative conclusion such as "the subaltern cannot speak," "minority discourse" analyses offer hope: their recognition of subordination (as evidenced in the word "minority" as opposed to "majority" or "mainstream") is accompanied by a persistent belief in the possibilities of expression, articulation, and agency (as evidenced in the word "discourse"). In terms of its capacity for understanding cultural diversities as discursive practices, "minority discourse" is an eminently *enabling* conceptual model. Under its rubric, "otherness" finds a variety of infinitely expanding and changing expressions—as differences performed by way of class, gender, sexual preference, religion, and so forth. Articulated together, these multifarious minority discourses could potentially become an effective coalition against the domineering legacy of the white Protestant heterosexual man of property.

As soon as different minority discourses begin to mushroom, however, it becomes clear that "otherness," as the site of opposition, alternative subject formation, and alternative value, is hardly a unified essence. Otherness-as-diversity soon becomes recognized not only from outside the West, in the margins of mainstream representation, but from within the apparatuses of Western imperialist domination as well. The cultures of imperialism as much as the cultures of the West's others, the white Protestant heterosexual man of property as much as the subaltern, are now considered anew as so many different kinds of "hybrids"—as the work of Homi Bhabha, among others, suggests.[8]

Even though these four types of analyses—Orientalism-critique, investigations of subaltern identities, minority discourses, and culture-as-hybridity—have generated a phenomenal variety of contents, what they demonstrate collectively is cultural studies' close relation to "theory" in the poststructural sense. To cite what is perhaps the most evident instance in that relation, an essay such as Jacques Derrida's "Sign, Structure, and Play,"[9] which deconstructs the metaphysics of the "center" as a kind of indispensable but ever-shifting function in human signification, could now be seen as a document that maps out, in theoretical terms, the potentialities that arise with the displacement of the West as the universal "center." Between the philosophical underpinnings of deconstruction's imperative to undo the West from within its own logocentric premises and cultural studies' insistent orientation toward pluralism, the structural affinities are more than obvious. One could go as far as arguing that cultural studies' chief characteristic, summarized by Simon During as the "affirmation of otherness and negation of metadiscourse,"[10] is genealogically made possible and necessary by the dislocation of the sign that inaugurated the "structuralist controversy"[11] of three decades ago. Cultural studies as we know it today would not have been conceivable without the radical reformulations of language and discourse, of the relation between high and low culture, and of the relation between representation and politics, which were enabled by poststructuralist theory. Even at its most empirical, therefore, cultural studies contains within its articulations this fundamental *theoretical* understanding of the need to challenge the center of hegemonic systems of thinking and writing.[12] And yet, if poststructuralist theory is, at least in the United States, in part what triggers the "new cultural politics of difference"[13] that has become such a global movement, why is it that so many of those who raced toward "theory" are now among the harshest critics of cultural studies and cultural criticism?

It seems to me that the answer to this question lies in cultural studies' status as, in effect, a kind of dangerous supplement to poststructuralist theory. For all its fundamental epistemological subversiveness, the dislocation of the sign as philosophized in the heyday of "high theory" could still be contained within a more or less European tradition. One could, for instance, trace the work of Derrida back to Lévi-Strauss, Saussure, Husserl, Heidegger, Nietzsche, and ultimately to Kant. This explains why, for nearly two decades in North America, an act as avant-garde and as radical as dislocating the sign was paradoxically practiced in the most elitist educational institutions, such as Yale, Johns Hopkins, and Cornell, where the followers of deconstruction enjoyed the best of both spiritual and material worlds, as mental radicals and as well-paid Ivy League professors. But that period was an Indian summer. The implications unleashed by the dislocation of the sign were soon no longer confinable within Europe or within Ivy League institutions. Soon, what teachers and students felt needed to be dislocated included Europe and the Ivy League institutions themselves—and the culture and pedagogical disciplinarity they represented.

Moreover, the turn toward otherness that seems to *follow* from the theoretical dislocation of the sign is, strictly speaking, the very historicity that *precedes* the poststructuralist subversion: the supplementary look at Europe's others reveals anew the violence that was there, long before the appearance of "theory," in the European imperialism of the past few hundred years. This violence that is now disturbingly unleashed in academic institutions is thus a kind of retroactive replay, a re-membering of the history of racial and cultural imperialism that lies at the "foundations" of the theoretical dislocation of the sign.[14] Because this violence can no longer be safely contained within the folds of a purely European tradition, it also renders the (illusory) articulatory self-sufficiency of that tradition untenable. Cultural studies, by its dogged turns toward the other not only within language and text but also outside language and text, in effect forces poststructuralist theory to confront the significance of race—and with it the histories of racial discrimination and racial exploitation—that is repressed in poststructuralist theory's claim to subversiveness and radicalism. By so doing, *cultural studies challenges poststructuralist theory's own position as the "other" of Europe, as the "other" within the European tradition.* And this, I think, is cultural studies' most significant threat to the once avant-garde theorists who, like Bloom, must literally junk it.

Culture and Area Studies

Once racial difference is introduced into the picture, it is possible to argue that the study of what is called culture, in particular the cultures of the non-West, is in fact not a novel event, at least not in North American universities. Since, after the Second World War, the United States has inherited Western Europe's former role as military-aggressor-and-cultural-imperialist-cum-savior around the world, the study of non-Western cultures has always been part of its universities' function as the support for United States foreign policy. Through "fieldwork," teaching in the classroom, and language training, social science disciplines such as anthropology, economics, and political science, and humanistic disciplines such as history, linguistics, and literature, have long participated in the massive information retrieval that constitutes the study of non-Western cultures under the establishment known in the United States as "area studies." In such study, what are continually being observed and analyzed by the mainstream practitioners of the various disciplines are not only monuments, documents, rituals, customs, practices, and narratives, but also the "peoples of color."[15]

Area studies, in other words, has long been producing "specialists" who report to North American political and civil arenas about "other" civilizations, "other" regimes, "other" ways of life, and so forth. To the extent that such "others" are now often also the objects of investigation for cultural studies, one could perhaps argue that cultural studies as a "new" discipline (or counterdiscipline) is merely a belated institutional form, a new name for certain well-established pedagogical practices. If, for area studies, the information target field is defined by way of particular geographical areas and nation states, such as South Asia, the Middle East, East Asia, Latin America, and countries of Africa, then for cultural studies, the information target field is something called "culture" or "ethnicity."

There is, however, a major difference: whereas the study of "culture" in the area studies establishment is frequently undertaken in the name of scientific objectivity, knowledge acquisition, cross-cultural understanding, and other such humanistic ideals which continue to belie the racist underpinnings of the establishment itself, cultural studies cannot similarly pretend that its tasks are innocent ones. However much the practitioners of cultural studies might subscribe to similar humanistic ideals, they are compelled by the theoretical premise of cultural studies—the affirmation of otherness and the negation of metadiscourse that are genealogically derived from or affined to poststructuralism—to acknowledge, if not directly address, the exploitative, asymmetrical relations inherent in the Western studies of non-Western cultures, relations that continue to be deemphasized if not altogether denied by many area studies specialists. Once these relations are acknowledged, the paths of inquiry taken by cultural studies toward its "objects" are bound to be different from those historically adopted in area studies. Meanwhile, because area studies and cultural studies do seem to overlap in terms of their objects, cultural studies, in order to demarcate its own pedagogical goals, must remain on the alert toward this persistent denial of racial inequities coming from area studies specialists. Otherwise, since such denial tends to reproduce and perpetuate itself, it could easily turn cultural studies into a reification of culture. This potential of cultural studies for turning against its own critical capacity is, I think, the foremost danger against which students of cultural studies must be repeatedly warned. To understand this point fully, we need, once again, to return to the relationship between cultural studies and theory, and show how this problem of (potential) culture-reification, too, is implicated in that relationship.

"Theory" against "Culture"—"Monolith" against "Pluralism"?

In spite of the disavowal of cultural studies' relation with theory, a disavowal that comes from *both* many of cultural studies' critics (who dislike cultural studies for being "untheoretical," "empiricist," and "garbage") and many of its supporters (who dislike "theory" for being "elitist," "abstract," and "universalist"), the mutual implications between theory and cultural studies are, as I mentioned in the foregoing pages, tenacious.[16] Accordingly, the position of those who feel they need to defend theory against cultural studies is a hypocritical one. When theory is upheld as some pristine, ultimate ideal that cannot be soiled by the "garbage of cultural criticism," or when multiculturalism is dismissed *en bloc* as a "cloud-cuckooland of egalitarianism and euphemism,"[17] the shape of the opposition to cultural studies inevitably resembles that of reactionary patriarchal attacks on feminized mass culture. In this instance, "theory" stands against "culture" as "mind" against "matter" or "masculinist" against "feminist," complete with all the repressive coercions typical of attempts to adhere to what has become historically defunct. However, even though such reactionary attacks on cultural studies are annoying, they are not, to my mind, its major problem. What is much more problematic is the disavowal of cultural studies' relation with theory that comes from the other direction—namely, the direction of those supporters of cultural studies who think that the study of "culture" means that there is no longer a need to engage with "theory."

At this point, my own experience as a teacher and writer provides some help in illustrating my arguments. As someone who is officially affiliated with the discipline of comparative literature and whose work has much to do with Asian cultures and literatures, my position contains within it major aspects which seem to contradict each other in the age of cultural studies: on the one hand, comparative literature is the hotbed of "theory" and the bastion of Eurocentric views of literature;[18] on the other, by virtue of the fact that I teach and write about the non-West, my work also unavoidably intersects with the "culture" study that is undertaken by the area studies establishment. Perhaps because of these two at times incompatible anchorings of my professional life, I tend to be more vigilant than some of my colleagues in either field against any kind of irresponsible dismissal of either "theory" or "culture," and more invested than most in pursuing the affinities between them. As a discipline, comparative literature is currently faced with a challenge both in terms of the form and content of its disciplinarity—form, because the question as to what kinds of comparative *relations* should be introduced and what kinds of media should be "compared" can no longer be taken for granted; content, because the kinds of literatures that need to be addressed have far exceeded the traditional Eurocentric parameters of the discipline.[19]

For those engaged in the study of comparative literature, then, this is a moment of opportunity, a moment when cultural studies has very interesting alternatives to offer in terms of the study of non-Western cultures and literatures, and of other kinds of media.[20] Instead of the traditional Eurocentric frameworks of the nation-state, national language, and geographical area that constitute area studies, cultural studies offers modes of inquiry that require students to pay attention to the cultural politics of knowledge production. Instead of reinforcing the kind of Orientalist methodology that is deeply entrenched in area studies, cultural studies would emphasize how the study of non-Western cultures as such cannot proceed as if modernity and tradition were simply a matter of "indigenous" continuity without taking into consideration the ideological consequences of Western imperialism or without addressing the asymmetrical relations between "master discourses" and "native informants."

On the other hand, precisely because of the obstinacy of the methods of area studies, this is also a moment of danger because the turn toward "other" cultures that is espoused in the name of cultural studies could easily be used to refuse and replace rather than strengthen the theoretical modes of inquiry that remain a valuable part of comparative literature. For instance, it is disturbing to hear a kind of claim that is now often made about the study of non-Western cultures in the age of multiculturalism: "Now we can go back to the study of indigenous cultures and forget all about 'Western theory'!" Even though this is a caricatural paraphrase, I believe it accurately sums up the sentiments that are involved in the *antitheoretical clamor for cultural studies*. Let me be more specific about why such sentiments are problematic.

In the age of the general criticism of Western imperialism, the study of non-Western cultures easily assumes a kind of moral superiority, since such cultures are often also those that have been colonized and ideologically dominated by the West. For the same reason, "theory," for all its fundamental questioning of Western logocentrism, has easily but effectively been lumped together with everything "Western" and facilely rejected as a non-necessity. This is evident in the manner in which the following type of question, for all its illogicality, continues to be in vogue among some practitioners of Asian studies: "Why should we use Western theory to study Asian cultures?" In the climate of multiculturalism, such practitioners find in cultural studies' obligatory turns toward pluralism a kind of rhetorical justification that works to their own advantage—for what better "reason" is there for the rejection of "Western theory" than the widely advocated study of "other" cultures? In the name of studying the West's "others," then, the *critique* of cultural politics that is an inherent part of both poststructural theory and cultural studies is pushed aside, and "culture" returns to a coherent, idealist essence that is outside language and outside mediation.[21] Pursued in a morally complacent, antitheoretical mode, "culture" now functions as a shield that hides the positivism, essentialism, and nativism—and with them the continual acts of hierarchization, subordination, and marginalization—that have persistently accompanied the pedagogical practices of area studies; "cultural studies" now becomes a means of legitimizing continual conceptual and methodological irresponsibility in the name of cultural otherness.

One prominent instance of such legitimation is the argument for returning to "indigenous" origins. As Spivak points out, the notion of a return to pure "indigenous theory" is not a viable one because of the history of imperialism:

> I cannot understand what indigenous theory there might be that can ignore the reality of nineteenth-century history. As for syntheses: syntheses have more problems than answers to offer. To construct indigenous theories one must ignore the last few centuries of historical involvement. I would rather use what history has written for me.[22]

To add to Spivak's point, it should be emphasized that the advocacy for a return to indigenous theory and culture usually masks, with the violence of "the West," the violence of the cultural politics that is *within* an indigenous culture.

Furthermore, the same untheoretical espousal of non-Western cultures leads some to think that cultural studies is something that can be conveniently localized and nationalized, and, by the same token, globalized and internationalized. We have, for instance, the new formula of "X cultural studies," with X being a nation, a place, or a particular group, the study of which is always simultaneously held to be "international" and "global" in its implications. If one of the major tasks of cultural studies is that of bringing the entire notion of "culture" into crisis rather than simply that of assembling different cultures for their mutual admiration, then a localist and nationalist strategy as such, which returns culture to the status of some origin, property, or set of attributes—such as "Chinese," "French," "American"—that everyone owns prior to language and discourse, would precisely put an end to the critical impetus of cultural studies. As Fazal Rizvi puts it in a different context:

> while multiculturalism may be viewed as intrinsically oppositional in nature, all cultural practices are thought to be valid within their own terms. These culturalist presuppositions support a rationalist peda- gogy that is both ahistorical and depoliticised. Ahistorical because it treats culture as something fixed, finished or final and depoliticised because it obscures the inherently political character of pedagogical practices.[23]

It is only because the gestures toward localism and pluralism—the two are virtually synonymous in this context—are ultimately essential- ist and positivistic that the study of culture could be imagined as a way of putting an end to "Western theory." Ironically, thus, a new rhetori- cal/pedagogical situation has arisen: at academic conferences and re- search gatherings as well as in print, very conservative practitioners of area studies can now safely endow their own retrograde positions with the glorious *multiculturalist* aura of defending non-Western traditions. Even those whose work has only to do with the most culturally chau- vinistic, canonical issues and nothing to with gender, class, or race, are suddenly able to claim not only for their objects of study but also *for themselves* the subject position of an oppressed, marginalized minority simply because they are the so-called "specialists" of a non-Western culture, because they are, as they always have been, straightforward Orientalists! In the words of Spivak, such specialists of non-Western cultures in fact help legitimize the position of those to whom they think they are opposed:

> There is a lot of name-calling on both sides of the West-and-the-rest debate in the United States. In my estimation, although the politics of the only-the-West supporters is generally worth questioning, in effect the two sides legitimize each other. In a Foucauldian language, one could call them an opposition within the same discursive formation. The new culture studies must displace this opposition by keeping nation and globe distinct as it studies their relationship, and by tak- ing a moratorium on cultural supremacy as an unquestioned spring- board.[24]

In sum, in contrast to the hostile critics who defend "theory" against cultural studies, the friendly supporters who applaud cultural studies on the moral high ground of recognizing diverse "contexts" and "histo- ries" present a very different, and to my mind much more insidious, kind of problem. This time, we are confronted not with the forgetting of the racial origins of theory (and their multicultural implications) but rather with the reification of culture in the name of opposing "theory" and opposing reification. For those who see in cultural studies the critical potential for examining and transforming institutionalized intellectual disciplinarity itself, the necessity to mobilize against such foreclosures of that potential by many enthusiastic supporters of "curriculum-diversification" cannot be sufficiently emphasized. Otherwise, in the name precisely of sponsoring the "marginal," the study of non-Western cultures would simply contribute toward a new, or renewed, Orientalism:

> As this [marginal] material begins to be absorbed into the discipline, the long-established but supple, heterogeneous, and hierarchical power-lines of the institutional "dissemination of knowledge" continue to determine and overdetermine its conditions of representability. It is at the moment of infiltration or insertion, sufficiently under threat by the custodians of a fantasmatic high Western culture, that the greatest caution must be exercised. The price of success must not compromise the enterprise irreparably. In that spirit of caution, it might not be inappropriate to notice that, as teachers, we are now involved in the construction of a new object of investigation—"the third world," "the marginal"—for institutional validation and certification. One has only to analyze carefully the proliferating but exclusivist "Third World-ist" job descriptions to see the packaging at work. It is as if, in a certain way, we are becoming complicitous in the perpetuation of a "new Orientalism."[25]

Culture and Power

Beyond the institutional boundaries of theory, area studies, and cultural studies, the much larger question that is lurking behind multiculturalism remains, finally, that of the relation between culture and power, between representation and social equality.[26]

Multiculturalism is, in many ways, the result of the putative end of metanarratives, an end that Jean-François Lyotard calls the "postmodern condition."[27] The apparent absence of metanarratives gives rise to the impression that every kind of expression, every kind of representation, and every kind of culture is as valid as others. This is one reason why the variety of objects that can be studied in cultural studies seems infinite and the criteria for judgment seem increasingly arbitrary. At the same time, if indeed multiculturalism is intent on promoting a liberalist politics of recognition, recognition is still largely a one-way street—in the form, for instance, of *white culture recognizing non-white cultures only.*[28]

For those groups on the side of non-white cultures, the problem presented by multiculturalism remains one of tactical negotiation. Negotiating a point of entry into the multicultural scene means nothing less than posing the question of rights—the right to representation and the right to culture. What this implies is much more than the mere fight (by a particular non-white culture) for its "freedom of speech," because the very process of attaining "speech" here is inextricably bound up with right, that is, with the processes through which particular kinds of "speeches" are legitimized in the first place. To put it in very simple terms, a non-white culture, in order to "be" or to "speak," must (1) seek legitimacy/recognition from white culture, which has denied the reality of the "other" cultures all along; (2) use the language of white culture (since it is the dominant one) to produce itself (so that it could be recognized and thus legitimized); and yet (3) resist complete normativization by white culture.[29] If this example using racial inequality is but one among the many, many kinds of tactical negotiations that inevitably take place in multiculturalism, then the issue of "culture" in cultural studies cannot in effect be divorced from the issue of power—of rights, laws, and justice. And, unless such fundamental power relations are carefully articulated alongside the politics of recognition, the "equality" principle of multiculturalism would simply be exploited to cover up the perpetuation of certain kinds of power. As Rizvi writes, a multiculturalism that preaches a "harmonious multicultural society in which all cultural traditions can be maintained" is

> really about a politics of assimilation concerned with domesticating egalitarian demands. By invoking the universalist ideal of a society governed by a set of social principles for a common humanity, in which we can all participate happily without reference to class, ethnicity, race or gender, multiculturalism obscures the issues of power and privilege. [A] curriculum based on these assumptions can only deal with differences by making them marginal; by being tokenistic.[30]

For the practitioners of cultural studies to address these issues of power, a type of theoretical intervention that continues to critique the legitimating structures inherent in the production of knowledge is absolutely necessary, especially at a time when everything seems equivalent and we could all happily return to our own "cultures," "ethnicities," and "origins." To put it in a different way, it is precisely at the time of multiculturalism, when "culture" seems to be liberalized in the absence of metanarratives, when "culture" seems to have become a matter of "entitlement" rather than struggle, that we need to reemphasize the questions of power and underscore at every point the institutional forces that account for the continual hierarchization of cultures. Instead of simply perpetuating what Spivak terms the "revolutionary tourism" and "celebration of testimony"[31] that seem to characterize so much of what goes on under the name of cultural studies these days, it is the meticulous investigation of such legitimating structures of power that would, in the long run, give cultural studies its sustenance and integrity as a viable pedagogical practice.

In the classroom, this means that students should not be told simply to reject "metadiscourses" in the belief that by turning to the "other" cultures—by turning to "culture" as the "other" of metadiscourses—they would be able to overturn existing boundaries of knowledge production that, in fact, continue to define and dictate their own discourses. Questions of authority, and with them hegemony, representation, and right, can be dealt with adequately only if we insist on the careful analyses of texts, on responsibly engaged rather than facilely dismissive judgments, and on deconstructing the ideological assumptions in discourses of "opposition" and "resistance" as well as in discourses of mainstream power. Most of all, as a form of exercise in "cultural literacy," we need to continue to train our students to read—to read arguments on their own terms rather than discarding them perfunctorily and prematurely—not in order to find out about authors' original intent but in order to ask, "Under what circumstances would such an argument—no matter how preposterous—make sense? With what assumptions does it produce meanings? In what ways and to what extent does it legitimize certain kinds of cultures while subordinating or outlawing others?" Such are the questions of power and domination as they relate, ever asymmetrically, to the dissemination of knowledge. Old-fashioned questions of pedagogy as they are, they nonetheless demand frequent reiteration in order for cultural studies to retain its critical and political impetus in the current intellectual climate.

TWO

The Fascist Longings in Our Midst

Evil is never done so thoroughly and so well as when it is done with a good conscience.

—*Blaise Pascal*[1]

Fascism is not the prohibition of saying things, it is the obligation *to say them.*

—*Roland Barthes*[2]

"FASCISM" IS A banal term. It is used most often not simply to refer to the historical events that took place in Hitler's Germany and Musso-lini's Italy, but also to condemn attitudes or behavior that we consider to be excessively autocratic or domineering.[3] Speaking in the mid-1970s, Michel Foucault referred to the popularized use of the term "fascism" as "a general complicity in the refusal to decipher what fascism really was." The non-analysis of fascism, Foucault goes on, is "one of the important political facts of the past thirty years. It enables fascism to be used as a floating signifier, whose function is essentially that of denunciation."[4] In this chapter, I attempt to study this—what amounts to a collective—"denunciation" of fascism by examining not only what is being denounced but also the major conceptual paths through which denunciation is produced. My argument is hence not exactly one that avoids the "floatingness" of "fascism" by grounding it in a particular time or space. Instead, I take fascism as a commonplace, in the many ways it is used to indicate what is deemed questionable and unacceptable. In the process, I highlight what I think is fascism's most significant but often neglected aspect—what I will refer to as its tech-nologized idealism. In my argument, fascism is not simply the disguised or naturalized "ideology" that is examined by Louis Althusser and Roland Barthes;[5] rather it is a term that indicates the production and consumption of a glossy surface image, a crude style, for purposes of social identification even among intellectuals. In lieu of a conclusion, I also comment on the affinities between fascism as a "large" historical force and the mundane events of academic life in North America in the 1990s by foregrounding the idealizing tendencies in what is called multiculturalism.

Monstrous Visions

For those of us who do not have personal experience of the period of the Second World War in Europe and Asia, the picture that comes to mind when we think of fascism is always a photograph, a scene from a film, a documentary, or some graphic account narrated by survivors. The visual association we have with fascism is usually one of horror and destruction. Several years ago, for instance, I had the chance to view a video called "Magee's Testament" (produced and distributed by the Alliance in Memory of the Victims of the Nanking Massacre, 1991) about Japan's invasion of the city of Nanjing during December 1937 to February 1938. These newsreel pictures of rape and massacre constitute the only known filmed document of the atrocities committed by Japanese soldiers during what the Chinese call "Nanjing da tusha," the Nanjing Massacre or the Rape of Nanjing. Shot by an American missionary, John Magee, and recently rediscovered after fifty-five years, the cans of amateur film from the 1930s have been incorporated into a thirty-minute video by the Chinese American filmmaker Peter Wang. According to Magee's account, about 300,000 Chinese were killed in a week. This number would be among the 15 to 20 million generally estimated to have been killed during Japan's aggression against China from 1931 to 1945.[6]

What comes across most powerfully in "Magee's Testament" is the aesthetics of Japanese brutality. I use the term aesthetics not in its narrow sense of principles of beauty or good taste, but in the broader, Kantian sense of principles of perception and cognition, principles that are in turn manifested in outward behavior, as behavioral style. Among the Chinese survivors interviewed some forty-five years after the war, the memories of that aesthetics unfold in narratives that are juxtaposed with pictures taken in 1937 and 1938 of heart-rending wounds, amputations, disabilities, and deaths. I was struck most of all by the pictures of a still-living woman, the back of whose neck had been sawed at with a bayonet. A large portion of the head, which must have at one time been dangling in mid-air without being completely chopped off, was surgically stitched back onto this woman's body. At the time the news-reel was made, it was as if the camera, simply because it captured so vividly the painful physicality of this event, was an accomplice to the original act of brutality. So was the doctor who manipulated the woman's head for the camera, and so were those watching the film.

No words would do justice to the monstrosity of such an aesthetics. But what exactly is monstrous? No doubt it is the calamitous destruction that descended upon the victims. And yet a monstrous aesthetics is also an aesthetics of *making* monstrous, of demonstrative magnification and amplification. As one writer points out, the Japanese soldiers who committed such acts of atrocities were able to do so because, like the Nazis, their loyalty to their ideology was so absolute that it freed them from all other restraints.[7] Unlike the Nazis, who were Christians mindful of the close relations between "body" and "spirit" and who regarded physical involvement with their victims' bodies as a form of spiritual contamination, the Japanese showed no such compunction. The point about their fascism was not enthusiasm in discipline but enthusiasm in unharnessed cruelty. It was thus not enough simply to extinguish the enemy's life *tout court*; they must torture and mutilate in ways that prolong and aggravate their victims' suffering and thus maximize their own pleasure. There was no sense of being contaminated by the enemy because the enemy was just raw material into which they poked their swords, or discharged their urine and semen alike.

Like all graphic records of fascist destructiveness, the images of "Magee's Testament" clarify two things about fascism. The first, which is the easier to grasp, is that fascism is a form of technology. This does not simply refer to the fact that fascism deploys technological means for its purposes, but also that fascism is a kind of demonstrative culture/writing whose magnitude—whose portent—can only be that of the technological. The Japanese soldier did not simply use technological weapons; he was a murder machine that happened to take the form of a man. The second thing about fascism, which is closely related to the first but not as readily acceptable, is that the most important sentiment involved in fascism is not a negative but a positive one: rather than hatefulness and destructiveness, fascism is about love and idealism. Most of all it is a search for an idealized self-image through a heartfelt surrender to something higher and more beautiful. Like the Nazi officer who killed to purify his race, the Japanese soldier raped and slaughtered in total devotion to their emperor and in the name of achieving the "Greater East Asia Co-Prosperity Sphere." Like the Nazi concentration camp official who was genuinely capable of being moved to tears by a Beethoven sonata being played by Jewish prisoners, the Japanese officer, we may surmise, was probably also genuinely capable of being moved by the delicate feelings inscribed in cultured practices such as haiku poetry, calligraphy, or the tea ceremony. In each case, what sustains the aesthetics of monstrosity is something eminently positive and decent.

Projection I: The Violence "in Us All"

The question of the relationship between the destructive and idealizing sentiments in fascism is thus much more difficult than it first appears. Let us think, once again, of Foucault's criticism that we have used the term "fascism" only to denounce others. On another occasion, in the preface to Gilles Deleuze and Félix Guattari's *Anti-Oedipus*, Foucault writes that the strategic adversary combatted by *Anti-Oedipus* is fascism, adding that by this he means "not only historical fascism, the fascism of Hitler and Mussolini . . . but also the fascism in us all, in our heads and in our everyday behavior, the fascism that causes us to love power, to desire the very thing that dominates and exploits us."[8]

By moving from events in the world outside back to the fascism "in us all," Foucault reminds us of an ancient piece of advice: "Know thyself." At the same time, by calling attention to the fascism "in us" as opposed to that outside us, Foucault articulates a specific conceptual mechanism used in many accounts of fascism, the mechanism of *projection* as defined by Freud. The function of projection is described by Freud as a *defense:* when we sense something dangerous and threatening in ourselves, we expel and objectify it outward, so as to preserve our own stability. The best social example of Freud's understanding of projection is anti-Semitism. The "Jew" is the name and the picture of all those things we cannot admit about ourselves; it is thus a symptom of our fears and anxieties.[9] Even though it is not always consciously stated as such, Freudian projection is crucial to some of the most sophisticated accounts of fascism.[10] However, what emerges interestingly from Foucault's brief comments on fascism is that *if the fascist discrimination against the "Jew" is a projection in Freud's sense, then our denunciatory use of the term "fascism," insofar as it remains a "floating signifier," is also such a projection.* "Fascism" has become for us the empty term, the lack, onto which we project all the unpleasant realities from which we want to distance ourselves. This is why fascism is associated alternately with colonialism, authoritarianism, mysticism, populism, socialism, banality, and so forth.[11] Ortega y Gasset summarizes fascism's emptiness perceptively when he writes that it is "simultaneously one thing and the contrary, A and not-A. . . ."[12] The extreme logical conclusion to this is that those who most violently denounce fascism—who characterize others as fascists—may be themselves exhibiting symptoms of fascism.

ETHICS AFTER IDEALISM

But what is it that we "cannot" admit about "ourselves"? Like many of his other concepts, Freud's definition of projection hinges on an act of negation: projection is the outward manifestation of a basic denial or refusal (of knowledge) in the individual organism. Once we focus on the indispensable negativity involved in projection, we notice that the premise for this projection is something like "human nature," which is treated as the source of the problems at hand. A critique of fascism by way of Freudian projection would hence always emphasize fascism as an expression of *our own repression*—our oppression of ourselves— and most critics of fascism, it follows, see fascism first of all as an inner or internalized violence from which we need to be "liberated." The belief in repression and liberation as such has the effect of turning even the perpetrators of fascism—those who rape, mutilate, and slaughter— into *victims* who are ultimately pardonable. For instance, in his classic study, *The Mass Psychology of Fascism,* Wilhelm Reich argues that fascism, like many forms of organized religion and mysticism, is the mass expression of orgiastic impotence or repressed sexual energies. Citing Hitler as his type case, Reich locates the social origin of fascism in the authoritarian patriarchal family, in which feelings of fear and rebellion toward the father are combined with those of reverence and submission.[13] While Reich's interpretation made up in a significant way for the neglect of sexuality that characterized most Marxist and economic approaches to fascism of his day, it nevertheless reads like a vulgarized use of Freud's notion of repression: fascism becomes the compensatory "sublimation" (in distorted form) of the energy that had nowhere else to go. Not surprisingly, therefore, the solution offered by Reich is finally that of "love" and "work"—the proper sublimation of sexual energies that should, he writes, govern our lives.

Similarly, in *Anti-Oedipus,* Deleuze and Guattari explain the repressive violence characteristic of Western society by way of Nietzsche's notion of *ressentiment.* For them, *ressentiment,* which is active life force turned inward, has a name—Oedipus. Freudian psychoanalysis, insofar as it helps perpetuate the ideological baggage of a metaphysics of interiority, is for Deleuze and Guattari the place to begin criticism of the everyday fascism of Western society.[14]

The "internalized violence" model is so persuasive that it captures even a Marxist political philosopher like Ernesto Laclau. In *Politics and Ideology in Marxist Theory,* Laclau's project is that of finding ways to articulate the popular forces that motivated fascism in Europe. While Laclau does not fail to see the problems in Reich's interpretation,[15] his own criticism of Nicos Poulantzas's well-known study of fascism[16] is precisely that Poulantzas reduced every contradiction to a class contradiction and failed to take into account the processes of subjectivization involved. Using Althusser's notion of "interpellation," Laclau thus reformulates fascism as a kind of populism that interpellated masses as "a people" in ways that went beyond their class distinctions. It does not seem problematic to Laclau that Althusser's notion of interpellation is still, arguably, dependent upon an outside (ideology) versus an inside (the individual), and that the moment the individual responds to the hailing "Hey, you!" is also the moment when the force of ideology is "internalized."

Despite the differences among these critics of fascism—Deleuze and Guattari mock and deterritorialize Freudian psychoanalysis while Reich, Althusser, and Laclau continue to adapt it to their own purposes—they all implicitly agree that fascism's effectiveness has to do with its being a violence—a *negative* force—that has been "internalized," a violence that is somehow "in us" by nature or by culture. This leaves us with the question of how exactly fascism is "internalized." What does it mean for fascism to be "in us"? Do we violate ourselves the way the Nazis and the Japanese violated the Jews, the Gypsies, and the Asians? How does the lack "in us" (in Freud's terms, fear and denial) turn into a concrete thing "outside" us? How does the nameless "in us" acquire the external name "Jew"? Conversely, how does that monstrous picture "out there" signify/become what is "in us"? How are we to understand that proclamation by Göring which epitomizes this basic problem of fascist projection—"I have no conscience. My conscience is Adolf Hitler"?[17]

In other words, when we move from acts of brutality to "internalized violence," or when we move from the lack that is supposedly "in us" to external atrocities, some change, presupposed and yet unexplained, has taken place. This change, which is the unarticulated part of all of these theories of internalized violence, is metaphorical, imaginary, and, as I will argue, technological. It indicates that which happens but which we cannot actually see or hear—and which we must therefore explain in terms *other* than itself. The filmic image, because it is obvious and palpable, offers a convenient way of staging these "other" terms.

But there is a more fundamental reason why fascism can be explained by way of film. Not that film "expresses" the images of fascism effectively. Rather, like film, fascism as an ideology has "its foundation in projection." I take this phrase from Alice Yaeger Kaplan's illuminating study of French fascism, *Reproductions of Banality.* Basing her notion of fascism not on the profound but on the banal and obvious,[18] Kaplan calls for a different kind of attention to be paid to fascism—not a convoluted search in the depths of our selves for the *ressentiment* imposed by religion or family, but attention to fascism as projection, surface phenomena, everyday practice, which does away with the distinction between the "inside" and the "outside": "The fascist ideal is being swallowed by the subject at the same time as it is being projected onto the leader. Projection and introjection are not always even that distinguishable."[19] The indistinguishability of introjection from projection means that there is a mutual implication between fascism and technology, including the technology that is psychoanalysis. When authors like Freud used terms such as "projection" and "screen memory," Kaplan writes, they were already speaking to the mediatized makeup of our experience.[20]

What is "internalized"—if the language of internalization still makes sense—is thus not so much the atrocious ideology of cruelty as its monstrous, propagandist form:

> The crowd comes to know itself as film. Subjects knowing themselves as film—that is, internalizing the aesthetic criteria offered in film— have a radically different experience, than if they knew themselves through film. In the film experience the spectators do not merely control a model that remains exterior to their untouched subjectivity; rather, their subjectivity is altered and enlarged by the film. . . .[21]

What is "internalized" in the age of film is the very *projectional* mechanism of projection. If individuals are, to use Althusser's term, "interpellated," they are interpellated not simply as watchers of film but also as film itself. They "know" themselves not only as the subject, the audience, but as the object, the spectacle, the movie. In his study of the cinema of Fassbinder, Thomas Elsaesser makes a similar argument about German fascism, namely, that German fascism was based in the state of being-looked-at, which cinema's proclivity toward visual relations conveniently exemplifies. Elsaesser holds that the Fassbinder trademark of exhibitionism—the persistent foregrounding of being-looked-at and its significance for the formation of social identity— should be understood in this light:

> What, Fassbinder seems to ask, was fascism for the German middle and working-class which supported Hitler? We know what it was for Jews, for those actively persecuted by the regime, for the exiles. But for the apolitical Germans who stayed behind? Might not the pleasure of fascism, its fascination have been less the sadism and brutality of SS officers than the pleasure of being seen, of placing oneself in view of the all-seeing eye of the State? Fascism in its Imaginary encouraged a moral exhibitionism, as it encouraged denunciation and mutual surveillance. Hitler appealed to the *Volk* but always by picturing the German nation, standing there, observed by "the eye of the world." The massive specularization of public and private life . . . might it not have helped to institutionalize the structure of "to be is to be perceived" that Fassbinder's cinema problematizes?[22]

In Elsaesser's phrase "to be is to be perceived," we see that projection, instead of being preceded by "being," is itself the basis from which "being" arises. What this means is a reversal of Freud's model of projection. While Freud begins with the "being" that is the individual organism—the inner something that, sensing something unpleasant, projects it outward—Elsaesser's reading of Fassbinder enables us to begin instead with the projection that is obviously "out there"—the projection that is "being perceived," the projection that is film. While the Freudian model describes projection as being based upon an original lack, as an externalized concretization or objectification of that lack, we can now ask instead: how does the projection that is film "become" us? How does visual technology inhabit the human shape?

In order to answer these questions, we need to recall the more conventional meaning of projection as an act of thrusting or throwing forward, an act that causes an image to appear on a surface. Despite the suggestive association of fascism with film, what remains unarticulated in Kaplan's (and to some extent Elsaesser's) account is the difference between this *obvious* sense of projection and Freud's definition. While the common conceptual path taken by most critics of fascism is projection in Freud's sense, that is, projection as a subject's refusal to recognize something in order to defend itself; film, as external image, operates with the more obvious sense of projection—as objects already out there, objects that may not necessarily be a compensation or substitution for an original (subjective) lack or inability. Once the premise of projection is changed from "inside" to "surface" in this manner, it becomes possible to think of projection as a *positing* rather than a negating function. It would also, I propose, be possible to rethink fascism away from the projection-as-compensated-lack model provided by Freud.

Projection II: Angels of Light

By turning to film and to the formal mutuality between film and fascism, I am not saying that film offers a means of illustrating the principles of fascism. What I am saying is that fascism cannot be understood without a certain understanding of the primacy of the image, *which is best exemplified by the relations of receptivity involved in film.* My point can be stated in a different way: film, because it is obviously imagistic, stands as a good way of analyzing the abstract problem of projection, which is also the problem of that imaginary and metaphoric change between external and internal violence that remains unexplained in the writers I mentioned earlier.[23]

It is hence not an accident that critics of fascism frequently turn to film for their discussions. Consider, for instance, Susan Sontag's classic "Fascinating Fascism," from which the title of the present chapter is taken.[24] In her essay, Sontag repudiates the judgment that the work of filmmaker and photographer Leni Riefenstahl, who received generous support from the German government for her productions during the Nazi period, is nevertheless in some significant manner "apolitical." By refusing to separate artistic technique from ideology, Sontag persuasively shows how the creation of beauty in Riefenstahl's films is intimately linked to fascist ideals. Toward the end of the essay, Sontag writes:

> it is generally thought that National Socialism stands only for brutishness and terror. But this is not true. National Socialism—or, more broadly, fascism—also stands for an ideal, and one that is also persistent today, under other banners: the ideal of life as art, the cult of beauty, the fetishism of courage, the dissolution of alienation in ecstatic feelings of community; the repudiation of the intellect; the family of man (under the parenthood of leaders).[25]

Insofar as she identifies the *positive* messages of fascism as an inalienable part of its functioning, I am in total agreement with Sontag. Her charge that the most widely appreciated qualities of Riefenstahl's work—its beauty, its technical refinement—are precisely what speak most effectively to "the fascist longings in our midst" is so perceptive that it is unsettling.[26] Yet peculiarly, in an essay that so clearly insists on the inseparability of art and ideology, Sontag nonetheless makes a distinction between art and ideology *as soon as she tries to contrast fascist art with communist art:*

> The tastes for the monumental and for mass obeisance to the hero are common to both fascist and communist art. . . .
> But fascist art has characteristics which show it to be, in part, a special variant of totalitarian art. The official art of countries like the Soviet Union and China is based on a utopian morality. Fascist art displays a utopian aesthetics—that of physical perfection. . . .
> In contrast to the asexual chasteness of official communist art, Nazi art is both prurient and idealizing. . . . The fascist ideal is to transform sexual energy into a "spiritual" force, for the benefit of the community.[27]

If Sontag's judgment about fascist art does away with the distinction between propaganda and aesthetics, her reading of the difference between communist and fascist art reintroduces it. We can only speculate that, as a Jewish intellectual writing in the United States of the 1970s, Sontag was absolutely clear-eyed about the fascism of the earlier decades, but like all left-leaning Eurocentric intellectuals of that period, she retained a sense of illusion about communism. Hence even though she writes that fascist art shares with totalitarian art the same tastes for the monumental and for mass obeisance to the hero, she seems to imply, ultimately, that because fascism beautifies and thus hides its totalitarian motives in aesthetically impeccable images, it is the more pernicious and dangerous of the two. Once ideology and art are distinguished as content and facade in this way, however, "aesthetics" returns to the more narrow and conventional sense of the beautiful alone.

By describing fascism as fascinating "aesthetics" in the narrow sense, Sontag, in spite of her own insights, rejoins the tendency of most discussions of fascism, in which attention is almost always focused, negatively, on the "deceptiveness" of fascist authorities: these fascists, it is thought, paint beautiful (that is, delusive) pictures about their ugly (that is, real) behavior. Such pictures, in other words, have the status of deliberate *lies*. Fascist atrocities thus become the "real" that sets the records straight, that exposes the "deceit" and "error" of fascist rhetoric.

But it is precisely in this kind of interpretive cross-over from rhetoric to deed, from "lies" to "truth," from "beautiful pictures" to "ugly reality" that critics have downplayed the most vital point about fascism— its significance as image and surface; its projectional idealism. The "false-true" dichotomization leads us to believe that good intentions cannot result in cruel behavior, and conversely, that the fact of cruelty can only be the result of hidden evil motives "dressed up" as beautiful pictures. We see how the substitutive or compensatory logic of Freud's notion of projection is fully at work here: the fascists, according to this logic, project what they (secretly) deny about themselves "outside"; we the critics thus have to negate their negation and rewind their projection from that false "outside" back into their hidden "inside." According to this logic, not only are intentions and behavior transparently linked; they are also linked through opposition and negation: hence, the "good" image is a cover for "bad" motives. But what if the declared ideals were not lies (projection in Freud's sense) but projections (projection in the common sense of throwing forward)? How then do we understand the relation between noble intentions and atrocious deeds?

Without the illusion about communism—that its propaganda, unlike the beautiful facade of fascism, has after all some real connection to a "utopian morality"—Sontag would in fact have come close to saying that the aesthetics of fascism (aesthetics in the broad sense of cognition and perception) resides precisely in images—not so much images-as-the-beautiful but images-as-the-positivistic-and-self-evident. The "beautiful" images are not images that "hide" (the content of horror); rather they are the cognitive form of the technological age, the surface or superficial phenomena that present themselves as evidence of themselves instead of some other, "inner" meaning. What is fascist about fascism's idealized images is not only that they are positive, but also that they pose and posit, and are positivistic. This positivity is the "projection" that the followers of fascism "internalize."

What Sontag correctly identifies as the "idealizing" tendencies of fascism can thus be explained by the projectional nature of film. To present something in "idealized" terms is literally to enlarge and embolden it—in short, to blow it up as a picture. While it takes its materials from everyday life, this picture, by its very positivity, also becomes mythic. It holds a promise and turns the everyday into the primitive and archetypal. In the process of consuming it, we become infantilized. As Kaplan writes, "the machinery of the media gave birth to a new kind of ideological vulnerability. It was mother bound."[28] In what amounts to the same argument: "When fascism took power, it took charge of the imaginary."[29]

André Bazin provides an astute analysis of these relations between film and idealism, relations that are based on projection, in an essay called "The Stalin Myth in Soviet Cinema."[30] Unlike Sontag, who still attributes to communist art a utopianism that would set it off from fascist art, Bazin calls attention precisely to the idealizing—that is, fascistic—logic in the Soviet films about Stalin. Writing around 1950, Bazin was amazed by the fact that these mythically positive images of Stalin—as a hyper-Napoleonic military genius, as an omniscient and infallible leader, but also as a friendly, avuncular helper to the common people—were made while the man was still alive. Bazin's point is that only the dead are larger than life: "If Stalin, even while living, could be the main character of a film, it is because he is no longer 'human,' engaging in the transcendence which characterizes living gods and dead heroes."[31] The glorifying films have the effect of mummifying and monumentalizing Stalin, so that it is the Stalin-image which becomes the ultimate authority, which even Stalin himself had to follow in order to "be."[32]

According to Bazin, thus, the idealizing power of cinema is not only positivistic but also *retroactive,* calling for a submission to that which has always, in the process of being idealized, already become past or dead. The Stalin myth in Soviet cinema commands an absolute surrender—an identification that is possible only with the cessation of history. Bazin illustrates the retroactive logic of fascist idealization with another, non-filmic example, the Stalinist trials. For Bazin, the major accomplishment of the trials is their success in remaking, that is, falsifying, history with the preemptiveness of retroaction:

> According to the Soviet "Stalinist" communist perspective, no one can "become" a traitor. That would imply that he wasn't always a traitor, that there was a biographical beginning to this treason, and

that, conversely, a person who became a menace to the Party would have been considered useful to the Party before becoming evil. The Party could not simply bust Radek to the lowest rank, or condemn him to death. It was necessary to proceed with a retroactive purge of History, proving that the accused was, since birth, a willful traitor whose every act was satanically camouflaged sabotage. Of course, this operation is highly improbable and far too serious to be used in every case. That is why the public *mea culpa* can be substituted concerning minor figures whose historical action is indirect—such as artists, philosophers, or scientists. These solemn hyperbolic *mea culpas* can seem psychologically improbable or intellectually superfluous to us if we fail to recognize their value as exorcism. As confession is indispensable to divine absolution, so solemn retraction is indispensable to the reconquering of historical virginity.[33]

By inserting this discussion of the logic of totalitarian interrogation in an essay about cinematic representation, Bazin enables us to see retroaction as the crucial common ground for both the Stalinist trials and the filmic construction of Stalin. Moreover, he enables us to see that retroaction works hand in hand with positivism: like the interrogative erasure of the history of communist "traitors"—an erasure (of counter-evidence) that, in effect, becomes the self-validating "evidence" of their guilt—the very (retroactive) idealization of Stalin's goodness in the form of (positivistic) images is part of a manipulation of history that *uses images as their own alibi* by making them appear self-evident. The effect is mass sacrifice—the sacrifice of the masses' own knowledge of history in submission to the mythic image.

Bazin's analysis offers us a way out of Freud's definition of projection. Instead of operating negatively as refusal, compensated lack, and defense mechanism, projection here is the positive instrument of transparency, of good intentions shining forth in dazzling light. Stalin as the angel of light—not only in the sense that he was bringing enlightenment to the people but also in the sense that he was himself transparent, thus allowing for an identification that dissolves the boundary between the inside and the outside—this was the magic of his image. It is therefore not by focusing on the atrocious deeds, the "evil" of fascists, but on their moments of idealism production, their good conscience, that we can understand the effectiveness of fascist aesthetics. The voice of Emperor Hirohito, heard for the first time by his people over the radio after the bombing of Hiroshima and Nagasaki, speaking solemnly of the sadness of national defeat, was one example of this aesthetics. The voice and image of Mao Zedong telling the Red Guards that "Revolution is not criminal, revolt is reasonable" in the form of massive street slogans and pamphlets was another. The sincere altruistic rhetoric we hear in U.S. presidential campaigns, complete with the candidates' demonstrations of their ordinariness (their love of family, for instance), is a third. In all of these cases, it is the force of light, transparency, and idealized image that works in the service of "interpellating" the masses, who receive the leaders as a mesmerizing film. To say that the leaders are "lying" to the masses would be to miss the point of our thoroughly mediatized feelings and perceptions, which accept this aesthetics without coercion, and which accept it as positive and good.[34]

That fascism is primarily a production of light and luminosity is an argument Paul Virilio makes, among other works, in *War and Cinema: The Logistics of Perception.*[35] Virilio's point over and over again is the fatal interdependence of the technologies of warfare and vision, "the conjunction between the power of the modern *war* machine . . . and the new technical performance of the *observation* machine."[36] Hitler and Mussolini clearly understood the coterminous nature of perception and destruction, of cinematic vision and war. While the former commented in 1938, "The masses need illusion—but not only in theatres or cinemas," the latter declared, "Propaganda is my best weapon."[37] These remarks show us the technical nature of fascism, not only in the sense that fascism deploys technological weapons, but also in the sense that the scale of illusion/transparency promised by fascism is possible only in the age of film, the gramophone, and the loudspeaker. The mediatized image and voice—machines in human form rather than humans using machines—are, in Heidegger's terms, fascism's *techne.* Virilio writes:

> If photography, according to its inventor Nicéphore Niepce, was simply a method of engraving with light, where bodies inscribed their traces by virtue of their own luminosity, nuclear weapons inherited both the dark room of Niepce and Daguerre and the military searchlight.[38]

To paraphrase Virilio, we might add that fascism is an engraving with light on people's "minds": fascist leaders inscribed their traces by virtue of their own luminosity; fascist propaganda inherited both the darkroom of Niepce and Daguerre and the military searchlight. . . .

The Story of O, or, the New Fascism

In the foregoing pages, I have tried to argue that fascism needs to be understood not only in its negative but more importantly in its positive aspects, and that fascism's production of idealism is a projectional production of luminosity-as-self-evidence. In an essay entitled "The Evidence of Experience," which does not at first seem to have anything to do with the topic of fascism, Joan Scott has made comparable observations about the use of "experience" in the North American academy today.[39] In the general atmosphere of a felt need to deconstruct universalist claims about human history, Scott writes, scholars of various disciplines have increasingly turned to personal experience as a means of such deconstruction. However, she argues, by privileging experience as the critical weapon against universalisms, we are leaving open the question as to what authorizes experience itself. Scott charges that the appeal to experience "as uncontestable evidence and as an originary point of explanation" for historical difference has increasingly replaced the necessary task of exploring "how difference is established, how it operates, how and in what ways it constitutes subjects who see and act in the world."[40]

For me, what is especially interesting is the manner in which Scott emphasizes the role of vision and visibility throughout her essay. Beginning her discussion with Samuel R. Delany's autobiographical meditation, *The Motion of Light in Water,* Scott notes that "a metaphor of visibility as literal transparency is crucial to his project." She concludes that, for Delany, "knowledge is gained through vision; vision is a direct apprehension of a world of transparent objects."[41] What Scott articulates here is the other side of Virilio's argument about the coterminous nature of visual perception and destruction—that is, the coterminous nature of visual perception and knowledge: "Seeing is the origin of knowing."[42] While the technology of seeing, or seeing-as-technology, has become an inalienable part of the operation of militarism and fascist propaganda, Scott shows how it has also come to dominate our thinking about identity, so much so that visibility and luminosity are the conditions toward which accounts of difference and alternative histories derived from "personal experience" now aspire.

This kind of aspiration, Scott implies, is an aspiration toward the self-evidence of the self's (personal) experience. *The self as evidence:* this means that the self, like the Stalin myth in Soviet cinema, is so transparent, so shone through with light, that it simply *is,* without need for further argument about its history or what Scott calls its "discursive character."

By alerting us to the technology (what she calls metaphor) of visibility, which is now engraved in the attitudes toward knowledge, history, and identity, Scott's argument provides a way of linking the "large" historical issues of fascism and totalitarianism we have been examining with the "small" sphere of North American academic life in the 1990s. In the remainder of this chapter, I will elaborate this linkage further with the help of a fictional scenario. As many readers will recognize, the features of this scenario are a composite drawn from the recent general trends of "multiculturalism" in the academy. By portraying these features in a deliberately exaggerated form, my point is not to slight the significance of the work that is being done by non-Western intellectuals on the non-Western world, but rather to deconstruct our increasingly fascistic intellectual environment, in which facile attitudes, pretentious credentials, and irresponsible work habits can be fostered in the name of "cultural pluralism." The heroine in my fictional scenario is ultimately a mock heroine, the victim of a dangerous collective culture which all of us working in the West perpetrate in different ways.

We will call this imaginary heroine O. A "person of color" from a "third world" country, O is enrolled in a graduate program in a North American university. Despite her upper-class background, O tells people that she is from poor peasant stock in order to enhance her credibility as a "third-world" intellectual. After muddling and bluffing through her coursework, O launches a "multidisciplinary" dissertation that deals with various types of social protest by underdogs in her culture of origin. For two or three years O does virtually nothing by way of serious reading and research, though she makes her presence known regularly by speaking extemporaneously at different conferences. Much as she holds "Western capitalism" in contempt and tirelessly brandishes slogans of solidarity with downtrodden classes in the "third world," O seems even more determined to get her share of fame, privilege, and material well-being in the "first world" by hook or by crook. But even while O has no qualms about faking her way through graduate school, and even while no one can, when asked, say what her project really is apart from repeating the vague generalities that O habitually recites, the support O receives from well-established academics across the United States is tremendous. Many of these supporters are white. Some of them assert that O is the most talented young intellectual from a "third world" country they have ever encountered. With their glowing recommendations, O eventually finds herself a job teaching at a U.S. university.

What is behind such sincere support of a great impostor from what are undoubtedly intelligent and accomplished people? A mass process similar to that described in the classic story of the emperor's new clothes is mobilized here, as someone willing to occupy the position of the emperor accidentally appears. Obviously, we cannot say to O's supporters: "But can't you see . . .?!" because another kind of seeing is taking place. By seeing a student of color, no matter how pretentious and fraudulent, as self-evidently correct and deserving of support, these supporters receive an image of *themselves* that is at once enlightenedly humble ("I submit to you, since you are a victim of our imperialism") and beautiful ("Look how decent I am by submitting to you"), and thus eminently gratifying.[43]

Even though O may be cheating her way through the system, therefore, *she alone is not to blame for this ridiculous situation.* As I already emphasized, it is our flagrantly irresponsible environment of "cultural pluralism" that nurtures her behavior and allows her to thrive.[44] In the white liberal enthusiasm for "peoples of color" that is currently sweeping through North American academic circles, something of the fascism we witnessed in earlier decades has made its return in a new guise. The basis for this fascism is, once again, the identification with an idealized other placed in the position of unquestionable authority. Like the fascism of the 1920s and 1930s, a feeling of rebellion is definitely present; like the old fascism also, there is a massive submission to a kind of figure of "experience" that is assumed to be, to use the terms of Scott's analysis, luminously self-evident. This time, what is "rebelled" against is, fashionably, the canon of the West or "Western imperialism," and the figure onto whom such feelings are projected is the "person of color," regardless of that person's actual personal or professional politics.[45]

Once fascism starts taking effect, it is useless to point out that the person being put in the position of the emperor wearing new clothes is a fraud. Debunking O as an impostor by pointing out her fraudulence—that she is actually ignorant, lazy, and deceitful, for instance—would be to miss the point that fascism happens when people willingly suspend disbelief in fraudulence and that, in fact, it is precisely with such fraudulence that they identify. The trait-of-identification between O and her supporters is the glossy surface image of a righteous "person of color" who, *simply by being (herself), simply by making loud proclamations against the West at all times,* brings justice to everyone who has suffered under Western imperialism. Since the identification is precisely with this truth/illusion about O—that she simply *is,* without work or effort—debunking it would reinforce rather than destroy O's appeal.[46] Fascism here is the force of an "in spite of" turning into a "precisely because": in spite of the fact that the emperor has no clothes on, people see him as the opposite: precisely because he has no clothes on, people *themselves* provide the vision that makes up for this lack. In this vision, an impostor like O looms with irresistible charm, as an angel of light. For those who love her with benevolence, O is a cipher, an automaton performing the predictable notions of the "third world" intellectual *they* desire.

This "story of O" is but one among many that characterize the "politically correct" atmosphere of the North American academy of the 1990s. In using the term "politically correct," what I intend is not the kind of conservative, rightwing bashing of how the academy has gone to hell with feminism, cultural pluralism, multidisciplinarity, and their like, but rather the phrase's original sense of a criticism of our own moral self-righteousness gone haywire. In this original sense, "political correctness" is a machinery of surveillance that encourages certain kinds of exhibitionism. To borrow from Elsaesser's study of Fassbinder, we may say that "in the face of a bureaucratic surveillance system ever more ubiquitous," the O's of the academy, like the German middle-class citizens in Fassbinder's films, take on "an act of terrorist exhibitionism which turns the machinery of surveillance . . . into an occasion for self-display."[47]

As a "person of color" from the "third world," as a student doing a project about lower classes in the "third world," O occupies a number of positions that are currently considered, in an *a priori* manner, as "other" and "marginalized." But are such positions alone, especially when they are self-consciously adopted and promoted simply in order to draw attention and in place of hard work, a genuine contribution to change? Does "otherness" itself automatically suffice as critical intervention? By subscribing to the "evidence of experience" as embodied by the likes of O, those who support "peoples of color" insult the latter a second time: this time peoples of color are not being colonized territorially and ideologically; rather they are uniformly branded as the "virtuous other" regardless of their own class, gender, race, and other differences, and are thus, to cite Edward Said, Orientalized all over again. To put all this in blunter terms, we can draw an analogy between what is happening to O and the much criticized white fantasy about the "sexuality" of, say, black people. According to this fantasy, the black man or woman simply *is* sex, primitive rhythm, unrepressed nature, and so forth. To this wish list we may now add "the oppressed," "revolution," and "political correctness" as well.[48]

The machines of surveillance here are not war airplanes but the media—the networks of communication, which, in the academic world, include the classroom, conferences, publications, funding agencies, and even letters of recommendation. With the large number of students (rightly) eager for alternative histories, of academic conferences (rightly) devoted to the constructions of differences, and of publishers (rightly) seeking to publish new, unexplored materials, fascism has reasserted itself in our era. And, as even my brief discussion shows, fascism's new mode is very much complicated by postcoloniality. The question facing intellectuals in the contemporary West is how to deal with peoples who were once colonized and who are now living and working in the "first world" as "others."[49] In the early days of colonialism, when actual territorial conquests were made and relocation from the "mother country" to the colonies was a fact of life for those from what eventually came to be called the "first world," the questions for white people finding themselves removed from home were questions of what Nancy Armstrong and Leonard Tennenhouse call "the imaginary puritan": how to preserve whiteness while in the brown and black colonies? How to stay English in America? How to fabricate a respectable national origin against the onslaught of barbaric natives—that is, how to posture as the invaded and colonized while invading and colonizing others? All in all, these questions amount to: how *not* to "go native"?[50] As Armstrong and Tennenhouse argue, the English novel, which was conceptually based not so much on previous cultural developments in Europe but rather on the captivity narratives that found their way back to Europe from the "New World," bears symptoms of this white anxiety about cultural purity. In this sense, the English novel is perhaps the earliest example—to use Fredric Jameson's classic pronouncement on "third world" literature—of a "national allegory."

Toward the end of the twentieth century, as the aftermath of the grand imperialist eras brings about major physical migrations of populations around the globe, it is no longer a question of white people going to the colonies, but rather of formerly colonized peoples settling permanently in their former colonizers' territories. The visible presence of these formerly colonized peoples in the "first world" leads to violent upheavals in "Western thought." The overriding preoccupation among first world intellectuals has now become: how to become "other"? How to claim to be a minority—to claim to be black, Native American, Hispanic, or Asian, even if one has only 1/64th share of these "other" origins? In other words, *how to "go native"?* Instead of imagining themselves to be a Pamela or Clarissa being held captive, resisting rape, and writing volumes in order to preserve the purity of their souls (and thus their "origins"),[51] first world intellectuals are now overtaken by a new kind of desire: "Make me other!" And so, with expediency, we witness the publication of essays which are studded with names of nations and territories in order to convey a profile of "cosmopolitanism"; journals which amass the most superficial materials about lesser known cultures and ethnicities in the name of being "public," "global," or "transnational"; and book series which (en)list "indigenous" histories and narratives in the manner of a world fair—all this, while so-called "postcolonial" criticisms of former European imperialist strategies of representing, objectifying, and exhibiting "the other" are going on.

If there is one thing that unites the early territorial colonialism and the contemporary white liberalist intellectual trends that I am describing, it is the notion of a clear demarcation between "self" and "other," between "us" and "them"—a demarcation that is mediated through the relations between consciousness and captivity. The myth, in the days of territorial colonialism, was that (white) consciousness had to be established in resistance to captivity—even while whites were holding other peoples and lands captive—so that (white) cultural origins could be kept pure. In the postcolonial era, by contrast, the myth is that (white) consciousness must itself "surrender to" or be "held captive by" the other—that (white) consciousness is nothing without this captivity called "otherness." In both cases, however, *what remains constant is the belief that "we" are not "them," and that "white" is not "other."* This belief, which can be further encapsulated as *"we are not other,"* is fascism *par excellence.*

Emerging in postcoloniality, the new "desire for our others" displays the same positive, projectional symptoms of fascism that I discussed in the preceding pages—a rebelliousness and a monstrous aesthetics, but most of all a longing for a transparent, idealized image and an identifying submission to such an image. Like the masses' embrace of a Hitler or a Mussolini, this fascism seeks empowerment through a surrender to the other as film—as the film that overcomes me in the spell of an unmediated "experience." The *indiscriminate* embrace of the peoples of color as "correct" regardless of their differences and histories is ultimately the desire for a pure-otherness-in-pristine-luminosity that is as dangerous as the fascism of hateful *discrimination* from which we all suppose we are safely distanced. The genealogical affinity of these two fascisms is perhaps best exemplified by the art of a Leni Riefenstahl, who progressed from embracing Nazi racism to embracing the beautiful Nuba men of the southern Sudan.[52]

If the controversial label "fascism" is indeed useful, as I think it is, for a radical critique of the contemporary intellectual culture in the West, it is because it helps us identify and problematize the good conscience and noble obligations of the new liberal fascism with its multiculturalist modes and its sophisticated enterprises of visibility. Some will no doubt want to disavow such ongoing fascist longings in our midst; others, hopefully, will not.[53]

THREE

Ethics after Idealism

---

*This chapter was originally written as a review of
the works of Gayatri Chakravorty Spivak and
Slavoj Žižek.*[1]

The Formalism of Negativity

GAYATRI CHAKRAVORTY SPIVAK and Slavoj Žižek are two of our most
energetic post-Marxist writers today. Both draw significantly on Marx
—in particular on Marx's analysis of the commodity—for their work
and both are concerned with the question of justice. In each case, we
find a rigorous formalism that derives its force from negativity. What
makes the juxtaposition of these two writers interesting is a basic antagonism that persists beyond what they have in common, while this
antagonism is at the same time the indicator of their equally compelling ethics. I want first to recapitulate important points of their arguments in order to foreground the analytic energy at play.

In the two long essays on Marx ("SSQV" and "SRM") as well as in
many of the conversations that make up *The Post-Colonial Critic* (PCC),
Spivak refocuses the attention of *cultural* politics on "value" and in
particular on the hitherto precluded "use value." Her reasons for doing
so are complex but justified: in the discursivist climate of "cultural
studies," economics has been too easily written off as "economic reductionism." This dismissal of the economic text is part of the old binary
opposition between "economics" and "culture," an opposition that is
so deeply entrenched that any attempt to reopen the "economic" question runs the risk of being mistaken for an embarrassing instance of
economic determinism. So why is it so important *not* to let go of this

question? One explanation is that the "economic" occupies a place in Spivak's reading that is similar to "center" in Jacques Derrida.

In contemporary poststructuralist critiques of Marx, what often happens is a rewriting of value as exchange value and exchange value alone. A notable example is the early work of Jean Baudrillard. In texts such as *For a Critique of the Political Economy of the Sign* and *The Mirror of Production*, Baudrillard's thesis is basically that, although Marx introduced the importance of exchange value, he nevertheless fell into the trap of (re)privileging "use" as what authenticates value. For Baudrillard, such a (re)privileging is the sign of an essentialism that lies at the heart of Western society's productionism, a productionism that Marxism further intensifies.[2] However, the sweeping dismissal of "the West" that Baudrillard makes as a consequence of this thesis, a dismissal that was typical of the generation of avant-garde intellectuals writing in France in the late 1960s and early 1970s, did not make him any less Orientalist or less imperialist in his approach to non-Western ("primitive") cultures. Even though his critique of "use value" remains theoretically pertinent, Baudrillard has not succeeded in providing any genuine alternative to the problems he describes. At the other extreme, we find Jean-Joseph Goux's attempt to account for the rise of money in "polysymbolic" ways. Goux's *Symbolic Economies after Freud and Marx* offers an understanding of the successful evolution of the general equivalent that is progressivist and respectably academic. Unlike Baudrillard, who *denounces* the West as a result of a similar kind of understanding, Goux *rationalizes* it by giving the ascendency of money the systematicity and inevitability of a philosophical tradition.[3] Spivak astutely calls Goux's type of account "continuist" ("SSQV," p. 155 ff.).

So how should that "slight, contentless thing" (Marx's way of describing value) be theorized? While we must, if we follow Marx, accept "value" as an index of "labor," Spivak objects to the view that value is simply labor's "representation." She maintains that to think of value in these terms is to relativize it—to analogize it with narrative, metaphor, language, etc., and thus to disavow its irreducible materiality. Such relativizing of value is mere postmodernist "culturalism" ("SSQV," p. 168). Spivak's alternative comes from Derrida, whom together with Jacques Lacan I shall take as the two major clichés—commonplaces—that structure the writings of the two authors under review.

Taking from Derrida's notion of writing as *différance*, Spivak concentrates on value not as the representation (i.e., completed replication) of labor but as difference:

> [T]he basic premise of the recent critique of the labor theory of value is predicated on the assumption that, according to Marx, Value represents Labor.

> Yet the definition of Value in Marx establishes itself not only as a representation but also as a differential. What is represented or represents itself in the commodity-differential is Value.... ("SSQV," p. 158)

"Value," in other words, functions in the same enigmatic manner as "writing." While it is supposed to be secondary (since it occurs as a result of labor, as writing is thought to occur after "natural" language—speech), it seems shamelessly usurping: it acts as a primary determinant, an agent that creates and stabilizes value/worth. Like writing also, value poses the question about origins: does the value/worth of value come from what "precedes" it, namely, labor, or does it come from itself? Isn't it scandalous to assume that value is self-originating when, supposedly, labor is? And yet we cannot think (labor) without thinking in value . . . and so on. Reading Marx after reading Derrida, Spivak is thus able to force a heterogeneous and improper "economic text" to emerge: like writing, money is both outside and inside ("SSQV," p. 162); its value comes from its being *inside* circulation/exchange, but in order to own it you have to take it *outside* circulation. It is both "Culture" (the agent of capitalism, the general equivalent overriding all others) and "Nature" (what is "originally" there), and it violates the clean conceptual boundary between the two.

The return of value to this originary openness is what Spivak calls the "insertion into textuality" of the economic. It is not to be confused with economic determinism, which it resembles simply because it refuses to let go of the significance of the economic "text." Not letting go of the economic means not accepting the privileging of one term over the other in the binary opposition between economic and cultural, and thus not accepting the happy stability of either economism and culturalism (the latter being merely an inverted version of economism). Economic/use value is therefore the equivalent to "center" in Derrida's philosophizing. It is a function, a catachresis that results from a series of constructions, and, even though we must deconstruct it, we cannot do without it: "Claiming catachreses from a space that one cannot not want to inhabit and yet must criticize is . . . the predicament of the postcolonial."[4]

The foregrounding of value as a problematic—as heterogeneity—enables Spivak to read Marx in a more nuanced way than he has hitherto been read:

> [I]t is in Marx's basic critique of the suppression of heterogeneity that the Derridean analogy is to be found. Derrida's analogy (and indeed all his work, most especially "White Mythology" and *Limited Inc*) discloses that the method of all logic . . . is allied to capitalism: exclusivism, a common mode represented as universal, suppression of heterogeneity. ("SRM," p. 51)

> The method of *Capital*—the title of a book—is the method of capital—
> the value form (as Marx points out) not by special dispensation but
> because making theory has something in common with capitalisation
> (as Derrida points out). ("SRM," p. 56)

What is special about Spivak's reading is not simply that it is nuanced,
but that it is through such nuancing that she returns us to the question
of *social* injustice that was the primary basis of Marx's inquiry. In her
reading, "heterogeneity" becomes a criticism not only of economic
and/or cultural reductionism but also of philosophy's demand for
purity. It is only when we give up the impulse to be philosophically
pure, she writes, that we can see the point Marx is making about the
social injustice brought about by capitalism, because there is nothing
in this injustice itself which is philosophically problematic:

> Marx questions philosophical "justice" and "elegance" (and neces-
> sity) even as he uses them to establish his analysis. Otherwise Marx
> could not write of the extraction of surplus-value, the condition of
> possibility of capitalist exploitation: "This circumstance is a piece of
> good luck for the buyer [of labour-power: the capitalist], but by no
> means an injustice towards the seller [of labour-power: the worker]"
> *Capital* 301). A purely *philosophical* justification for revolutionary prac-
> tice cannot be found.
>
> It is because this heterogeneous concatenation of "knowing" and
> "doing", this possibility of a radical critique of philosophical justice,
> is most often recuperated within a reading *in terms of* philosophical
> justice and consistency, that the deconstructive moment in Marx
> is seen as a blind condemnation of what, according to Marx's
> own system, is philosophically just. ("SRM," p. 50; emphases in the
> original)

The interest of this reading of Marx is that there is something philosophy cannot account for, no matter how "consistent" it is—or precisely
because it is so "consistent." This something is the asymmetry between
capital and labor, the accounts of which have to be settled outside the
bounds of philosophy's sense of justice. In this regard, "Marx's use
of the word 'value' may be seen as catachrestical to the philosophical
usage."[5]

While Spivak reads the asymmetry between capital and labor as
catachrestical *différance*—the excess that is "outside" the system and
that at the same time keeps it functioning, Žižek, following Lacan
rather than Derrida, calls this asymmetry the "symptom" invented by
Marx. This is the way Žižek describes it in *The Sublime Object of Ideology*
(SOI):

> How, then, can we define the Marxian symptom? Marx "invented the
> symptom" (Lacan) by means of detecting a certain fissure, an asym-

metry, a certain "pathological" imbalance which belies the universalism of the bourgeois "rights and duties." This imbalance, far from announcing the "imperfect realization" of these universal principles—that is, an insufficiency to be abolished by further development—functions as their constitutive moment: the "symptom" is, strictly speaking, a particular element which subverts its own universal foundation, a species subverting its own genus. In this sense, we can say that the elementary Marxian procedure of "criticism of ideology" is already "symptomatic": it consists in detecting a point of breakdown *heterogeneous* to a given ideological field and at the same time *necessary* for that field to achieve its closure, its accomplished form. (SOI, p. 21; emphases in the original)

While Spivak would focus on the question of value—the place where the fissure and heterogeneity of the "equation"/"equivalence" between capital and labor occurs—Žižek too would return the "symptom" to the way Marx analyzes the commodity. Žižek's reference here is Alfred Sohn-Rethel, who argues in *Intellectual and Manual Labour: A Critique of Epistemology* that the groundbreaking point made by Marx with regard to commodities is that abstraction is located not in human minds but in the social relations conducted between human beings through the commodity.[6] Sohn-Rethel's point, however, is not that the commodity "conceals" the social exchange between men, but that the exchange is possible only with a certain non-knowledge, non-awareness. It is the action of exchange itself that is abstract. Sohn-Rethel thus not only overthrows the idealist assumption that mental activities are "abstract" but also the materialist assumption that actions are "concrete." Instead, real abstraction has nothing to do with what we assume to be "inner" or mental reality. As Žižek puts it: "the abstraction appertaining to the act of exchange is in an irreducible way external, decentred" (SOI, p. 19).

Belaboring this point about abstraction is part of Žižek's effort to put across the thesis of his book, that there is a kind of abstraction/materiality which is neither simply mind nor simply matter, but which is a "sublime object." Using money as his primary example, Žižek writes in a way that reminds us of Saussure's description of language:[7]

> [W]e have touched a problem unsolved by Marx, that of the *material* character of money: not of the empirical, material stuff money is made of, but of the *sublime* material, of that other "indestructible and immutable" body which persists beyond the corruption of the body physical. . . . This immaterial corporeality of the "body within the body" gives us a precise definition of the sublime object. (SOI, p. 18; emphases in the original)

Beginning with Marx's analysis of money, then, both Žižek and Spivak concentrate on that asymmetrical situation between the supposedly reciprocal exchange between labor and capital and both point to surplus value as the "origin" of the social (the social as exploitation or the social as symptom). But while Spivak would go on from here to deconstruct value, i.e., to return value to *différance*, to emphasize the indispensability of "use value" as a "master word," and to critique this indispensability, Žižek would concentrate on surplus itself as the locus of the impossible encounter between rationality and trauma.

To paraphrase Žižek, we may say that there is a traumatic kernel (the Real) which we cannot comprehend, but this non-comprehension is also what enables us to function. The negativity of this "kernel"—negative because we do not and cannot know it—is what gives our life its positive consistency (our ability to make sense of the world). Survival means a non-knowledge of the "Real"; conversely, knowing is lethal. This non-knowledge-cum-living-well is our symptom: it is at once what sustains us and what (potentially) can destroy us. The symptom itself might be a nauseous, verminous open wound such as the one growing luxuriantly on the child's body in Kafka's "A Country Doctor" (SOI, p. 76), but it's also probably all you have—it's what makes you "you," what is "in you more than yourself."

His elegant style notwithstanding, Žižek's message hits home primarily because of his repetitiveness and his at times dogmatic insistence on the force of "negativity." Whether he is reading literature, film, jokes, comics, science fiction, philosophy, or anything else, Žižek is seldom interested in the problem of aesthetic form and its relation to (the construction of) subjectivity as such. Rather, he is always looking for the moment when the symptom erupts, when the paradox reveals itself. Neither is he interested in the distinction between the individual and the social: the working of the symptom applies to individual organisms and collective bodies alike. This is why he describes the functioning of capitalism in the same terms he would describe individual consciousness:

> [T]he evolutionist reading of the formula of capital as its own limit is inadequate: the point is not that, at a certain moment of its development, the frame of the relation of production starts to constrict further development of the productive forces; the point is that *it is this very immanent limit, this "internal contradiction", which drives capitalism into permanent development.* (SOI, p. 52; emphasis in the original)

By contrast, Spivak is concerned with subjectivity (which she sometimes calls "soul-making") in relation to its various forms of collective predication (e.g., philosophical, historiographic, literary, aesthetic, and economic). The rough and unfinished quality of her rhetorical style is the sign of an impatience with deliberate conceptual refinement or coherence of any kind. This impatience stems from the old-fashioned Marxist view that the social rather than the personal is the place of struggle.

The Roles of Error

This recapitulation of the formalisms of Spivak and Žižek allows us to approach a major question in their texts, namely, the roles of "error." For Žižek it is simple: error is not a problem. In his texts we often find a kind of defense of the *truthful* role of error and of deception. Among his favorite stories about lying is the Freudian joke often quoted by Lacan, in which a Jew reproaches his friend: "Why are you telling me that you are going to Cracow and not to Lemberg, when you're really going to Cracow?" (SOI, p. 197). The Lacanian point is that we are so deeply ingrained in the belief that "truth" is something hidden, that even when it is frankly displayed in front of us, we will take it as a lie. Because of our *perverse* relation to truth—i.e., our tendency to believe only in the "truth" *we* have a hand (consciousness) in establishing—there is little need for us to "expose" errors deliberately. Instead, we should trust that truth will always reveal itself through (the distortions of) human language/behavior, while deliberate exposure of error may often do no more than hide and distort the truth further. For Žižek, it is through that "surplus," that extra something which is not consciously calculable and which works as a limit from within (an organism and a system), that truth "unveils" itself.

For Spivak it is not so simple. Her relation to error is more contradictory. ("I don't have a problem with something being a contradiction. I think contradictions can be productive" [PCC, p. 127].) On the one hand, she sounds like Žižek when she insists that deconstruction is *not* ideology-critique, that is, it is not interested in the exposure of error:

> The problem with the idea of deconstruction as a form of ideology-critique is that deconstruction is not really interested in the exposure of error. . . . Derrida is interested in how truth is constructed rather than in exposing error. . . . Deconstruction can only speak in the language of the thing it criticises. So as Derrida says, it falls prey to its own critique, *in a certain way.* That makes it very different from ideology-critique. (PCC, p. 135; emphasis in the original)

Indeed, in the writings of proper deconstructionists like Paul de Man, it is the errors—the misreadings, the aporias, and the failures—that are language's most truthful revelations. And yet if deconstruction is, as Spivak says, not interested in the exposure of error, from where does her ethical charge come? The burden that Spivak places on deconstruction—not that of reifying the text but that of producing difference and thus alternative histories, such as those of women and the oppressed in the "third world"—is often indistinguishable from the burden of a critical awareness and a permanent wakefulness. Her frequent use of the word "vigilance" warns that the critic must always be on the alert, especially against her own (privileged) slippages. In spite of Spivak's disclaimers, thus, her use of deconstruction can indeed be seen as a form of ideology-critique (as, for instance, the critique of "first world" imperialism) that is in keeping with the reconstructive and reinventive spirit of the Enlightenment.[8] *There is nothing wrong with such a use*, but there is a problem. The problem is that, caught between the deconstructive demand to be nuanced with regard to textual heterogeneity (a demand that is negative in force because such is the force of language) and the rationalist demand to be "vigilant" to "errors" committed exploitatively against the disenfranchised, Spivak's writing must become more and more "self-conscious"—self-referential and self-subverting at once—even as, ironically, some of her readers charge her for being too theoretical and elitist (i.e., deconstructionist) while others criticize her for being heavy-handed (i.e., not paying enough attention to the fine turns of philosophical texts).

The problem indicated by Spivak's contradiction (a contradiction for which she is not personally responsible but which the intensities of her readings exemplify) is succinctly described by Žižek in what he considers to be the problem of poststructuralism. (However, it is important to remember that Žižek makes no distinctions among terms such as "poststructuralism," "deconstruction," and "discourse analysis.") Žižek thinks that the problem of poststructuralism springs from its (excessively) painstaking scrutiny of language. While poststructuralism denies that there is something called "metalanguage"—that is, a language which takes another language as its object, thus making itself the mastering subject—it nonetheless continues to speak *as one* (since this is the way language operates). And yet, precisely because of this denial of metalanguage (a "master narrative"), the poststructuralist "subject" must *also* speak as if it is fully conscious of itself, of its "position," of its limits—hence the endless self-referential digressions, qualifications, apologies, anticipations of criticisms, and so on. What Žižek advocates, therefore, is that no matter how self-conscious (that is, responsible) we try to sound, we will always be speaking in the metalinguistic mode about others as objects. The flip side of this is that we cannot completely control how our language would sound, nor can we always anticipate and thus outsmart the criticisms of others:

> [T]he only way to avoid the Real is to produce an utterance of pure metalanguage which, by its patent absurdity, materializes its own impossibility: that is, a paradoxical element which, in its very identity, embodies absolute otherness, the irreparable gap that makes it impossible to occupy a metalanguage position. (SOI, p. 156)

Interestingly, this is also Spivak's attitude toward language. Despite her "error-exposing" tendency, Spivak's *other* point is precisely that we need from time to time to risk essentialism. In no way can we

absolutely avoid making "essentialist" or "universalist" statements
(i.e., avoid talking metalinguistically), because "universalisation, final-
isation, is an irreducible moment in any discourse" (PCC, p. 11). Moreover, the ability to talk essentialistically, precisely because it ignores the
puritanical demand of theory, can be politically useful:

> You pick up the universal that will give you the power to fight against
> the other side, and what you are throwing away by doing that is your
> theoretical purity. Whereas the great custodians of the anti-universal
> are obliged therefore simply to act in the interest of a great narrative,
> the narrative of exploitation, while they keep themselves clean by not
> committing themselves to anything. In fact they are actually run by
> a great narrative even as they are busy protecting their theoretical
> purity by repudiating essentialism. (PCC, p. 12)

This fearlessness vis-à-vis speaking "the universal"—a fearlessness
that is firmly grounded in an understanding of the dangers of essentialism and metalanguage—is one of the most crucial traits in both Spivak's
and Žižek's ethics. Both are, in the sense described by Marx, ruthless.[9]

The Critique of Idealism

Beneath the jokes and anecdotes in Žižek's book is a consistent
critique of idealism. Two senses of the word "idealism" are important
here: (1) idealism as in idealist philosophy, which holds that the object
of external perception consists of ideas (Marx's critique of German
idealism, for instance, is that it privileges the mind); (2) idealism as the
act of idealizing—of envisioning and asserting goodness and perfec-
tion in the thing or person perceived. While the first of these senses
is familiar to those who know Marx and Marxist criticism, it is, I think,
the second sense of idealism that makes Žižek's work a timely response
to the cultural politics of the post-Marxist world. We can define this
response in the same terms that Žižek uses to describe Ernesto Laclau
and Chantal Mouffe's *Hegemony and Socialist Strategy*:[10] as a "political
project based on an ethics of the real . . . , an ethics of confrontation with
an impossible, traumatic kernel not covered by any *ideal* (of the unbro-
ken communication, of the invention of the self)."[11]

It would be impossible to understand this criticism of idealism-as-
idealization without coming to terms with the distinction Žižek makes
between imaginary and symbolic "identification."[12] Imaginary identification is identification with the image, or identification based on an
imagined resemblance with the image that can be seen. Symbolic identification, on the other hand, is identification with the gaze, with the
place from which we appear in a certain way—likeable or contempt-

ible—to ourselves. Because it does not rely on imagistic resemblance, the significance of symbolic identification is often neglected. For Žižek, however, symbolic identification is the more profound of the two. The distinction between symbolic and imaginary identification leads him to call authors such as Dickens, who wrote about the common people in an idealized form, false:

> [W]e find the Dickensian admiration of the "good common people", the imaginary identification with their poor but happy, close, un-spoiled world, free of the cruel struggle for power and money. But (and therein lies the falsity of Dickens) from where is the Dickensian gaze peering at the "good common people" so that they appear like-able; from where if not from the point of view of the corrupted world of power and money? (SOI, p. 107)[13]

Žižek's point is that the truth reveals itself negatively, *not* in the visible picture or image of Dickens's discourse, but in the place where there is no image, the place from which such "good" images of the common people are seen. This is the place of those who need to legitimize their domination and exploitation of others, those who disguise their ag-gressivity through the active invocation of a positive image that be-comes, for Žižek, the symptom, the excess, the secret enjoyment of their lives.

Another example of Žižek's way of problematizing identification is his interpretation of Judas. For Žižek, Judas, "the bad guy," is the real tragic hero in the Jesus story because he is the negative limit necessary for the Jesus character to unfold in its positivity. Without Judas's "be-trayal," the Jesus story could not be told. And Judas's sacrifice is pure: unlike Jesus, who gets to stay on in our hearts as the hero who saves us from our sins, Judas does not receive an afterlife. Judas dies twice—first physically and then symbolically, as the traitor in the grand narrative of Christianity. We only identify with the good image—Jesus—whom we are supposed to emulate.[14]

Žižek's critique of idealism as idealization does not pertain only to writers and artists like Dickens and Brueghel nor only to Christianity, but also to totalitarianism. The ingenuity of Žižek's critique lies in the way it speaks equally compellingly to the operational fantasies of com-munist regimes as it does to that of "democratic" ones. Moving charac-teristically back and forth between the "symptoms" of the religious and the secularized worlds, Žižek draws parallels between them such as the following, in which Judas in the Jesus story is likened to the victims forced to confess to their "crimes" under Stalin:

> Jesus used Judas as a means to attain his goal, knowing very well that his own suffering would be transformed into a model imitated by millions (*imitatio Christi*), while Judas's sacrifice is a pure loss without

any narcissistic benefit. Perhaps he is a little like the faithful victims of the Stalinist monster trials who confessed their guilt, proclaimed themselves miserable scum, knowing that by so doing they were accomplishing the last and highest service to the Cause of the Revolution. (SOI, p. 128)[15]

A subtitle of Žižek's book could have been something like "an analysis of fascism from Church to Party." The most obvious criticism of fascism in the book is, of course, his analysis of anti-Semitic discourse, in which the "Jew" is evil personified. (I will return to this in the last section.) Equally important, however, are his countless jokes, comments, and anecdotes about what was traditionally fascism's opposite—communism. In a way that would certainly make leftist intellectuals in the liberal West squirm (since the criticism of fascism often means, for such intellectuals, an affirmation of communism), Žižek's text gives us example after example of the absurdity of totalitarian regimes that reign under the name of Marx and the common good, as for instance the Yugoslav student who was ordered to sign a free oath (SOI, p. 165), Rosa Luxemburg's description of the revolutionary process (SOI, p. 84), and the invincible Stalinist Communist who operates with the same fantasy logic as the cat in the Tom and Jerry cartoons ("a cat whose head is blown up by a dynamite and who, in the next scene, proceeds intact his pursuit [*sic*] of his class enemy, the mouse") (SOI, p. 145).

Totalitarianism suits Žižek's critique of idealism more aptly than it suits anti-Semitism, not only because it relies on positive images, but also because it relies on *the image as positivistic evidence* for its manipulation. Typical of totalitarian rule's self-representation and self-legitimation is a kind of language, verbal or visual, which proclaims/presents a noble, respectable idea/image of "the people." The point of this kind of language is to seduce—to divert attention away from the rulers' violence and aggressivity at the same time that sympathy/empathy with the good idea/image is aroused. Totalitarianism thus exemplifies the problematic of privileging imaginary identification that for Žižek lies at the heart of idealism. This idealism functions as if the *conscious* level of articulation/representation is all there is: We say/show this (good image), therefore we are this (good). The success of such idealism comes from the collaboration of those who spontaneously identify with the things they consciously hear/see.

Naming

As Žižek understands it, totalitarianism is not an anomaly but rather the most palpable instance of the way ideology works in the secularized modern world: "the case of so-called 'totalitarianism' demonstrates what applies to every ideology, to ideology as such: the last support of the ideological effect (of the way an ideological network of signifiers 'holds' us) is the non-sensical, pre-ideological kernel of enjoyment" (SOI, p. 124). The closeness between Žižek's and Althusser's understanding of ideology—a closeness that has its roots in Lacan—is unmistakable. Like Althusser, Žižek explains the "interpellation" of the subject through Pascal, who is for both a major reference in thinking about Marxism. Althusser puts it this way:

> [We] are indebted to Pascal's defensive "dialectic" for the wonderful formula which will enable us to invert the order of the notional schema of ideology. Pascal says more or less: "Kneel down, move your lips in prayer, and you will believe." He thus scandalously inverts the order of things. . . .
> . . . where only a single subject (such and such an individual) is concerned, the existence of the ideas of his belief is material in that *his ideas are his material actions inserted into material practices governed by material rituals which are themselves defined by the material apparatus from which derive the ideas of that subject.*[16]

The point of what Žižek calls the Pascalian-Marxist argument is this: even if I cannot prove that there is a God/Great Leader, my (material) acting *as if* there were one would give me great practical benefits. I pray, then I believe; I support the Great Party Leader, then he exists. The submissive practices of the believers—what Althusser refers to as "material"—are what authenticate the "idea" of the Leader. Hence, Žižek writes,

> it is as if the totalitarian Leader is addressing his subjects and legitimizing his power precisely by referring to the . . . Pascalian-Marxian argument—that is, revealing to them the secret of the classical Master; basically, he is saying to them: "I'm your Master because you treat me as your Master; it is you, with your activity, who make me your Master!" (SOI, p. 146)

Žižek goes further: this "People" on which the Leader bases his power does not really exist except in the form of a fetish, the fetish precisely of the Party and its Leader. In other words, totalitarianism functions in the form of a kind of circular definition of "the People": "in the Stalinist universe, 'supporting the rule of the Party' is 'rigidly designated' by the term 'People'—it is, in the last analysis, *the only feature which in all possible worlds defines the People*" (SOI, p. 147; emphasis in the original).

But if Žižek's argument resembles Althusser's up to this point, he also parts company with Althusser in that he is not primarily interested in the subject. For Žižek, the subject's ideological interpellation is simply a way of illustrating something else—the surplus he calls "desire." How does he arrive at desire?

In the phrase "the People always support the Party," the word "support" operates linguistically as well as symbolically. Besides the meaning of upholding a ruler, "support" is also synonymous with the "rigid designator," the term Žižek takes from antidescriptivist philosophy to refer to that act of *naming* which depends for its authentication on something more than the objective properties of the thing named. Using Saul Kripke's arguments in *Naming and Necessity*,[17] Žižek explains the traditional division between the descriptivists and antidescriptivists as follows: while descriptivists regard "names" as referring to the immanent meanings of things, antidescriptivists regard "names" as referring to an external causal link, which allows things to be transmitted from subject to subject (SOI, p. 90). Žižek sides with the antidescriptivists not because he thinks they are entirely right but because their theory contains "libidinal" implications (SOI, p. 91). Although Kripke does not deal with affect as such, his understanding of naming as *more than* a straightforward correspondence between name and thing is a sign that there is more involved in naming than pure designation. This "more" is what Žižek calls "desire."

The introduction of desire in the act of naming enables Žižek to make what I think is his most important argument, which is that naming, an act that is radically contingent, is a *retroactive constitution of identity*. Naming constitutes (a thing's or a person's) identity, beyond ever-changing descriptive features, *backward in time*. This point about naming is the point at which all of Žižek's arguments come together:

First, we can now say that the "traumatic kernel," "surplus enjoyment," "excess," and "symptom" correspond to the name/designator/determinant that, while being entirely arbitrary and contingent (that is, nothing), nonetheless *stabilizes* and constitutes identity in a (chronologically) retroactive and/or (spatially) extimate fashion. ("L'extimité"—external intimacy—was a term coined by Jacques-Alain Miller.)

Second, the "name" is that *objet petit a* which, while enabling the subject to enter the symbolic (by taking something from him, by "barring" or crossing him), remains afield, afloat, accidental. Rather than the object catching the name, it is the name that catches (the object) and makes "it" an object.

Third, the "name" is also that visible, material practice/behavior that confers meaning on *nothing;* it is the act of praying that makes me believe; it is the "People" that "supports" the Party and its Leader.

Finally, the "name" is the sublime object, the "matter" that has a body/materiality other than its physical qualities, a reality that is conjured retroactively—literally, after the act/name.

Furthermore, naming is the place where both Žižek and Spivak attempt to plot an *alternative* ethics. And yet, because of the tricky nature of the problem, it is also the place where the greatest confusion arises.

Žižek, by associating Kripke with Laclau and Mouffe, thinks that Kripke's theory of the "rigid designator" offers a theory similar to Laclau's "anti-essentialism":

> We can now see how the Kripkean theory of "rigid designator"— of a certain pure signifier which designates, and at the same time constitutes, the identity of a given object beyond the variable cluster of its descriptive properties—offers a conceptual apparatus enabling us to conceive precisely the status of Laclau's "anti-essentialism." (SOI, p. 98)

Here, in spite of his dislike for poststructuralism, Žižek talks rather like an antiessentialist poststructuralist, when in fact *his own point*, that the "rigid designator" constitutes the identity of an object beyond its nameable properties, *does not call for dispensing with the name, a kind of "essence," itself*. (This is why he always emphasizes, as does Lacan in his later writings, the importance of the Thing: some form of identity always takes place.) Even though it is impossible in its "designation," the act of "naming" is also, we may say, unavoidable. (We do not have a choice not to name.) That *this*, rather than Laclau and Mouffe's "anti-essentialism," is Žižek's real argument is indicated by the example he often uses, that of the name "democracy." Laclau and Mouffe's point is that while the name "democracy" seems to designate a certain kind of reality, it is impossible to know what democracy *is*. But for Žižek, this does not mean that we should throw out the name, because, as Winston Churchill put it, democracy is our worst possible system, but none of the others is better (SOI, pp. 5; 148).

When it comes to naming, Spivak, a strong advocate of our necessity from time to time to "risk essentialism," also makes odd-sounding statements:

> A deconstructive awareness would insistently be aware that the masterwords are catachreses . . . that there are no literal referents, there are no "true" examples of the "true worker," the "true woman," the "true proletarian." (PCC, p. 104)

> Basically I learned first from de Man and then from Derrida the importance of reading absolutely literally. And of course the word "literally" is like the word "history." Like any master word, it is a catachretical word. (PCC, p. 163)

> The subaltern is all that is not elite, but the trouble with those kinds of names is that if you have any kind of political interest you name it in the hope that the name will disappear. That's what class consciousness is in the interest of: the class disappearing. What politically we want to see is that the name would not be possible. (PCC, p. 158)

As I was saying when you asked me, didn't I ally myself with the subaltern. I said by no means, I noticed myself as a namer of the subaltern. The subaltern is a name as "woman" in Derrida, or "power" in Foucault, and the name comes with an anxiety that if the political program gets anywhere the name will disappear. (PCC, p. 166)

In these passages, names—catachreses or master words—are regarded as merely strained, inadequate expressions; the supposition is that naming would lead to its opposite—the disappearance of the names. This, however, is quite different from the kind of argument Spivak otherwise makes *when she is not specifically talking about naming.* Consider the following passage, for instance:

As Derrida says, and now I am quoting, "Logocentrism is not a pathology," it is the thing that enables us—except, if because it enables us, we say that it is correct, it would be a mistake. That is all he is saying. So that, in fact, all that he looks at is the way in which the subject centers itself. He is not decentering the subject. . . . There is no way that a subject can be anything but centered . . . the fact that the subject is centered begins with that kind of an un-endorsable error. That doesn't mean that the subject can be decentered. There is no such thing as the decentered subject. There is no such thing. (PCC, p. 146)

Isn't the point of this passage that the center is always necessary? Isn't Spivak's argument for risking essentialism that the essentialist moment is the irreducible part of any discourse? And isn't "naming" precisely the centering, the essentializing act? For a deconstructionist, names are not "simply" catachreses; catachreses are not "simply" catachreses:

Whenever someone attempts to put together a "theory of practice" where the intending subject as absolute ground is put into question, catachrestical master-words become necessary, because language can never fully bypass the presupposition of such a ground. The particular word is, in such a case, the best that will serve, but also, and necessarily, a misfit. . . . It must be said, however, that these master-words are misfits only if the ordinary use of language is presupposed to have fully fitting cases.[18]

In other words, since "misfit" is the general condition of all language, catachreses, while embodying this general condition, also perform the additional but indispensable task of posing as the "absolute ground." And yet, in spite of her careful articulations of the way language works, when it comes specifically to naming, Spivak, like Žižek, becomes strangely "antiessentialist," thus letting poststructuralism's discursivism, of which both of them are otherwise so astutely critical, gain the upper hand.

Between Love and the Void

The ambivalence about "naming," it follows, is also an ambivalence about "history." Here Spivak and Žižek embark on completely different journeys.

In a moment when she is defending deconstruction, Spivak criticizes the popular view that deconstruction is decadent and negative, while Marxism is activist and about class struggle (PCC, p. 130). She shows, for instance, how the seeming negativity of Derrida's critique of anthropomorphism can in fact lead one back into history:

> When Derrida criticized Sartre's anthropomorphic re-reading of Heidegger, that critique of anthropomorphism was picked up in two ways, and over the last almost twenty years, we've seen it going in two directions within the deconstructive establishment. One has been for the critic to say, "Do not look in it for a *human* story, but rather for the text's constitution of its own textuality or narrativity." Another, which has been Derrida's track, has been to say: "Look here, it is almost as if the sign, anthropos, has no history." (PCC, p. 53; emphasis in the original)

In other words, either antianthropomorphism can lead to a reification of the text, or it can alert us to the limits of a specifically constructed history and thus to the possibility of other histories. Here, in her most persuasive defense of deconstruction, Spivak reintroduces something that one does not usually associate with it—a (Marxist) humanism for which man is the original subject and object. The deconstruction of human history that Spivak calls for does not depart from the basic belief in humans as animals whose "productive" activity distinguishes them from the rest of the universe. Depending on the type of philosopher, that activity can be construed as "sensuous experience" or "consciousness," as "manual labor" or "intellectual labor," as "agriculture" or "language." But no matter how emphatic it is about the human condition as a "perverse" condition,[19] deconstruction's stern gaze at words—human verbal language—means that it continues to operate within the parameters of a subscription to the primacy of human endeavor, human consciousness, human language, and human history.[20]

It is therefore not an accident that Spivak sees the absolute relevance of deconstruction to the work of the Indian Subaltern Studies historians. As writing, the lives of the subalterns are paradigmatic of the logic of "the dangerous supplement," the sign that not only adds but also substitutes.[21] Even though Spivak must read the Subaltern Studies historians against their grain and demonstrate how, despite their apparently positivistic intention—to restore the voices of the oppressed classes and thus to instigate an alternative history of postcolonial India—these historians are already being thoroughly deconstructive,[22] the affinity between deconstruction and Subaltern historiography is clear once we understand that *the practice of deconstruction itself is potentially humanistic*. The writing of an alternative history from the perspective of the subalterns does not detract from the basic view of humans as the primary creators/producers of value. Rather than alerting us to humans as destructive instead of productive forces, or to the frequent indistinguishability between human productiveness and destructiveness—as would be the case when deconstruction is exercised on issues such as ecological concerns or animal rights—the welding of deconstruction and historiography means that the negativity of deconstruction takes on a positive function. This is how Spivak speaks of Derrida's more recent "affirmative deconstruction": it is a deconstruction that obliges you to "say yes to that which interrupts your project," to the "political" that interrupts "theory" (PCC, p. 47). Most important, affirmative deconstruction enables the continual practice of "history."[23]

Žižek's view of politics and history is decidedly different. He does not give the negativity of his formalism a positive affirmation. Instead, what he affirms is negativity itself—or what he calls, after Laclau and Mouffe, antagonism. For Žižek negativity is an internal limit, a hindrance intrinsic to an organism and its drive. "Positive" social happenings in history are what give shape and form to this *immanent negativity*. Understanding the immanent nature of this negative limit amounts to an ethics that refuses to idealize the reconciliation of social antagonisms and that, instead, accepts their permanence. The ultimately irreducible character of such antagonisms is for Žižek the traumatic Real.

Žižek's insistence on the immanence of negation is a compelling way of critiquing the "excesses" of human history. The paradigmatic case here is anti-Semitism, in which what we cannot afford to admit about ourselves, we personify externally as the "Jew." In this age-old custom of *collective* discrimination, the Jew is the embodiment of whatever we must insist we are not. Like "woman" in Lacan, the Jew is for Žižek the figure of the impossible, the "symptom" of the reflexive determinant that is "man" or "non-Jew." We can add to the list of such "symptoms" the Japanese, the Moslems, patients with AIDS, and so forth. The point is, their "secret" lies in *our* desire not to recognize something about ourselves.

The strength of Žižek's work, then, lies not in his offering us a model with which to think and act, but in his *absolute* (general) attack on *specific* historical instances (anti-Semitism, fascism, totalitarianism). Because his point is not "history" in its specific forms (such as nations, periods, genders, classes, etc.), it would be uselessly tautological to fault him on that count. Instead, his point is a transhistorical one, namely, that there is a lack in the Other. It is transhistorical in the sense that this "lack" is present whenever history (in its specific forms) is present. This is how he puts it:

> Today, it is a commonplace that the Lacanian subject is divided, crossed-out, identical to a lack in a signifying chain. However, the most radical dimension of Lacanian theory lies not in recognizing this fact but in realizing that the big Other, the symbolic order itself, is also *barré*, crossed-out, by a fundamental impossibility, structured around an impossible/traumatic kernel, around a central lack. Without this lack in the Other, the Other would be a closed structure and the only possibility open to the subject would be his radical alienation in the Other. So it is precisely this lack in the Other which enables the subject to achieve a kind of "de-alienation" called by Lacan *separation:* not in the sense that the subject experiences that now he is separated for ever from the object by the barrier of language, but that *the object is separated from the Other itself,* that the Other itself "hasn't got it", hasn't got the final answer—that is to say, is in itself blocked, desiring; that there is also a desire of the Other. This lack in the Other gives the subject—so to speak—a breathing space, it enables him to avoid the total alienation in the signifier not by filling out his lack but by allowing him to identify himself, his own lack, with the lack in the Other. (SOI, p. 122; emphases in the original)

Žižek's is an ethics of limits, which is based on the understanding of the fundamental schism between God and man (and between man and language) as we find it in Judaism:

> [I]s not the Jewish God the purest embodiment of this *"Che vuoi?"*, of the desire of the Other in its terrifying abyss, with the formal prohibition to "make an image of God"—to fill out the gap of the Other's desire with a positive fantasy-scenario? . . . The basic position of a Jewish believer is, then, that of Job: not so much lamentation as incomprehension, perplexity, even horror at what the Other (God) wants with the series of calamities that are being inflicted upon him. (SOI, p. 115)

The "lack" of the Other is not simply a lack in the sense of an empty hole; it is also the impossibility/refusal of answer, the absolute limit that separates us and the Other, making the question *"Che vuoi?"* an unanswerable one. This "lack" of the Other is a question of/about the Other that remains fathomless and untamable, irreconcilable with and indifferent to symbolization, gentrification, or domestication through sacrifice and love as we find it in the dogmatic, missionary versions of institutionalized Christianity.

We may safely say that Žižek is, ultimately, not so much concerned with "history" and "politics" as with human nature. Consider the notion of "antagonism," which he takes over from Laclau and Mouffe, who use it to say "the social doesn't exist." The notion of "antagonism," we must remember, operates ambivalently, both as a negative *charge* and/or as a *voiding*. It is, I think, the latter sense that speaks most closely to Žižek. This is why he emphasizes the distinction between social and radical antagonism:

> We must then distinguish the experience of antagonism in its radical form, as a limit of the social, as the impossibility around which the social field is structured, from antagonism as the relation between antagonistic subject-positions: in Lacanian terms, we must distinguish antagonism as *real* from the social *reality* of the antagonistic fight. And the Lacanian notion of the subject aims precisely at the experience of "pure" antagonism as self-hindering, self-blockage, this internal limit preventing the symbolic field from realizing its full identity: the stake of the entire process of subjectivation, of assuming different subject-positions, is ultimately to enable us to avoid this traumatic experience.[24]

Radical antagonism is the pure Real that cannot be negated:

> [T]he Real is something that cannot be negated, a positive inert datum which is insensitive to negation, cannot be caught in the dialectics of negativity; but we must add at once that it is so because the Real itself, in its positivity, is nothing but an embodiment of a certain void, lack, radical negativity. *It cannot be negated because it is already in itself, in its positivity, nothing but an embodiment of a pure negativity, emptiness.* (SOI, p. 170; emphasis in the original)

To put it another way, the reality of *social* antagonism is only a partial manifestation of radical antagonism. The historical and political events of conflict and struggle are mere fantasies that at once shield the Real and shield (protect) us from it:

> [I]t is not the external enemy who is preventing me from achieving identity with myself, but every identity is already in itself blocked, marked by an impossibility, and *the external enemy is simply the small piece*, the rest of reality upon which we "project" or "externalize" this intrinsic, immanent impossibility.[25]

In ways that remind us of the non-being/nothingness that is often taught in Eastern philosophies such as Buddhism, radical antagonism would thus seem to be the void of social/material life itself. But unlike the case argued by Laclau and Mouffe, "the social doesn't exist" not because the antagonisms persisting among social spheres are multiple and infinite, but because the sentient aspects of human life, the joys and sufferings we inevitably experience as parts of our *social* existence, are themselves illusory.

According to institutional records of Buddhist history, it was precisely by alluding to this basic void of human life that the Chinese monk Hui Neng (better known as Wei Lang, 638–713 c.e.) proved that he had attained the Essence of the Mind. Hui Neng, an illiterate seller of firewood in South China, had travelled far to pay respects to the Fifth Patriarch at the time when the latter was looking for someone to hand over the robe (the insignia of the Patriarchate) and the Dharma (the esoteric teaching of the Dhyana School). The Fifth Patriarch's require-ment was that this person had to have understood the Essence of the Mind. Shen Xiu, one of his outstanding disciples, tried to demonstrate his attainment of spiritual insight by writing the following stanza:

> The body is the Bodhi-tree,
> The mind is the bright mirror-stand.
> Take heed always to wipe it clean,
> So that no dust collects on it.

By drawing an analogy between the material and immaterial aspects of life, Shen Xiu, we might say, establishes an ethics of achieving enlight-enment through active intervention. In spite of Shen Xiu's brilliance, however, the Fifth Patriarch did not consider him to have attained the Essence of the Mind. By contrast, when the commoner Hui Neng unex-pectedly composed his stanza, the Fifth Patriarch knew he had, and made him the Sixth Patriarch. Hui Neng's stanza goes as follows:

> The Bodhi-tree is originally not a tree,
> Nor is the bright mirror originally a stand.
> Since there is originally no-thing,
> From where arises all this dust?[26]

The ethics established by Hui Neng's stanza is that of achieving en-lightenment through recognizing the no-thing-ness of the world rather than through doing something to correct the world's problems. Accord-ing to legend, then, it is Hui Neng's intuitive grasp of our original void that distinguished him from others. We might interpret the point of this story to be that life is beyond all human interventions, including (espe-cially) well-intentioned and morally righteous ones. Hui Neng's stanza ends not with a truth but with a question. Žižek would call this "the eternal philosophical question," to which he thinks Lacan makes a response:

> [I]n the final years of Lacan's teaching we find a kind of universaliza-tion of the symptom: almost everything that is becomes in a way symptom, so that finally even woman is determined as the symptom of man. We can even say that "symptom" is Lacan's final answer to the eternal philosophical question "Why is there something instead of nothing?"—this "something" which "is" instead of nothing is indeed the symptom. (SOI, p. 72)

The symptom, we might say, is the *avoiding of the void* through desire. But as we also learn from the ancients, the void is unavoidable. That is why desire, which is often the desire to possess (things) as such, is always insatiable.

Perhaps it is the perception of the unavoidability of the void—which also means, paradoxically, the eternal return of the symptom—that prompts Spivak to look to history for a possible freedom from the void's tyranny. History here is no longer the master narrative; instead it is *différance*, supplementary writing, and other-ing.[27] History offers, however temporarily, the hope of reconstruction, reinvention, redemption. Hence even though her characteristic move when talking about texts, including the original texts of Marx, is that of voiding—of emphasizing postponement, deferral, failure, non-fulfillment, and "impossibility" ["SSQV," p. 175; "SRM," p. 58]—Spivak's final message is one of an ethical affirmation of the historical and social as the site of struggle against exploitation.

This affirmative ethics leads Spivak to describe her own relation to both deconstruction and Subaltern historiography in terms of love:

> [D]econstruction . . . is the critical moment, the reminder of cata- chresis, the reminder of the politics of the open end, or of the politics of great-narrative, depending on what the moment asks for, the re- minder of the fact that any really "loving" political practice must fall a prey to its own critique. (PCC, p. 111)

> The only things one really deconstructs are things into which one is intimately mired. It speaks you. You speak it. (PCC, p. 135)

> I really read the Subalternists with that kind of love that I was talking about . . . so that some of the opponents of Subaltern Studies in India think of me as a Subalternist; on the other hand the Subalternists realize . . . that I don't endorse everything in their project. (PCC, p. 142)

> This relationship of love, which is the deconstructive relationship— you cannot deconstruct something which is not your own language. (PCC, p. 164)[28]

With equal energy, Žižek would call his relationship to the void/the Real one of "enthusiastic resignation":

> [T]he signifying field is always structured around a certain funda- mental deadlock. This deadlock doesn't entail any kind of resigna- tion—or, if there is a resignation, it is a paradox of the *enthusiastic resignation:* we are using here the term "enthusiasm" in its strict Kantian meaning, as indicating an experience of the object through the very failure of its adequate representation. Enthusiasm and resig- nation are not then two opposed moments: it is the "resignation"

itself, i.e., the experience of a certain impossibility, which incites enthusiasm.[29]

In other words, the apprehension of the world as void does not lead to existentialist angst and revolt, or thereby a new assertion of the meaningfulness of human endeavor. Rather, the void stands as the source of a distinct form of passion, the passion of an indomitable "as if": although defeat is imminent, one goes on enthusiastically as if one doesn't know it—indeed, as if one's entire life force actually comes from this defeat.

Between love and the void, between affirmative deconstruction and enthusiastic resignation, the question is neither one of choice nor of alliance. It is the confrontation of perhaps ultimately incompatible but equally insuppressible logics, whose intensities are, at every juncture, provokingly instructive.

FOUR

The Politics of Admittance: Female Sexual Agency, Miscegenation, and the Formation of Community in Frantz Fanon

> *Male subaltern and historian are . . . united in the common assumption that the procreative sex is a species apart, scarcely if at all to be considered a part of civil society.*
>
> —Gayatri Chakravorty Spivak, "Subaltern Studies: Deconstructing Historiography"

> *Whenever women continue to serve as boundary markers between different national, ethnic and religious collectivities, their emergence as full-fledged citizens will be jeopardized.*
>
> —Deniz Kandiyoti, "Identity and Its Discontents: Women and the Nation"

> *As long as woman is excluded from the community, it is not really* common.
>
> —Mieke Bal, Lethal Love

A LEADING FEATURE that connects the many studies of the black psychiatrist Frantz Fanon since the first publication of his work in the 1950s is undoubtedly the politics of identification. As Henry Louis Gates, Jr.

writes, "Fanon's current fascination for us has something to do with the convergence of the problematic of colonialism with that of subject-formation."[1] Beginning with Jean-Paul Sartre, critics have, when examining Fanon's texts, focused their attention on the psychic vicissitudes of the black man's identity. While Sartre, writing in the heyday of a leftist existentialism, draws attention to those vicissitudes in terms of a third-world nationalism in formation, a collective revolt that could be generalized to become the revolt of the world proletariat,[2] contemporary critics, geared with lessons in poststructuralism, have alternately reformulated those vicissitudes by way of Derridean deconstruction, Lacanian psychoanalysis, and gender politics involving the representations of white women and the issues of homosexuality.[3] If these critics have rightly foregrounded the tortuous ambiguities that inform the politics of identification in the contexts of colonization and postcolonization, their discussions tend nonetheless to slight a fundamental issue—the issue of community formation. Once we put the emphasis on community, it would no longer be sufficient simply to continue the elaboration of the psychic mutabilities of the postcolonial subject alone. Rather, it would be necessary to reintroduce the structural problems of community formation that are always implied in the articulations of the subject, even when they are not explicitly stated as such.

As the etymological associations of the word "community" indicate, community is linked to the articulation of commonality and consensus; a community is always based on a kind of collective inclusion. In the twentieth century the paradigm of ideal community formation has been communism, which is the secular version of a holy communion with a larger Being who is always beyond but with whom man nonetheless seeks communication.[4] At the same time, however, there is no community formation without the implicit understanding of who is and who is not to be admitted. As the principle that regulates community formation, admittance operates in several crucial senses.

There is, first, admittance in the most physical sense of letting enter, as when we say we are admitted to a theater, an auditorium, a school, a country, and so forth. The person who is or is not admitted bears on him or her the marks of a group in articulation. This basic, physical sense of admittance, of being allowed to enter certain spaces, governs a range of hierarchically experienced geographical and spatial divisions in the colonial and postcolonial world, from the segregation of black and white spaces in countries such as the United States and South Africa, to the rules forbidding local people to enter "foreign concessions" in their own land during the heyday of the "scramble" for Africa and China, to the contemporary immigration apparatuses in politically stable nations that aim to expel "illegal immigrants" from such nations' borders. Meanwhile, to "let enter" is, as can be surmised from these examples, closely connected with recognition and acknowledgment, which is the second major connotation of admittance. Admittance in this second sense is a permission to enter in the abstract, through the act that we call validation. To be permitted to enter is then to be recognized as having a similar kind of value as that which is possessed by the admitting community. Third, there is admittance in the sense of a confession—such as the admittance of a crime. Insofar as confession is an act of repentance, a surrender of oneself in reconciliation with the rules of society, it is also related to community.

To this extent, I feel that the work in cultural studies that has followed poststructuralist theory's close attention to issues of identification and subjectivity is both an accomplishment and a setback: an accomplishment, because such work—which I shall call "subject work"—enables the subject to be investigated in ever more nuanced manners across the disciplines, holding utopian promise often by concluding that the subject, be it masculine, feminine, gay, postcolonial, or otherwise, is infinitely "unstable" and therefore open-ended; a setback, because nuanced readings of the subject as such also tend to downplay issues of structural control—of law, sovereignty, and prohibition—that underlie the subject's relation with the collective. Much "subject work" has, in other words, too hastily put its emphasis on the "post" of "poststructuralism," (mis)leading us to think that the force of structure itself is a thing of the past. I believe that these neglected other issues, which are the issues of admittance, pertain even more urgently to the kind of conceptualization of community that begins as a revolt against an existing political condition, such as the condition of colonization. In turning to the texts of Fanon, then, the questions I would like to explore are not questions about the colonized or postcolonized subject per se, but rather: how is community articulated in relation to race and to sexuality? What kinds of admittance do these articulations entail, with what implications?

Race and the Problem of Admittance[5]

Fanon's discussions of the existential dilemmas facing the black man, which he interprets with the explicit purpose of liberating the black man from himself, are well known. From the feelings of "lust" and "envy" that accompany the historically inevitable violence toward the white man in *The Wretched of the Earth*, we move to the picture of an "infernal circle" of shame and longing-for-recognition in *Black Skin, White Masks*:

> I am overdetermined from without, I am the slave not of the "idea" that others have of me but of my own appearance. . . .

> Shame. Shame and self-contempt. Nausea. When people like me,
> they tell me it is in spite of my color. When they dislike me, they point
> out that it is not because of my color. Either way, I am locked into
> the infernal circle. (BSWM, p. 116)

> Man is human only to the extent to which he tries to impose his
> existence on another man in order to be recognized by him. As long as
> he has not been effectively recognized by the other, that other will
> remain the theme of his actions. It is on that other being, on recogni-
> tion by that other being, that his own human worth and reality de-
> pend. It is that other being in whom the meaning of his life is con-
> densed. (BSWM, p. 217)

These compelling passages indicate that for the black man, selfhood
and communal relations are entirely intertwined with skin color and
race. If the forced coexistence with the white man is impossible as a
basis for community, it is because the white man, with his attitudes of
racist superiority, does not *admit* the black man as an equal. Significantly, admittance here operates in the first two senses I mentioned:
first, in the sense of letting enter; second, in the sense of validation and
acknowledgment. The physical sense of admittance connotes in a vivid
manner the process of acceptance by permission, and hence the process
of identification as the successful or failed acquisition of a particular
kind of entry permit. And yet, being "admitted" is never simply a
matter of possessing the right permit, for validation and acknowledgment must also be present for admittance to be complete. The existential burden that weighs on the black man is that he never has admittance in these first two, intimately related senses of the word: his skin
color and race mean that even if he has acquired all the rightful permits
of entry into the white world—by education, for instance—he does not
feel that he is acknowledged as an equal.

For Fanon, the conceptualization of a community alternative to the
colony is thus inseparable from a heightened awareness of race as a
limit of admittance. If the black man is not admitted by the white man
because of his skin color, then this very skin color would now become
the basis of a new community—the basis of entry into and recognition
by the postcolonial nation. But how does race operate as a new type of
admittance ticket, a new communal bond? On close reading, it would
seem that race, in spite of the fact that it is imagined at the revolutionary
moment as the utopian communion among people who suffer the same
discrimination, nonetheless does not escape the problems structural to
all processes of admittance. The issue of admittance—of legitimate
entry and validation—becomes especially acute when we introduce
sexual difference—when we read the different manners in which Fanon
describes the black man and the black woman.

Fanon's analyses of the woman of color are found in a chapter of *Black Skin, White Masks,* the chapter entitled "The Woman of Color and the White Man." The title signals, already, that identification for the woman of color is a matter of exchange relations, a matter of how the woman of color is socially *paired off* or *contracted.* Unlike the black man, who is considered a (wronged) sovereign subject, the woman of color is first of all an object with exchange value. Fanon's views are based in part on his reading of fiction—such as the stories *Je suis Martiniquaise,* by Mayotte Capecia, and *Nini,* by Abdoulaye Sadji—even though it is clear that his reading is intended beyond the "fictional" contexts. Fanon describes the woman of color in terms of her aspiration toward "lactification" and summarizes her "living reactions" to the European in this manner:

> First of all, there are two such women: the Negress and the mulatto. The first has only one possibility and one concern: to turn white. The second wants not only to turn white but also to avoid slipping back. What indeed could be more illogical than a mulatto woman's acceptance of a Negro husband? For it must be understood once and for all that it is a question of saving the race. (BSWM, pp. 54–55)

> For, in a word, the race must be whitened; *every woman* in Martinique knows this, says it, repeats it. Whiten the race, save the race, but not in the sense that one might think: not "preserve the uniqueness of that part of the world in which they grew up," but make sure that it will be white. Every time I have made up my mind to analyze certain kinds of behavior, I have been unable to avoid the consideration of certain nauseating phenomena. The number of sayings, proverbs, petty rules of conduct that govern the choice of a lover in the Antilles is astounding. It is always essential to avoid falling back into the pit of niggerhood, and *every woman* in the Antilles, whether in a casual flirtation or in a serious affair, is determined to select the least black of the men. Sometimes, in order to justify a bad investment, she is compelled to resort to such arguments as this: "X is black, but misery is blacker." I know a great number of girls from Martinique, students in France, who admitted to me with complete candor—completely white candor—that they would find it impossible to marry black men. . . . (BSWM, pp. 47–48; my emphases)

In the light of these extended remarks, Fanon's later remark regarding the woman of color, "I know nothing about her" (BSWM, p. 180), can be taken only as a disclaimer of definitive views that he has, in fact, already pronounced. To this extent, critics who, despite their critical sensitivity, accept Fanon's "I know nothing about her" at face value are simply sidestepping a problem that would interfere with the coherence of their own interpretations. This is the problem of the sexuality of the woman of color, the legitimation and delegitimation of which is crucial to the concept of a postcolonial national community.[6] The predominant impression given by the passages just quoted is that women of color are *all alike:* in spite of the differences in pigmentation between the Negress and the mulatto, for instance, they share a common, "nauseating" trait—the desire to become white—that can be generalized in the form of "every woman." In an account of black subjecthood that is premised on the irreducible (racial) difference between black and white people, thus, Fanon's descriptions of the women of color are paradoxically marked by their non-differentiation, their projection (onto femininity) of qualities of indistinguishability and universality.[7] Before we examine Fanon's descriptions of the sexuality of women more specifically, however, I would like to dwell for a moment on the theoretical linkage between community formation and sexual difference by turning to a classic text about community formation—Sigmund Freud's *Totem and Taboo.*

Community Formation and Sexual Difference:
A Double Theoretical Discourse

In *Totem and Taboo,* Freud offers a theory of community formation that is drawn from anthropological, sociological, and religious studies of "primitive" societies. As is well known, Freud, instead of contradicting the findings of early studies, supports them by focusing on two interrelated aspects of community formation.[8] First, participation in a common bond is achieved through the murder and sacrifice of the primal father, who is afterward venerated and raised to the status of a god, a totem. Second, this bond is secured through the institution of a particular law, the law against incest:

> Thus the brothers had no alternative, if they were to live together, but—not, perhaps, until they had passed through many dangerous crises—to institute the law against incest, by which they all alike renounced the women whom they desired and who had been their chief motive for dispatching their father. In this way they rescued the organization which had made them strong—and which may have been based on homosexual feelings and acts. . . .[9]

The two principles at work in community formation are thus the incorporation of kin (the primal father is being eaten and internalized as law) and the exportation of sex (the women are being banned and transported outside). Freud's model is thought provoking because it signals the crisis-laden nature of the relationship between community and sexual difference. Here is an area, his text suggests, where things are likely to be explosive. If the potential destruction of the group is likely to result from heterosexual relations within the group, then precisely those relations must be tabooed—hence the prohibition of incest.

But what is dangerous about incest? In his explication of taboos, Freud emphasizes that touching or physical contact plays a major role in taboo restrictions because touching is "the first step toward obtaining any sort of control over, or attempting to make use of, a person or object."[10] In other words, the taboo has as its power the force of contagion—the force of passing from object to person and then from person to person—through physical contact. If a taboo is not only a thing or an act, but also the person who has violated the taboo, then the person who *embodies* "touching" and "physical contact" must be looked upon as the taboo as well. Women, because they have the capability of embodying physical contact—of giving material form to "touching," to the transgression of bodily boundaries—in the form of reproduction, are always potentially dangerous; and incest, which could result in such reproduction within the same tribe, is thus danger raised to the second degree and the cultural taboo par excellence. Even though Freud's account leaves many questions unanswered, what stands out from his text is the unmistakable recognition of female sexuality as a form of physical power. It is this physical power, this potentiality of transmission, confusion, and reproduction through actual bodies, that could break down all boundaries and thus disrupt social order in the most fundamental fashion. Because of this, female sexuality itself must be barred from entering a community except in the most non-transgressive, least contagious form.

The implications of Freud's theory are eventually extended, among others, by Claude Lévi-Strauss, who argues that the incest taboo is the origin of human culture because it ensures the practice of exogamy and thus the social relations among different groups of men. Following Marcel Mauss's theory of gift-giving as what sustains the equilibrium of power in tribal society, Lévi-Strauss reads women as the gifts in the kinship system: women are exchanged between families so that kinship as an elaborate network can function.[11] But even though they facilitate *communication* and thus *community relations,* women themselves are not considered as initiators of communication or active partners in community formation. As Gayle Rubin comments in her classic essay, "The Traffic in Women":

> If it is women who are being transacted, then it is the men who give and take them who are linked, the woman being a conduit of a relationship rather than a partner to it. . . . If women are the gifts, then it is men who are the exchange partners. And it is the partners, not the

presents, upon whom reciprocal exchange confers its quasi-mystical power of social linkage. . . it is men who are the beneficiaries of the product of such exchanges—social organization.[12]

Moreover, one could argue that this exchange of women as gifts—this "admittance" that in fact preempts women from having the same rights as men—operates not only as the content but also as the structure of Lévi-Strauss's theorizing. For, once the problem of female sexuality is displaced onto the regulation of kinship structures, it is kinship structures that become the primary focus, while the potential significance of female sexuality as a transgressive force becomes subordinated and thus minimized. By barring female sexuality from entering their writings as a disruptive force, Freud's followers such as Lévi-Strauss thus uncannily repeat, with their acts of theorizing, the story of *Totem and Taboo:* even though these male theorists have, following Freud, identified the handling of sexual difference as what makes a community work,[13] seldom do they bother to elaborate sexual difference itself beyond the point that it serves to support the community formation that is, in the final analysis, a veneration of the father. The continual incorporation/internalization of the voice/narrative of the father (in this case, Freud) and the exportation of the "touch" of sexual difference represented by women mean that the paradigm of community building doubles on itself even as it is being enunciated as theory: we have, in the (psychoanalytic, anthropological, sociological) writings about community formation, a metacommunity building that can be named the solidarity of "male homosocial readings." We must note that in this metacommunity building, this solidarity forming through interpretation, women are never being erased but always given a specific, corollary place: while not exactly admitted, neither are they exactly refused admission. To interrupt this metacommunity building, it would therefore not be enough simply to take sexual difference into consideration; what is more crucial is moving sexual difference beyond the status of "corollary" or "support" that Freud and his followers allow it. Instead of the incorporation of the father and the community among men, then, we need to look at what is "exported," the taboo that is female sexuality itself.

Another problem with *Totem and Taboo* is that, as is characteristic of many of Freud's writings, it is most suggestive in its explanation of the mechanics—the displacements, negations, and emotional ambivalences—*within* a group. And yet if this text is eminently useful as a reminder of the linkage between community formation and sexual difference, it is inevitably inadequate in a situation where more than one community is involved. The postcolonized situation, in which a formerly colonized group seeks to establish its new status as a national community that is alternative to the one in preindependent times, necessarily complicates Freud's binarist, interiorist model. The most outstanding feature in the postcolonized situation is not one group of men and women (and the problem of sexuality within their community), but the conflictual relations between the colonized subject, his own ethnic/racial community, and the lingering effects of the colonizer. The presence of what are at the very least two groups—colonizer and colonized—rather than one, as well as the persistent hierarchical injustices brought about by the domination of one over the other, means that any consideration of community formation in the postcolonial aftermath must exceed the model of the *in-house* totemism and taboo as suggested by Freud.

It is, thus, with a twin focus on female sexuality and on the *double* theoretical discourse of admittance and nonadmittance regarding female sexuality that I return to the problem of community formation in Fanon. The question here is not whether Fanon gives us more or less satisfying answers, but how, precisely because Fanon's texts are explicitly political and aimed at revolutionizing thinking about the social bases of identification—from the stage of colonization to national culture, from white imperialist domination to the reclamation of black personhood and agency—they offer a demonstration of the problems that are inherent in all masculinist conceptions of community formation more starkly and thus more disturbingly than most. My aim, in other words, is not to belittle the epochal messages of a seminal political thinker. Rather it is to argue, first, the ineluctability of considering female sexuality and sexual difference as *primary* issues in a discussion of community formation; and second, how, once introduced, female sexuality and sexual difference at both the empirical and theoretical levels interrupt community formation with powerful fissures. Ultimately, my question is: could female sexuality and sexual difference ever be reconciled with community? Are these mutually exclusive events? To begin to answer these questions, we will now examine the specific kinds of analyses Fanon gives of female sexuality.

What Does the Woman of Color Want?

Unlike his analyses of the black man, with their intent of foregrounding the existential ambivalences of the black male psyche, Fanon's depictions of women of color are, as we see in the passages quoted earlier, direct and with little doubt: the women of color *want* to have sexual relations with white men because it is their means of upward social mobility, their way of so-called "saving the race." If Fanon's manner of dealing with what the woman of color wants sounds somewhat familiar in its confident tone, it is because it reminds us of the manner in which Freud describes the little girl's acquisition of sexual identity. As feminists have often pointed out, Freud's portrayals of the psychic labor spent by the little girl and little boy in acquiring their respective sexual identities are remarkably different. While the little boy's psyche is full of the complexity of belated or retroactive consciousness—he does not understand the meaning of the female genitalia and hence sexual difference until he is threatened with the possibility of castration—the little girl, by contrast, "behaves differently. She makes her judgment and her decision in a flash. She has seen it and knows that she is without it and wants to have it."[14] As portrayed by Freud, the little boy is an *innocent victim* of his cultural environment, whereas the little girl is an *active agent* in her grasp of the politics of sexuality. Similarly, in Fanon's portrayals, we sense that the black man is viewed as a helpless victim of his cultural environment, whereas the woman of color is viewed as a knowledgeable, calculating perpetrator of interracial sexual intercourses. If the black man's desire to elevate himself to whiteness is a plea for what Fanon affirms as "active understanding" (BSWM, p. 81), the similar desire on the part of the woman of color is not given as complex a treatment. To paraphrase Freud, the woman of color simply "has seen it and knows that she is without it and wants to have it."

By refusing the woman of color any of the kind of emotional ambivalence that is copiously endowed upon the psyche of the black man, what Fanon accomplishes is a representation—representation both in the sense of portraying and in the sense of speaking for[15]—of the woman of color as potentially if not always a whore, a sell-out, and hence a traitor to her own ethnic community. Women of color are, in other words, shameless people who forsake their own origins ("the uniqueness of that part of the world in which they grew up") for something more "universally" desirable and profitable—association with the white world. Rather than living and working alongside her black kinsmen and sharing their ordeals, the woman of color jumps at any opportunity for getting out of her ghetto. While the black man is sympathetically and empathetically portrayed as filled with existentialist angst, as subjected to a state of psychic castratedness that is nonetheless a sign of his honor, his integrity as a cultural hero, the choices and actions of the woman of color are rather associated with efficiency, with determination, with confidence, even with "candor"—qualities which, however, become signs of her dishonor, her natural degeneracy. And it is as if, because of these qualities, the woman of color is unworthy of the careful *analytic* attention that is so painstakingly bestowed on her male counterpart.

In contrast to the view that the woman of color has been made to disappear or is deprived of her agency, therefore, I would argue that Fanon in fact gives her a very specific kind of appearance and agency. To confront the issue of female sexuality in Fanon, what is required is not exactly an attempt to "restore" the woman of color by giving her a voice, a self, a subjectivity; rather we need to examine *how* the woman of color has *already* been given agency—by examining the form which this attributed agency assumes. To use the terms of our ongoing discussion, this is, once again, a question about admittance. What kind of admittance does Fanon extend to the woman of color—what kind of entry permit and what kind of acknowledgment?

Fanon describes the woman of color in terms of her conscious wishes and her unconscious desires. This distinction does not in the end amount to a real difference because, as we shall see, whether conscious or unconscious, the woman of color is headed toward the same fate.

We will begin with her conscious wish, her supposed desire for the white man. Since the white man is the oppressor of black people, is this colored female agency, this desire for the white sexual partner, a masochistic act? Viewed as a way to climb up the social ladder in a world where white is superior, it would, at first, not seem so: the woman of color is in fact benefiting rather than bringing pain to herself from such an act. Unlike her black brother, Fanon suggests, she has everything to gain from her association with the white world. But the matter of masochism is not so clear once we juxtapose Fanon's description of the woman of color with yet another counterpart—this time the white woman. This juxtaposition reveals a much more disturbing perspective on the so-called "unconscious" of women *in general.*

In a manner paralleling his description of the woman of color, Fanon's description of the white woman fixes her with a determined sexual agency. The white woman, too, "wants it": she desires to have sex with the Negro in her fantasy. Moreover, this time what the woman "wants" is definitely a part of her masochism—her wanting to be raped:

> First the little girl sees a sibling rival beaten by the father, a libidinal aggressive. At this stage (between the ages of five and nine), the father, who is now the pole of her libido, refuses in a way to take up the aggression that the little girl's unconscious demands of him. At this point, lacking support, this free-floating aggression requires an investment. Since the girl is at the age in which the child begins to enter the folklore and the culture along roads that we know, the Negro becomes the predestined depository of this aggression. If we go farther into the labyrinth, we discover that when a woman lives the fantasy of rape by a Negro, it is in some way the fulfillment of a private dream, of an inner wish. Accomplishing the phenomenon of turning

against self, *it is the woman who rapes herself.* (BSWM, p. 179; my emphasis)

From this analysis of the white woman Fanon shifts to a speculation about women in general:

> We can find clear proof of this in the fact that *it is commonplace for women, during the sexual act, to cry to their partners: "Hurt me!"* They are merely expressing this idea: Hurt me as I would hurt me if I were in your place. *The fantasy of rape by a Negro is a variation of this emotion:* "I wish the Negro would rip me open as I would have ripped a woman open." (BSWM, p. 179; my emphases)

This passage indicates that all women fantasize being hurt in the sexual act and that this fantasy, which women project onto their sexual partners, is ultimately a fantasy of women *themselves hurting themselves.* ("It is the woman who rapes herself.") Accordingly, there is no such thing as a man hurting a woman; there is no such thing as rape. The implicit assumption that women are fundamentally unrapable is perhaps the reason, as critics have pointed out, in spite of his sensitivity to interracial sexual violence, Fanon has not attempted/bothered to deal with the prominent issue of the rape of women of color by white men.[16] Instead, women's essential unrapability means that the rape of women must be inverted to become women's desire and that the violence committed against women must be inverted to become the women's violence against themselves. And, since such violence is a condition characteristic of *all* women, the white woman's desire for her racial other, the black man, is merely "a variation of this emotion," to which (the emotion) skin color is but an accident.[17]

The above description of white female sexuality is then followed by the line in which Fanon claims his lack of knowledge about the woman of color. Revealingly, even as he makes this disclaimer, he adds an observation that in effect shows not exactly his lack of knowledge but (in accordance with the logic of his immediately preceding discussion) his understanding that black and white women are universally alike. If his preceding discussion shows the white woman to "want" rape by a Negro (since all women "want" rape), he now shows that black women, too, "want" the Negro who is socially inferior to them:

> Those who grant our conclusions on the psychosexuality of the white woman may ask what we have to say about the woman of color. I know nothing about her. What I can offer, at the very least, is that *for many women in the Antilles—the type that I shall call the all-but-whites—the aggressor is symbolized by the Senegalese type, or in any event by an inferior (who is so considered).* (BSWM, pp. 179–80; my emphasis)

In an account that ultimately minimizes if not effaces the racial and ethnic differences between black and white women, Fanon portrays women's sexuality in the main as characterized by an active, sado-masochistic desire—to be raped, to rape herself, to rip herself open. Furthermore, as in the case of the women in the Antilles who fantasize sex with Senegalese men, this sadomasochistic desire is implicated in class, as it is enacted through fantasies of relations with a socially inferior male. Not only is sex with a woman always a kind of rape generated by herself, but her essential femininity/depravity is proven by her desire for a man of the lower class.

We have by this point two seemingly contradictory descriptions of the woman of color: on the one hand, she wants the white man because he is socially *superior;* on the other hand, she wants certain types of black men because they are socially *inferior.* The first description pertains to the greed for upward social mobility; the second pertains to the realization of lewd sexual fantasies. However, from the perspective of the woman of color, the effect produced by both types of descriptions is the same. This is the effect of the construction of a female sexual agency that is entirely predictable and already understood, conscious or unconscious. Most crucially, this construction, because it admits women *as* sexuality and nothing more, leaves no room for the woman of color to retain her membership among her own racial/ethnic community. In terms of the community formation that is based on race, the admittance that Fanon gives the woman of color is solely based on sex.[18] Fanon's reading means that the woman of color is either a *black traitor* (when she chooses the white man) or a *white woman* (when she chooses a black man).[19] Fanon's admittance of the sexual agency of the woman of color signifies her inevitable expulsion from her community. Between her conscious actions and her unconscious desires, between her wish for "lactification" and her fantasy of being raped "by a Negro," the woman of color is thus, literally, *ex-communicated* even as she is being acknowledged, attacked and assaulted even as she is being "admitted."

In contrast to the agency given to the woman of color, the black man is, as I mentioned, portrayed much more sympathetically as a victim of multiple forces—of colonialism, of his own tormenting emotional responses to history, and ultimately of the infidelity and "whiteness" of "his" women. Instead of a concrete agency, conscious or unconscious, the black man is throughout enhanced with what I will call *the privilege of ambivalence,* a reaction that is defined as the impossible choice between whiteness and blackness. If ambivalence is a privilege, it is because it exempts the black man from the harsh requirements imposed upon the woman of color. Whereas the women of color are required to stay completely within boundaries, the black man is allowed to waver between psychic states and ethnic communities, to be "borderline." The black man is allowed to go in and out of his community—to mate with white women, for instance—without having his fidelity questioned.[20] If unconditional admittance to his ethnic community is what distinguishes the black man from the woman of color, it is because, in the texts of Fanon at least, the black man alone holds "ambivalence" as his entry and exit permit.

The Force of Miscegenation

Clearly, Fanon's descriptions of women do not depart significantly from the traditional masculinist view that equates women with sex. In contrast to men, who are defined by violence and ambivalence, Fanon's construction of womanhood is a construction through notions of sexual chastity, purity, fidelity, depravity, and perversion. Such notions of female sexuality are then welded onto the conceptualizations of the colonized subject and thus inevitably of the prospective communities to come after colonization. But why is the sexual agency of women such a prohibitive concern in the aftermath of colonization?

As can be glimpsed already in Freud's text, any conceptualization of community is by implication a theory about reproduction, both biological and social. Female sexuality, insofar as it is the embodiment of the "touching," the physical intimacy that leads to such reproduction, is therefore always a locus of potential danger—of dangerous possibilities. If the creation of a postcolonial national community is at least in part about the empowerment of the formerly colonized through the systematic preservation of their racial and ethnic specificities, then such an empowerment could easily be imagined to be threatened by miscegenation, the sexual intermixing among the races. Such sexual intermixing leads to a kind of reproduction that is racially impure, and thus to a hybridization of the elements of the community concerned.

Miscegenation leading to the mixing of races and cultures, the threat of impurity, the danger of bastardization—this much is common knowledge. Is this the reason why women's sexual agency is tabooed and excommunicated—since, as Fanon portrays it, women are consciously or unconsciously prone to miscegenation?[21] What dangers does a *female* tendency toward miscegenation hold for a theory of community formation in the aftermath of colonialism?

This is the juncture where two readings of Fanon's texts are, I think, possible. The first is that Fanon is just like any other man—that he is simply a patriarch who cannot tolerate differences and impurities. Instead of letting in Fanon's concerns as specifically the concerns of a person of color, such a reading would read him exclusively by way of his sexuality. The second reading, which is the one I would follow, is less straightforward and perhaps more contradictory, because it tries to admit the implications of Fanon's race as well as sexuality. This reading would show that what makes the women's conscious or unconscious desires for miscegenation such a traumatic event in Fanon's theory is that such *"sexual"* desires in fact share with the male intellectual's *race*-conscious, anti-colonialist message a common goal—the goal of ending the compartmentalized, Manichean division of the world into colonizer and colonized, us and them, that is colonialism's chief ideological legacy. In place of a pure grouping, racial sexual intermixing is the very force—the force of biological procreation and of social connotation—that gives rise to alternative groups of people whose origins are all bastardized and whose *communal bond* can henceforth not be based on the purity of their status as black or white. These groups would be the actual externalizations, the actual embodiments, of the psychical ambivalences, the split between being white and being black, that torment the black man as Fanon describes it. What such groups would have in common—what would make them a community—is paradoxically what they do *not* absolutely have in common in terms of blood, skin color, or ethnicity.

This other, alternative kind of community, a community in which the immanence and specificity of corporeality would coexist with a democratic, open-ended notion of collectivity, is the foreseeable consequence of a kind of sexual agency that disrupts the existing boundaries that mark different racial groups apart. It is also, theoretically speaking, the utopian transformative vision that underlies the clear pronouncements made by Fanon against the domineering racist practices of European imperialism. But the difficulty for Fanon is precisely the difficulty inherent to all events of community formation: admittance (into a group) by necessity implies exclusion. What and who must be excluded and why? This fundamental law about community formation is further exacerbated by the postcolonial situation, in which utopian vision and political reality do not exactly correspond. Even though the passionate imagining of a national culture must, in theory, oppose the segregational assumptions inherent in colonialism, the practical implementation of the postcolonial nation as such cannot but mark new boundaries and reinforce new exclusions. The (female) force of miscegenation, with its seemingly opportunistic oblivion to the injustices of a racist history, must be barred from entering the new realm of political necessity.

For Fanon at the postcolonized moment of nation formation, female sexuality is a traumatic event because it poses the danger of a double transgression. What disturbs him is that the women of color, instead of staying put in their traditional position as "gifts," as the conduits and vehicles that facilitate social relations and enable group identity, actually *give themselves.* By giving themselves, such women enter social relationships as active partners in the production of meanings rather than simply as the bearers of those meanings. And, if such sexual giving constitutes a significant form of transgression, this transgression is made doubly transgressive when women of color give themselves *to white men.* In the latter case, the crossing of patriarchal sexual boundaries crosses another crossing, the crossing of racial boundaries. The women of color are, accordingly, the site of *supplementary* danger—of the dangerous supplement (Jacques Derrida's term)—par excellence, adding to the injustice of race the revolt of sex (and vice versa), and substituting/transforming the meaning of both at once.

In the typical dilemma facing nationalist discourse once nationalist discourse encounters gender, thus, Fanon's discourse is beset with the contested issues of identity, agency, and sovereignty. Deniz Kandiyoti comments on this dilemma succinctly:

> A feature of nationalist discourse that has generated considerable consensus is its Janus-faced quality. It presents itself both as a modern project that melts and transforms traditional attachments in favour of new identities and as a reaffirmation of authentic cultural values culled from the depths of a presumed communal past. It therefore opens up a highly fluid and ambivalent field of meanings which can be reactivated, reinterpreted and often reinvented at critical junctures of the histories of nation-states. These meanings are not given, but fought over and contested by political actors whose definitions of *who* and *what* constitutes the nation have a crucial bearing on notions of national unity and alternative claims to sovereignty as well as on the sorts of gender relations that should inform the nationalist project.[22]

If the woman of color can be of value to her ethnic community only as a gift and a defenseless victim, then her assumption of any agency would in effect invalidate her and deprive her of admittance. The ultimate danger posed by the Negress and the mulatto is hence not their sexual behavior per se, but the fact that their sexual agency carries with it a powerful (re)conceptualization of community—of community as based on difference, heterogeneity, creolization; of community as the "illegitimate" mixings and crossings of color, pigmentation, physiognomy—that threateningly *vies with the male intellectual's.* The fact that the women are equal, indeed avant garde, partners in the production of a future community—is this not *the* confusion, the most contagious of forces, that is the most difficult to *admit,* to permit to enter, to acknowledge, and to confess? The ultimate taboo, it would seem, is once again the "taboo against the sameness of men and women," the "division of labor by sex."[23]

The woman of color, by virtue of being both female and colored, having entrance points into and out of the community through sex and through ethnicity, becomes extremely suspect in a situation when supposedly only the black man has such privilege of "ambivalence" and when supposedly only "race" as the black man experiences it matters in the articulation of community consciousness. Once we put our focus on this "tabooed" area of female sexuality, we see that female sexuality is what interrupts the unidirectional force of existential violence that is otherwise justified in Fanon's theory of postcolonial nation-building.[24] At this point, the three senses of admittance I mentioned earlier come together. The strategies of simplification and reduction Fanon adopts toward the woman of color (in the many forms of "she wants it") are, in this light, not exactly attempts to refuse her *entry* but rather signs of an implicit, though reluctant, *acknowledgment* of her claim (equal to his) to being the progenitor of the community to come. At the same time, if this acknowledgment could also be seen as a kind of *confession*, it is nonetheless only a confession that reconciles (the male intellectual) with the community of color *and* with male sexuality but not with the women of color; a confession that surrenders to the demands of race and to the distinctions of sex but not to the supplementary transgression of colored female agency.

Because women are, with their sexual behavior, powerful agents in the generation of a different type of community, the male intellectual senses that he cannot trust—cannot bond with—them. He cannot trust them because he cannot control the potentiality that ensues from their acts of miscegenation. But how is the future community to be conceived without women? Fanon, like all revolutionary male thinkers, would bond instead with "the people," which is the figure that empowers him in this *competition between the sexes* for the *birthing* of a new community. Community formation thus takes on, at the theoretical level, the import of a sexual struggle—a seizing of the power to reproduce and procreate. It is in this sense that the "native"—etymologically linked to "nation" and also to "birth"—becomes the progeny of the male postcolonial critic. The exclusive bond with this progeny allows for the fantasy of undoing and outdoing woman.

Interestingly, then, the "native" and the "people" in Fanon's texts are, like the black man, signs that waver with ambivalence. The people waver between complete deprivation—having nothing and thus nothing to lose—and an essential "resistance" toward colonialism.[25] The descriptions of the native/people as possessing nothing and something at once raises fundamental questions. On the one hand, if colonialism is an all-encompassing environment, leaving the native with utterly nothing, where does the native get his readiness to attack, to fight back? This could only mean either that there is an essential something (nature, history) that allows the native to resist, in which case the native is not "nothing"; or that there are gaps and fissures within the colonial system itself that allow the native some room to resist, in which case colonialism as a system of domination is less than airtight.[26]

By portraying the "native" and the "people" in this ambivalent light—now totally deprived, now possessed of resistive energy; now entirely at the mercy of colonial domination, now definitely the source of rebellion against the colonizer—Fanon retains them as empty, mobile figures, figures of convenience onto which he, like other revolutionary male thinkers, can write his own script.[27] Because the "native" and the "people" are fundamentally empty, they accommodate the revolutionary intellectual with a rhetorical frame in which to hang his utopian vision, whereas women, because they are understood to possess a potent sexual agency, stand as an obstinate stumbling block in the path of revolutionary thought. As a result, while the "native"/the "people" continue to be exonerated in the imagined community of the new nation, women are admitted only with reservation—and only as "sex."

Community Building among Theorists of Postcoloniality

Once introduced, female sexuality, because it foregrounds the difference in the kinds of admittance extended to men and women, complicates the entire question of how a new community is conceptualized in the postcolonial aftermath. If, in terms of the inequality of race, Fanon correctly identifies the "infernal circle" of shame and longing-for-recognition as the condition that traps the black man, who is not exactly refused entry yet not exactly given his due recognition by the white world, he also uncannily inflicts a similarly "infernal" circle on the woman of color. If the black man's "skin color" is the place where he can never be sure of his admittance into the world of the "other" men, the white men, then for the woman of color, sexuality as much as skin color is what renders admittance by all communities, *especially that of her own "race,"* problematic.[28]

As in the case of Freud, the politics of admittance works not only at the level of the content and structure of Fanon's articulations, but also at the level of his works' reception. In choosing not to discuss the obviously fraught issues of sexuality in Fanon, in choosing to pass over this significant part of his texts with silence, many postcolonial critics are themselves implicitly building a type of discursive community that repeats the ambivalences and neuroses of Fanon's articulations.[29] This kind of silence is often justified by way of "the more important" issues of racism and colonialism, and by way of the implicit assumption that any discussion of sexuality as such is, like the sexual behavior of Fanon's woman of color, a suspect move toward "lactification." In the collective incorporation of the rhetorical violences of the sexually troubled male intellectual, we see something of the "longing for the father" that Freud describes as the foundation of totem formation. Totemism in the context of postcolonial theory is a revolutionary male narcissism writ large, instigating the male revolutionary figure as the "primal father" who bestows meaning on the postcolonial horde,[30] while the sexuality of women, in particular the women who "belong" to the father—the women of color, the women of the tribe—continue to have their agency prohibited, exiled, and deferred—this time by postcolonial critics.

On the other hand, what I specify as female sexual agency in this essay is a name for that which is *equivalent* in potentiality to male intellectual agency, and which the latter must therefore ward off with *ambivalence*, as primitive peoples ward off particular powers through specially instituted taboos. Since female sexual agency is a taboo—a prohibited area of potential contagion, miscegenation, and danger—its admittance would always be at a major cost. Admitting female sexual agency would mean that a more purist notion of community cannot but dissolve.

Ultimately, Fanon's opinions about female sexual agency could also be read as a parable about the *inadmissible* position occupied by the "intellectual of color" in the postcolonial situation. Here I can merely allude to the many anxieties and displeasures expressed about such intellectuals' "selling out" to the West in oblivion of the "real" historical tasks at hand. The much criticized use of "Western theory," for instance, could, in the light of this parable, be rewritten as a licentious mixing with the white folks, an *intellectual miscegenation* shall we say, that is, for many, not unlike the depraved sexual behavior of Fanon's woman of color. "The most painful sting of patriarchy," writes one feminist critic, is "the solidarity *against* the other."[31] The fear and accusation of "compradore" mentalities, of intellectual whoredom, and of the lethal infidelities of *others* would thus always remain part and parcel of the patriarchal gestures of community building, and a discursive community—in the academy in particular—is no exception.[32] As we have seen with Fanon, however, such fears and accusations contain an implicit acknowledgment of the alternative agency that the "women of color"—the black whores—possess with their condemned behavior. Perhaps, as in the case of Fanon's reading, what cannot be admitted in the community of postcolonial theorists is that such depraved behavior of intellectual miscegenation, too, shares with those who condemn it similar emancipatory goals. This argument, obviously, will need to be elaborated on a separate occasion.[33]

FIVE

The Dream of a Butterfly

[L]ove is of such a nature that it changes man into the things he loves.

> —*Martin Heidegger (citing Meister Eckhart),* "The Thing"

[I]nescapably, I passed beyond the unreality of the thing represented, I entered crazily into the spectacle, into the image, taking into my arms what is dead, what is going to die. . . .

> —*Roland Barthes,* Camera Lucida

The mystical is by no means that which is not political. . . . What was tried at the end of the last century . . . by all kinds of worthy people . . . was an attempt to reduce the mystical to questions of fucking.

> —*Jacques Lacan,* "God and the Jouissance of the Woman"

THESE DAYS WE have become complacent about our ability to criticize the racist and sexist blunders inherent in the stereotypical representations of our cultural "others." "Our" here refers to the community of intellectuals, East and West, who have absorbed the wisdom of Edward Said's *Orientalism* and who are on the alert to point out the discriminatory assumptions behind the production of cultural artifacts, in particular those that involve Western representations of the non-West. But Said's work, insofar as it successfully canonizes the demystification of

Western cultural pretensions, is simply pointing to a certain direction in which much work still waits to be done—namely, the direction in which we must examine in detail the multifaceted psychical and philosophical implications of the conflict, confusion, and tragedy arising from "cross-cultural exchange" when that exchange is conditioned by the inequities and injustices of imperialist histories. This work that needs to be done cannot be done simply by repeating the debunking messages that Said has already so clearly delivered in his book. Rather, we need to explore alternative ways of thinking about cross-cultural exchange that exceed the pointed, polemical framework of "antiorientalism"—the lesson from Said's work—by continually problematizing the presumption of stable identities and also by continually asking what else there is to learn beyond destabilized identities themselves. In this chapter, I read the 1993 film *M. Butterfly* (directed by David Cronenberg, screenplay by David Henry Hwang) as an instance of such a badly needed alternative approach to the problematic of Orientalism.[1]

Let me emphasize at the outset that I am not discrediting or de-emphasizing the continual need for the criticism of Orientalism. Far from it: I am saying that precisely because Orientalism has many guises—both decadent and progressivist, in the form of sexual adventures and textual devotion, *and also* in the form of political idealization, fascination with subaltern groups and disenfranchised classes, and so forth—what we need to examine ever more urgently is fantasy, a problem which is generally recognized as central to orientalist perceptions and significations.

My task is made all the more challenging because the problem of fantasy, even though it is a predominant consideration of the stage play on which the film was based, is usually dismissed moralistically, in this case also by playwright Hwang. In responding to the real-life story of the French diplomat whose affair with a Chinese male opera singer gave him his inspiration for the play, for instance, Hwang writes confidently: "I . . . concluded that the diplomat must have fallen in love, not with a person, but with a fantasy stereotype."[2] Hwang's interest in this bizarre story is, one might say, primarily didactic, as he expresses it clearly in these remarks:

> *M. Butterfly* has sometimes been regarded as an anti-American play, a diatribe against the stereotyping of the East by the West, of women by men. Quite to the contrary, I consider it a plea to all sides to cut through our respective layers of cultural and sexual misperception, to deal with one another truthfully for our mutual good, from the common and equal ground we share as human beings.
>
> For the myths of the East, the myths of the West, the myths of men, and the myths of women—these have so saturated our consciousness

that truthful contact between nations and lovers can only be the result of heroic effort. Those who prefer to bypass the work involved will remain in a world of surfaces, misperceptions running rampant.[3]

And yet, because the question of fantasy as stated here is already part of a conclusive understanding, of a plea for truthful human contact devoid of "misperception," there is something inherently superfluous about the representation of the story: if these layers of cross-cultural "misperception" are a fact of such crystal clarity, why not simply state it as such? Why, in other words, do we need to have a play in the first place? As a moral fable that was designed to preach a lesson well understood in advance—the lesson about the laughable "fantasy" and ludicrous "false consciousness" of the imperialist Western man— Hwang's play, it would seem, is a gratuitous act. Is the play's over-whelming success in the West due perhaps precisely to this gratuitous, stereotypical, and thus absolutely safe mockery of fantasy and false consciousness? But this success—this approval received by an Asian American playwright in the West for correctly reprimanding Western imperialist fantasies—is it not itself a sign and a warning, not of how the West has finally learned its lessons, but rather once again of the very Orientalism which Hwang intends to criticize, and to which non-Western peoples nonetheless continue to be subjected today?[4]

My interest in the film *M. Butterfly* begins where Hwang would have us stop. Rather than being my conclusion, fantasy is the beginning of my inquiry, which is framed by two major questions.

First, if fantasy is not simply a matter of distortion or willful exploi-tation, but is rather an inherent part of our consciousness, our wakeful state of mind,[5] what are the possibilities and implications of achieving any kind of sexual and racial identification in a "cross-cultural" ex-change? Further, if the most important thing about fantasy is not the simple domination of an other but, as Laplanche and Pontalis argue, the variable positionality of the subject, whose reality consists in a constant shifting between modes of dominance and submission,[6] what could be said about the relations between East and West, woman and man, that is perhaps alternative to the ones they are assumed, in antiorientalist discourse, to have?

The second major question that concerns me, after fantasy has been sufficiently understood to be a kind of structuring and setting that is indispensable to any consideration of subjectivity, is how the film *M. Butterfly* also moves *beyond* subjectivity to philosophical issues of phe-nomenology and ontology. What is of particular interest is the manner in which the film relates the question of "cross-cultural" fantasy not simply to homosexuality, heterosexuality, or race, but also to the larger, open-ended question of the limits of human vision. As I will attempt to demonstrate, the film probes this other question by exploring the phenomenological effects of the image and the gaze.

"East Is East and West Is West, and Ne'er the Twain Shall Meet"

For me, what is most remarkable about the *M. Butterfly* story is, to put it in the simplest terms, the fact that it is a stereotype, in which a Western man believes he is romantically involved with an oriental woman. The story goes briefly as follows. It is 1964 in Beijing, China. René Gallimard, an accountant working at the French consulate, has just been to a performance of excerpts from Giacomo Puccini's opera *Madama Butterfly* (1904), staged at one of the foreign embassies. Gallimard finds himself drawn to the Chinese opera singer, Song Liling, who plays the role of Madame Butterfly. When he relates his fascination to his wife, who dismisses the Chinese with the familiar attitude, "East is East and West is West, and never the twain shall meet," he finds that she does not share his enthusiasm. In the rest of the film she is to become less and less significant as he embarks on a clandestine relationship with the opera singer. Song later tells Gallimard she has become pregnant; eventually she shows him a baby boy who is supposedly his son. As the Cultural Revolution progresses, the lovers are separated: Gallimard is sent back to Paris and Song put in a labor camp. Just as he is abandoning all hope, she shows up again unexpectedly in Paris outside his apartment. The lovers are happily reunited until they are arrested for passing secret information of the French government to China. But for Gallimard, the most devastating consequence of this exposure is the revelation by the French government that Song, who has all these years been his "Butterfly," is actually a male spy whose involvement with him has been for the purpose of extracting information for the Chinese government.

Precisely because of its stereotypical structure, the relationship between Gallimard and Song allows us to approach it as a kind of myth. In this myth, Gallimard occupies the role of the supposedly active and dominant white male, and Song, the role of the supposedly passive and submissive oriental female. The superimposition of the racial and sexual elements of this relationship creates the space in which the story unfolds.

In order to heighten the story's mythical quality on film, director Cronenberg dispenses with many of the complexities that characterized both the real-life story and the stage play. For instance, while in the real-life story, the "Chinese woman" that the French diplomat fell for always appeared as a man but told his beloved that he was really a woman, in the film Song always appears as a woman until the final scenes. And, while the stage play contains many farcical moments that present the Frenchman as the obvious object of ridicule, the film trims away such moments, preserving the story instead in an elegant mode, against an often hazy and darkish background, and frequently melancholic music. In thus stripping and reducing the story, Cronenberg makes its macabre structure stand out starkly. In the same vein, the usual elaborate manner in which a leading "feminine" character is fetishized is kept to a minimum. Instead of filling the movie screen with lavish physical, cosmetic, and sartorial details—such as is the case with the film with which *M. Butterfly* is often compared, *Farewell My Concubine,* by Chen Kaige—the portrayal of Song is low-keyed and unglamorous. Her singing and her stage performance, in both Western and Chinese theaters, are presented only briefly and appear to have been rather unremarkable. Some critics, predisposed toward a sensational and extravagantly colorful approach whenever a non-Western culture is represented, are quick to criticize *M. Butterfly* on the basis of *verisimilitude:* they point out disparagingly, for instance, that John Lone, who plays Song, does not look like a woman and that he and Jeremy Irons are unconvincing as lovers, and so forth.[7]

In thus missing the significance of the purposefully restrained design of the film, such critics also miss its status as the uncluttered sculpting of a stereotypical story, the artful experimenting with a familiar myth. What they have utterly failed to grasp is that, as in the case of the Chinese Beijing opera, what we see is not so much realistic props as suggestive ones, which are meant to conjure and signify rather than resemble an entire ambiance.

As the effects of verisimilitude give way to those of simplified plot, sparse detail, and minimalist characterization, the object of the story—fantasy itself—becomes intensified. The film becomes literally the *setting* that typifies fantasy.[8] With little sensational visual detail to distract us, we are compelled to focus on the absurd question: what happens when a man falls in love, not with a woman or even with another man, not with a human being at all but with a thing, a reified form of his own fantasy?[9] In the context of this film, this question is mapped over the question of Orientalism, so that it becomes: what happens when a Western man falls in love with a reification of the orient, with that mysterious thing called the "oriental woman"?

In many ways, we can say that the film teaches the lesson which is summarized in that platitudinous phrase repeated by Mme. Gallimard, "East is East and West is West." The conclusion that "never the twain shall meet" could, obviously, be interpreted in accordance with the argument against Orientalism, with *M. Butterfly* serving as a piece of didacticism. Gallimard, a Frenchman working in the exotic East, harbors the typical Western male fantasy about the East and in particular about submissive oriental women. He is so enamored of this fantasy of his that he cannot tell a fake oriental woman from a real one. This fantastical relation to "the other" could then be said to be symptomatic of a deep-rooted racist, sexist, and homophobic imperialism; and Gallimard could be called a symbol of the West, with a downfall that is well deserved, and so forth.

This kind of moral is, as I already suggested, indeed what the stage play tries to point at explicitly. For Hwang, the significance of fantasy is that of a content that needs to be changed; it needs to be changed because, by using other people as objects and things, fantasy dehumanizes them. Cronenberg, on the other hand, refuses this approach to fantasy and, as in the case of most of his other films, notably *Videodrome, The Fly, Dead Ringers,* and *Naked Lunch,* explores instead the possibilities and implications of fantasy precisely as a process of dehumanization—of deconstructing the human.[10] Instead of entirely dispensing with the antiorientalist didacticism, however, Cronenberg's film makes it part of its dramatization of the Gallimard-Song relationship. In this dramatization, the film no longer simply offers a diatribe against the stereotyping of the East by the West, or of women by men, but rather raises questions about the fundamental misrecognition inherent to processes of identification, *which the encounter between an oriental woman and a Western man magnifies and thus exemplifies.* The didactic, antiorientalist criticism of the West, then, remains a significant part of the story, but it is no longer its central focus.

Consider, for instance, the scene of the lovers' first encounter, wherein Song, instead of acting flattered, reprimands Gallimard for thinking that the story of Madame Butterfly is a beautiful one. It is only because he is so grossly ignorant of the history of the atrocities committed by Japan in China, Song says, that he could think that a Chinese actress playing a Japanese woman could be convincing. Further, if the races of the roles had been reversed—if it had been a Western woman sacrificing herself for an unattractive Japanese man—the judgment would most likely be that the woman is deranged rather than beautiful:

> Song: It's one of your favorite fantasies, isn't it? The submissive Oriental woman and the cruel white man.
>
> Gallimard: Well, I didn't quite mean. . .
>
> Song: Consider it this way: what would you say if a blonde homecoming queen fell in love with a short Japanese businessman? He treats her cruelly, then goes home for three years, during which time

she prays to his picture and turns down marriage from a young Kennedy. Then, when she learns he has remarried, she kills herself. Now, I believe you would consider this girl to be a deranged idiot, correct? But because it's an Oriental who kills herself for a Westerner—ah!—you find it beautiful.

While Song's words are undoubtedly historically astute, they also serve to fuel Gallimard's imagination of the "oriental woman" rather than cure it. In other words, the fact that this piece of antiorientalist criticism is inserted in the film as part of the first dialogue between Gallimard and Song means that the film has a relationship to the didactics of antiorientalism that is not direct but mediated. Rather than simply endorsing such a didactics, the film explicitly stages Orientalism as a psychic, interpersonal structure that unfolds with a specific logic. The Western man caught in a fantasy about oriental women is here portrayed as a version of Pavlov's dog: conditioned to respond according to certain artificially induced stimuli, such creatures can, at the mere ringing of a bell or the mere appearance of an oriental woman, be expected to behave in a predictable manner—so predictable, in fact, that their behavior cannot be altered simply by an explicit exposure of the conditions that enable it. These creatures would salivate and come alive *for real* even if the stimulus had nothing "real" behind it. In Gallimard's case, the stimulus is the stereotype of the "inscrutable oriental" in the female form—and the more inscrutable she is, the more charmed he is. Simply by playing "herself," by playing her stereotypical, inscrutable role, the "oriental woman" sets the Western man's mind afire.

There is, however, another twist that makes the film decidedly different from the play. Even though she may be the relentless scheming "woman" working for the Chinese Communist Party, and even though she is fully capable of giving Gallimard lectures about the political incorrectness of his "imperialist" fantasies, Song is, as Lone plays the part, herself attracted to Gallimard. As she tells him at the end of their second encounter before saying good-bye, "sometimes, the fascination could be mutual." Is this a response spoken from her heart? Or is it also part of her role-playing? We have no way of knowing until the very end. What is crucial, nonetheless, is that this suggestion of mutual fascination takes the film beyond the one-sided antiorientalism "message" that Song verbally enunciates. And what is mutuality here if not precisely the problematic of the "meeting" between East and West, and woman and man? As I will go on to argue, mutuality in this film occurs exactly in the form of nonreciprocity, so that together, mutuality and nonreciprocity constitute a symbiotic process of fantasy which, as it draws the lovers together, also ensures that they will never meet.

"The Beauty . . . of Her Death. It's a . . . Pure Sacrifice."

Why is Gallimard so fascinated by the Madame Butterfly character? He explains: he is moved by the beauty of her death. It's a pure sacrifice, he says, for even though the man she loves is unworthy, she sacrifices herself for him. To this Song responds, as I mentioned, by pointing out the imperialist implications of his fascination. But there are other possibilities of understanding this "pure sacrifice" of the "oriental woman."

At the most immediate level, this "pure sacrifice" describes exactly the role that Song plays even as she speaks. In the course of their amorous relationship, Song does, we may say, sacrifice herself for Gallimard, a man who is not worthy of her love, by living up to his fantasy. In this instance, the "pure sacrifice" of the "oriental woman" has the status of what Lacan calls lure—that lack of a coincidence between the eye and the gaze, a lack of coincidence that, however, is often what constitutes love:

> From the outset, we see, in the dialectic of the eye and the gaze, that there is no coincidence, but, on the contrary, a lure. When, in love, I solicit a look, what is profoundly unsatisfying and always missing is that—*You never look at me from the place from which I see you.*
> Conversely, *what I look at is never what I wish to see.*[11]

In this well-known passage, Lacan shows that the essential ingredient in love is misrecognition—a circular pattern of wishing, solicitation, frustration, and desire which stems from the belief that there is something more behind what we see (in the beloved). What Lacan calls lure, Jean Baudrillard calls, in a slightly different manner, seduction. To seduce, Baudrillard writes, is to divert the other from his own truth, from the secret (of himself) that escapes him.[12] In the film, by giving Gallimard the lure, the illusion of the self-sacrificing "oriental woman," Song leads Gallimard astray from his own truth. (I will specify what I think this truth is toward the end of this chapter.) But this process of seduction is, as Song says, mutual: while she successfully lures Gallimard, Song herself is also being seduced by Gallimard in that she has been drawn into his area of *weakness*—his weakness precisely for the beauty of the self-sacrificing Madame Butterfly. As Baudrillard writes, comparing seduction and challenge:

> Challenge and seduction are quite similar. And yet there is a difference. In a challenge one draws the other into one's area of strength, which, in view of the potential for unlimited escalation, is also his or her area of strength. Whereas in a strategy (?) of seduction one draws the other into one's area of weakness, which is also his or her area of

weakness. A calculated weakness; an incalculable weakness: one challenges the other to be taken in. . . .

To seduce is to appear weak. To seduce is to render weak. We seduce
with our weakness, never with strong signs or powers. In seduction
we enact this weakness, and this is what gives seduction its strength.[13]

If Song seduces Gallimard with the artifice/sacrifice of the submissive "oriental woman," Gallimard seduces Song with his naïveté, his
capacity for fascination, and ultimately his gullibility. In spite of her real
status as a spy for the Chinese government, therefore, she too seems to
have genuinely fallen in love with him.

What seduces, in other words, is not the truth of the other—what he
or she really is—but the artifact, the mutual complicity in the weaving
of a lure, which works as a snare over the field of encounter, ensuring
that the parties meet at the same time that they miss each other, in a kind
of rhythmic dance.

Furthermore, because the "pure sacrifice" of the "oriental woman" is
the thing that propels and sustains the lure, the act (such as Song's in the
earlier scene) of pointing out that it is a *mere* imperialist fantasy does not
only not succeed in destroying this lure; it actually enhances it—makes
it more alluring. Meanwhile, if the point of the film is not a straightforward antiorientalism, it is not simply homosexual love either: as in the
case of the criticism of imperialist fantasy, the lure cannot be destroyed
by pointing out that Gallimard is really a bisexual or closeted gay man.

A "homoerotic" reading that is intent on showing what Gallimard's
sexual preference really is runs a parallel course with the "antiorientalist" reading in the sense that both readings must rely on the belief
in a kind of repressed truth—repressed racism or repressed homosexuality—for their functioning. In both cases, the assumption would be
that we need to look beyond the surface structure of the lure in order to
locate what is "behind" or "beneath" it. In effect, critics who read this
story as the story of a confused sexual identity would be lending themselves to the lure set up by the film itself, in that they would be seduced
into going after the real penis, the visible body part, the "fact" of Song
being a male; their re-search would be echoing the re-search of the
antiorientalist critics, who are seduced into going after the real penis,
the visible body part, the "fact" of Gallimard being a white man. Be it
through the route of race or the route of sexual preference, such critics
would be trapped by their own desire for a secret—the secret of cross-
cultural exploitation or the secret of homosexual love, which they might
think they are helping to bring to light, when in fact it is they themselves
who have been seduced. In each case what seduces (them) is, shall we
say, the "purity" of a secret—an indubitable Orientalism or an indubi-

table homoeroticism—the way the indubitable love, the pure sacrifice, of an "oriental woman" seduces Gallimard.[14]

The film *M. Butterfly*, on the other hand, is much more cunning. We can see this, for instance, in the interesting scene in Song's bedroom where she is confronted by a party cadre about her decadent behavior. Dressed in a beautiful traditional Chinese woman's jacket, reclining on her bed by herself, and reading girlie magazines featuring oriental women, Song is surprised by the visit of Comrade Chin, her connection to the party authorities. Comrade Chin contemptuously reprimands Song for indulging in "decadent trash." This scene reveals for the first time that Song is working for the Chinese Communist Party and that her relationship with Gallimard is a means to uncover American military plans in Indochina. Is Song not merely playing a role for the sole purpose of getting information from Gallimard? So why, Comrade Chin demands, is she behaving in such a degraded manner when Gallimard is not even present? Song's response to these moralistic charges are remarkable:

> Song: Comrade, in order to better serve the Great Proletarian State, I practice my deception as often as possible! I despise this costume, yet, for the sake of the Great Helmsman, I will endure it along with all other bourgeois Western perversions!

> Comrade Chin: I am not convinced that this will be enough to redeem you in the eyes of the Party.

> Song: I am trying my best to become somebody else.

Significantly, deception, as it is described by Song, has shifted from the status of dishonesty to that of honor: the seductive "oriental woman," as we are now given to understand, is not only a romantically but also a politically self-sacrificing figure, who gives up herself—her "real" identity—for the cause of the revolution, so much so that she sacrifices even her private moments in order to immerse herself in this cause entirely, purely. The greatest deception, then, is also the greatest act of loyalty—to the people, to the country, to the "Great Helmsman." Even though, as the audience, we cannot but sense that these words of loyalty are spoken with irony—that Song's loyalty to the party is dubious precisely because she is so eloquent about it—this scene reveals that the myth of the self-sacrificing "oriental woman" far exceeds the "imperialist fantasy" that has been commonly used to decode it, and that in her artificial role, Song is faithfully serving in the intersection of two cultural symbolics—the nationalistic as well as the erotic, the intracultural as well as the intercultural.

Song does not rebel against her intended and prescribed role in either situation; rather she plays it, indeed lives it, with her truest emotions. In the relationship with Gallimard, the disguise, lure, and veil of the "oriental woman" serve the purpose of gaining access to the realm that is his trust, love, and imagination. In Gallimard's words, thus, her love is pure: she performs her artificial role to the hilt and thus sacrifices herself—gives up her "real" identity—for a man who, as he notices in the story of Madame Butterfly, is unworthy of that love. At the same time, with the revelation of Song's relationship with the party, a supplementary dimension of the myth of Madame Butterfly unfolds. In this supplementary dimension, we see for the first time that the Song-Gallimard story, which plays on the stereotype of "imperialist male fantasy," is itself the mere instrument of espionage, a means of gaining access to the forbidden realm of another country's military secrets. Gallimard's words about Madame Butterfly, then, were an unwitting description of Song's role-playing in this *other* political realm as well: for is not the "man unworthy" of her love not only Gallimard, her imperialist aggressor, her foreign enemy, but also her party leader, the Great Helmsman himself?

If, as we already said, the fascination between Gallimard and Song is mutual, we see now how this mutuality is simultaneously structured as a nonreciprocity. While the "oriental woman" remains an erotic object on the side of Gallimard, on the side of Song it is much more complex. For Song, the "oriental woman" is a means to exploit a foreigner as part of her service to the party. Gallimard, then, is not simply an erotic object or subject; rather he has been identified as a political object, a plaything that would unconsciously help Song give the party what it wants.

The Force of Butterfly; or, the "Oriental Woman" as Phallus

The foregrounding of this supplementary, political dimension of our Madame Butterfly story enables us to read the Gallimard character in a very different manner from the one originally intended by Hwang and followed by most critics. The fateful encounter between East and West takes place at a critical moment of twentieth-century world politics. For France, it is the end of the imperial empire, when Indochina was recently lost and Algeria has become independent. The emptiness of diplomatic life in Beijing is clear: officials cheat on expense accounts; women have illicit affairs; dinner parties and other gatherings are perfunctory and boring. Like a character from a Kafka novel, Gallimard has an uninspiring, low-ranking job as an accountant, but it is one that he takes seriously, so seriously that his corrupt colleagues become annoyed with him for continually exposing them. The high point of this rationalistic bookkeeping existence is tracking down the documentation from people who try to falsify their expense accounts. While we may say that Gallimard is the perfect example of the disciplined individual whose body and mind have, as Michel Foucault shows us in a work such as *Discipline and Punish,* been produced for the efficient, utilitarian functioning of its society, it is equally important to note that Gallimard is clearly a "flunky" in terms of the unspoken rules of political society. His tireless efforts to track down documentation for dubious expense accounts mean that he is out of tune with the smooth debaucheries that constitute the substance of the bureaucratic world. Precisely because he takes his job of accounting seriously, he reveals himself to be someone who does not know how to play the game. At a dinner gathering, as Gallimard sits down at the same table with his colleagues, they sneer and remind him: "You are nobody. You are worse than nobody: you are an accountant. If you are not careful we'll break all your pencils in half." To this Gallimard responds by leaving the table, clumsily dropping his silverware as he does so.

In terms of his relation to the cultural symbolic that is the world of politics, therefore, Gallimard occupies a place that is not dissimilar to that of Song in that he, too, is a bureaucratic informant, a submissive "woman" to the "man not worthy of her love"—the French government, to which he gives his loyal service. The affinity between Gallimard and Song lies in that both are manipulable and useful instruments of their respective political orders, and both respond to these orders with dedication. Gallimard's political usefulness is soon recognized by the ambassador, who sees in him the qualities of a head servant who is not smart enough to cheat and who can therefore be entrusted with the task of "coordinating a revamped intelligence division," that is, of policing the other employees. But it is obvious that in this world of complex political "intelligence," Gallimard is not at home at all as *a person in command.* As he receives, in the ambassador's office, the surprising news of his own promotion to vice-consul, we can see that he does not possess the suave body language to respond appropriately; instead his posture remains awkward and stiff, marking his destiny as someone who will remain marginal and insignificant in French diplomatic culture. When he finally sits in his office as vice consul, he lacks the presence to command the respect of those who are supposedly working for him. Instead of speaking to them with the air of mastery, he reads woodenly from a prewritten script as if he were someone being cross-examined.

It is into this impersonal but overpowering world of bureaucracy, which is echoed by a routine domestic life complete with an uncomprehending wife, classic pajamas, and bedtime tooth-brushing, that "Butterfly" intrudes with an irresistible force. Gallimard, we remember, stumbles upon "Butterfly" unexpectedly. Before the performance of the aria "Un bel dì" from Puccini's opera begins, Gallimard tells his neighbor, Frau Baden, with whom he will later have a casual affair, that he has never seen *Madama Butterfly*, even though his lack of culture is unsuspected by most people.[15] In the position of an outsider to his own European culture, then, Gallimard's eyes catch the "oriental woman" on stage, even though the situation—of a contemporary Chinese opera singer performing the role of a fetishized Japanese heroine from an Italian opera—cannot be more bizarre. If the "entrance of Butterfly" (as printed on the musicians' scores) represents a decisive marking of cultural identity and its concomitant confusion, what it marks first of all is in fact Gallimard's alienation from his own culture. Rather than simply notice the foreignness, the exoticness, of the spectacle in front of him, Gallimard finds in "Butterfly" a kind of anchorage for *himself*. (This is the reason why his behavior takes on a noticeably greater air of self-assurance from this point on.)

Because it is not fully attainable even as it is consumed through sexual contact, the fantasy of the "oriental woman" keeps the Frenchman *afloat with life* by inscribing in him an unanswerable lack. Song exists for Gallimard as the phallus in Lacan's sense of the term—that is, the Other that is always assumed to be more than it appears and that has the power to give us what we want and also to take it away. Lacan, we remember, emphasizes that the phallus functions only when it is veiled and that, once revealed, it becomes shame.[16] Song's tactic, however, includes precisely this "unveiling" of shame by deliberately calling attention to it in a letter to Gallimard: "What more do you want?" she writes. "I have already given you my shame." By feigning loss of dignity, thus, Song preserves her power as phallus, while the "shame" that has been revealed—the oriental woman's love—continues to be a sham veiling the male body that is beneath it.

The manner in which the "oriental woman" functions as a phallus is made even more clear by the fact that Gallimard seems content in love without ever experiencing Song completely naked. (Later in court, responding to the inquiry about this incredible fact, Song will describe Gallimard as a lover who has been very responsive to his "'ancient oriental ways of love,' all of which I invented myself—just for him.") The one time Gallimard comes dangerously close to stripping her, Song tells him at the crucial moment that she is pregnant, thus shifting his sexual desire into a more paternal frame. Meanwhile, Gallimard can have what he calls an "extra extramarital affair" with Frau Baden without its intruding into his fantasy. In the scene in which he and Frau Baden are in their hotel room, Gallimard, coming out of the bathroom in his hygienic-looking undershirt, is shown to be somewhat taken aback by the sight of Frau Baden sitting casually naked on the edge of the bed. Instead of the typical sexual excitement one would expect with an illicit affair, the following matter-of-fact exchange takes place between the would-be copulants:

> Gallimard: You look . . . just like I thought you would under your clothes.
>
> Frau Baden: What did you expect? So come and get it!

While Gallimard's remark highlights the complete coincidence between the eye and the gaze, and therefore the lack precisely of a lure in his relationship with this other woman, Frau Baden's notion of "getting it" complements his observation by containing sex entirely within the satiable and short-term realm of physical need. Sex with her is but a casual meal, in which the physical body, because it is completely available, remains a *mere* body. The force of the phallus—and with it fantasy, the lure, and seduction—does not come into play at all.

"Under the Robes, beneath Everything, It Was Always Me"

One of the most moving and unforgettable scenes in this film is the one in which, after the costume farce in the French courtroom, Song and Gallimard, both in men's suits, sit face to face alone in the police van taking them to prison. As the two men stare at each other, Song is the first to break the silence: "What do you want from me?" he asks. In psychoanalytic terms, this question is an indication of the fundamental issue in our relationship with an other—demand. However, even though Song has brought up this fundamental issue, he has, nonetheless, posed his question imprecisely, because he still thinks in terms of Gallimard's wanting something *from him*. Instead, as Lacan has taught us, the significance of demand is never simply what can be effectively enunciated by way of what the other can literally give us; rather, it is what remains resistant to articulation, what exceeds the satisfaction provided by the other.[17] To pose the question of demand with precision, therefore, Song would have had to ask: "What do you want, by wanting me? What is your demand, which you express through me?"

Gallimard, on the other hand, responds to (the philosophical implications of) this question precisely: "You are my Butterfly."

With this exchange, what takes place between the former lovers is now a new kind of nonreciprocity. If, in the past, their nonreciprocity was a matter of their playing their respective roles in the game of erotics and politics, a nonreciprocity that enabled them to meet through the lure, the new nonreciprocity has to do rather with Song's attempt to change the very terms of their relationship. Instead of playing "Butter-fly" the way he has for Gallimard all these years, Song does something he has never done before: he undresses, challenging Gallimard to see for the first time what he has always wanted but somehow always failed to see. Kneeling completely naked in front of Gallimard, Song pleads for a rekindling of the affection that once existed between them. As he gazes tenderly up at his former lover, Song says, in a manner that reveals that he has indeed loved the Frenchman all along: "Under the robes, beneath everything, it was always me."

If, until this tragic moment, the lure has been kept intact because it is upheld on both sides, Song, by the very gesture of undressing with which he tries to regain Gallimard's love, has destroyed that lure for-ever. While Song intends by this brave and defiant gesture a new beginning for their relationship—a beginning in which they can face each other honestly as they really are, two men physically and emotion-ally entangled for years—what he actually accomplishes is the death of that relationship. Song fails to see that what Gallimard "wants" is not him, Song, be he in the definitive form of a woman or a man, but, as Gallimard says, "Butterfly." Because Gallimard's desire hinges on nei-ther a female nor a male body, but rather on the phallus, the veiled thing that is the "oriental woman," Song's candid disclosure of his physical body can only be lethal. Like Frau Baden, who, having dis-clothed herself, invites Gallimard frankly to "come and get it," Song's gesture of undressing serves not to arouse but extinguish desire.

The naked body destroys the lure once and for all by demonstrating that what lies under the veil all these years is nothing, no thing for fantasy. With the veil lifted, the phallus shows itself shamefully as merely a man, a penis, a pathetic body in all its banal vulnerability, which Gallimard rejects in abhorrence. (As many have pointed out, this moment in *M. Butterfly* is comparable to a similar one in *The Crying Game*, in which the man, in love with a transvestite whom he supposes to be a female, vomits at the sight of his beloved's actual genitalia. What has to be thrown up literally is the repugnant reality of the physical.) Song's naked body must therefore be understood ultimately as the traumatic Real that tears apart the dream of "Butterfly," forcing Galli-mard to wake up in the abyss of his own self. In the two men's *parting* conversation, we see how, instead of rescuing Gallimard, Song's sincere love finally brings about the nonreciprocity that is their absolute part-ing of ways:

> Gallimard: You, who knew me so well—how could you, of all people, have made such a mistake?
>
> Song: What?

The Dream of a Butterfly

Gallimard: You've just shown me your true self—when all I loved was the lie. A perfect lie—it's been destroyed.

Song (genuinely hurt): You never really loved me?

Gallimard: I'm a man who loved a woman created by a man. And anything else—simply falls short.

"It's Not the Story; It's the Music"

From Gallimard's perspective, the disappearance of that "lie" he loves, that very thing in which he has found a means of anchoring his identity, means a traumatic self-awakening that is the equivalent of madness. Before examining this awakening/madness closely, I think it is necessary to discuss one more aspect of this "thing"—the music from *Madama Butterfly*—which, as much as the fetishized "oriental woman," serves as Gallimard's anchorage.

It is possible to think of the operatic music as a kind of big Other, to which the human characters submit in such a manner as to create their "fate." This fate is predicted by a remark made by Song in an early conversation with Gallimard, in regard to his fascination with the Madame Butterfly story: "The point is," she says, "it's not the story; it's the music." Indeed, one could argue that, as much as the "oriental woman," the music is the agent that engenders the plot of the story, so that it is the story which follows the lead of the music rather than the reverse. From the initial performance at the foreign embassy of "Un bel dì," which establishes contact between Gallimard and Song, we move through scenes in which the music of *Madama Butterfly* continues to haunt the characters, as if always to recall them to the primal moment of their fateful encounter. For instance, even Gallimard's wife, when she hears about his captivation by Song's performance, bursts into a spontaneous performance complete with hand gestures. In the mirror reflection that follows, we see Gallimard looking bewildered and uneasy at his wife's uncanny mimicry of the "other woman." He goes on to place a special order for the record album of the opera, noticing, upon its arrival, its cover illustration of the "oriental woman" in a submissive posture to her Western lover.

Crucially also, Gallimard's amorous relationship with "Butterfly" takes place at a time when both *Madama Butterfly* and Chinese opera singers are considered to be relics of the past.

In the China of the mid-1960s, not only were imported items such as Western operatic music considered bourgeois and imperialist; even indigenous traditional art forms such as the Beijing opera were deemed feudal and corrupt. The revolution demanded that all such ideologically suspect relics be purged and replaced by new, progressive practices. The second time Gallimard visits the Chinese theater where Song used to perform, a Maoist "model play" is being staged with a different kind of dramatic semiotics and a noticeably different didactic sentience. Such ostensible state intervention in aesthetic forms, together with the massive burning of traditional artifacts, the forced trial and punishment of intellectuals, writers, and artists, and the coerced surrender of personal ideals for the common good, made up the new reality of Chinese political life. In the film, the communist revolution establishes itself in Chinese society as a new big Other with its power to interpellate ordinary citizens with the call to repudiate the past and labor for the future. As Gallimard is finally sent back to France (since, as he is told, his foreign policy predictions about Vietnam and China were all wrong), Song is seen working with other intellectuals in a labor camp, where loudspeakers blare away with "reeducation" messages to cleanse people's souls.

If the loudspeaker of a labor camp is the apparatus for a new type of fantasy—the fantasy of revolutionized subjectivity, of proletarian agency, of nationalist progress—it is shown to compete rather weakly with that other, older and "corrupt" apparatus of interpellation, the operatic music of *Madama Butterfly*. As Song looks up strained and exhausted from her labor, she seems to hear another voice from afar, which gradually takes over the audible space hitherto occupied by the loudspeaker. As this voice becomes louder, we recognize it to be the familiar music from *Madama Butterfly*, and the grayish backdrop of the labor camp changes into Paris, 1968, when Gallimard is watching a performance of *Madama Butterfly*, with tears slowly trickling down his face, at the Paris Opera. Song and Gallimard are thus, we might say, reunited through this persistent "corrupt" big Other of "Butterfly," which was what brought them together in the first place.

This dream of a Butterfly, of an unforgettable erotic and emotional experience, inserts itself in a Paris that, as Gallimard's acquaintance in a bar tells him, is looking more like Beijing, with students shouting Maoist slogans and rioting in the streets. The juxtaposition at this point of the erotic and the political, the "personal" and the "historical," raises a question that *M. Butterfly* merely hints at but that nonetheless is crucial to any consideration of fantasy: is "revolution" itself, the film seems to say, not simply another type of "fantasy stereotype"—the fantasy stereotype that exploits in the name of the collective, the people? If we mobilize, as we must, criticism against Western "orientalist" and "imperialist" fantasies about the East, then should the cruelties committed by way of this *other* fantasy stereotype not also be under attack?

The pro-Chinese communist fervor in France of the 1960s—is it an awakening from Western imperialism and Orientalism, or is it not simply the other side of that dream called Butterfly, which fetishizes the East this time not in the form of an erotic object but in the form of a political object, not in the form of the beautiful "oriental woman" but in the form of the virile oriental man, the Great Helmsman, Mao Zedong?

In his indifference to the political revolution, Gallimard will listen again to the music from *Madama Butterfly* in his own private space, away from the clamor of the streets. An evening alone in his minimalist, orientalist apartment, where a meal consists of mere bread and broth, he sits forlornly accompanied by the "Humming Chorus" played on his MCA record. As if by miracle, "Butterfly" again enters: in the midst of the melancholic music, Song has mysteriously reappeared.

Madame Butterfly, C'est Moi

After this scene of reunion, the music from *Madama Butterfly* will be heard one final time—as an accompaniment to Gallimard's performance in jail. Played on a cassette, the music has by this time become a portable object, very much like the other things that Gallimard consciously displays *on himself* in this scene. How then are we to bring together the music, the "pure sacrifice" of the "oriental woman," and Gallimard's gory suicide?

In this final one-man show, which progresses as Song is meanwhile released and sent back to China, Gallimard begins by commenting on his own "celebrity" and then proceeds to tell the story that led up to it. Gradually but steadily, as he describes his vision of the slender "oriental women" in "cheongsams and kimonos, who die for the love of unworthy foreign devils," Gallimard performs a transformation into Madame Butterfly herself. The camera shows him putting on the sash for his kimono, followed by white foundation across his face, eyelining, shiny red lip gloss, and finally a wig. As his transformation becomes complete, the transvestite pronounces: "At last, in a prison far from China, I have found her. . . . My name is René Gallimard! Also known—as Madame Butterfly!"

This scene of dramatic transformation offers, I think, one of the most compelling and complex moments in cinematic history. Because of this I must emphasize that the readings I provide below are much more experimental explorations than exact renderings of its significance.

First, what is effected in these last moments of the film seems to be a merging of two separate identities. This merging returns us, once again, to the theme of the self-sacrificing "oriental woman" discussed above, with a new twist. If Gallimard is Madame Butterfly, then this performance of his transformed identity should perhaps be described as a retroactive enactment, a slow-motion replay, of a story whose meaning has become visible only now—for the first time. In this story, Gallimard the "oriental woman" has been sacrificing himself (herself) for a man (Song) who, as Gallimard points out, is not worthy of his (her) love. This merging and swapping of identities, through which Gallimard turns into "Butterfly," is what Hwang intends as the basic "arc" of his play: "the Frenchman fantasizes that he is Pinkerton and his lover is Butterfly. By the end of the piece, he realizes that it is he who has been Butterfly, in that the Frenchman has been duped by love; the Chinese spy, who exploited that love, is therefore the real Pinkerton."[18] To return to the point of seduction I made earlier, we may add, paradoxically, that in seducing Gallimard, Song in fact led him temporarily away from his own truth—the truth of a fantasy that is not a fantasy of the other but rather *of himself as the suicidal "oriental woman."* In desiring Song, Gallimard was desiring not exactly to have her but to be her, to be the "Butterfly" that she was playing. While being the setting and structuring of fantasy, therefore, the encounter with Song served in effect to displace and postpone the fulfillment of Gallimard's wish for his own immolation. The "Butterfly" that was Song, in other words, shielded Gallimard from the "Butterfly" that is himself.

But if the relationship with Song has been a screen against the Real by giving Gallimard a conventional anchorage—a relation with a physical other and within the acceptable symbolic of heterosexual sociality—the revelation of Song's banal maleness means that this screen, which protected him but also prevented him from seeing, has evaporated. With the screen also disappear the fixed positions that are usually ascribed to man and woman, occident and orient. In a manner similar to Laplanche and Pontalis's argument about fantasy, what Gallimard's fantasy of "Butterfly" accomplishes in this final scene of monstrous transformation is ultimately a belated staging of a field of relations with multiple entry points, a field where positions of dominance and submission, of male and female, of aggressor and victim, are infinitely substitutable and interchangeable. Gallimard's transformation continues, in tandem, the series of vertiginous transvestist masquerades that began with Song.

Second, while this interpretive narrative of interchangeable racial and sexual subjectivities that I have just offered is perhaps the one most likely to be favored by critics who are invested in the utopian potential of destabilized identities, there are other elements in this transformation that far exceed such a narrative. For one thing, the conclusion that Gallimard finally discovers himself to be Madame Butterfly does not explain the power of the *visual* play of this last series of shots. How, in other words, might we understand his transformation in terms of the dynamics, the power structure of vision—of the relations between the image and the gaze? What does the interplay between Gallimard the Frenchman, Gallimard the performer, and Gallimard the Madame Butterfly signify *in terms of visuality?* For my own aid, I turn at this point to Lacan's reading of a story which has much genealogical affinity with ours.

I am referring to Lacan's consideration of the Chinese philosopher Zhuang Zi's well-known butterfly dream. Zhuang Zi wrote that one day, he dreamt that he was a butterfly happily flitting and fluttering around. He did not know he was Zhuang Zi. On waking up, he was, of course, once again solidly and unmistakably himself, but he did not know if he was Zhuang Zi who had dreamt that he was a butterfly, or a butterfly dreaming he was Zhuang Zi.[19] Lacan's analysis, which foregrounds the relations of visuality, goes as follows:

> In a dream, he is a butterfly. What does this mean? It means that he sees the butterfly in his reality as gaze. What are so many figures, so many shapes, so many colours, if not this gratuitous *showing,* in which is marked for us the primal nature of the essence of the gaze. . . . In fact, it is when he was the butterfly that he apprehended one of the roots of his identity—that he was, and is, in his essence, that butterfly who paints himself with his own colours—and it is because of this that, in the last resort, he is Choang-tsu [Zhuang Zi].[20]

What fascinates Lacan, I think, is that the dream, in which the "I"/eye of Zhuang Zi becomes this Other, the butterfly, returns Zhuang Zi for a moment to a state of nondifferentiation in which the Other exists as pure gaze.[21] In this state of nondifferentiation, one is not conscious of oneself as consciousness, as thought. This dream is so powerful that even when he wakes up, Zhuang Zi is not sure whether "he" is not simply (a lost object) dreamt by the butterfly. For Lacan, Zhuang Zi's butterfly dream is a glimpse into the truth: "it is when he was the butterfly that he apprehended one of the roots of his identity—that he was, and is, in his essence, that butterfly who paints himself with his own colours—and that it is because of this that . . . he is Choang-tsu." The conscious identity of Zhuang Zi, the "I"/eye of waking life, in other words, is the result of the butterfly's "causing" him to exist or marking him with the grid of desire.[22] Waking from this dream back into consciousness is therefore an unsettling awakening into the fact that in one life's as *cogito,* one is a captive butterfly, captivated by nothing but the inescapable law and structure of human cognition.

Lacan's reading of Zhuang Zi's dream brings us one step closer to unraveling the visual dynamics of Gallimard's transformation. Accordingly, we could see Gallimard's transformation as an equivalent to Zhuang Zi's dream, in which he, Gallimard, becomes a "Butterfly." The very image of the "oriental woman" in her strange shape and figure, in her bright colors, is then the gratuitous *showing* that Lacan mentions as the primal nature of the essence of the gaze. This gaze returns Gallimard to the roots of his identity by showing, by giving to the eye, (the knowledge) that "Butterfly" is what causes him to exist by marking him with desire. As in Zhuang Zi's story, therefore, the question implicit in Gallimard's performance is: how do "I," Gallimard, know that I, with my fantasy, my longing for the "oriental woman," am not merely an object dreamt by "Butterfly," the gaze that I (mis)took for an image? Instead of being Gallimard dreaming of a "Butterfly," might I not myself be the dream of a "Butterfly"?

Third, just as Lacan writes that Zhuang Zi is, in his essence, "the butterfly who paints himself with his own colours," so Gallimard, strictly speaking, does not simply perform but rather *paints* himself into Madame Butterfly—or more precisely, paints himself with her colors. Once this emphasis is introduced, we are able for the first time to view this scene of transformation as about a process of painting, with philosophical implications to be deduced from the relationships between the act of painting, the painted image, and the gaze.

Lacan, contrary to conventional thinking and following philosophers such as René Caillois and Maurice Merleau-Ponty, writes that painting is not really mimicry or imitation in the sense of creating a secondary, derivative form on the basis of a pre-existing one. Rather, if it is indeed mimicry or imitation in the sense of producing an image, this image is part of a process in which the painter enters a specific relation with the gaze—a relation in which the gaze (especially as embodied by the spectator) is tamed:

> To imitate is no doubt to reproduce an image. But at bottom, it is, for the subject, to be inserted in a function whose exercise grasps it. . . .
>
> The function of the picture—in relation to the person to whom the painter, literally, offers his picture to be seen—has a relation with the gaze. This relation is not, as it might at first seem, that of being a trap for the gaze. It might be thought that, like the actor, the painter wishes to be looked at. I do not think so. I think there is a relation with the gaze of the spectator, but that it is more complex. The painter gives something to the person who must stand in front of his painting which, in part, at least, of the painting, might be summed up thus— *You want to see? Well, take a look at this!* He gives something for the eye to feed on, but he invites the person to whom this picture is presented to lay down his gaze there as one lays down one's weapons. This is the pacifying, Apollonian effect of painting. Something is given not so much to the gaze as to the eye, something that involves the abandonment, the *laying down*, of the gaze.[23]

These passages indicate that painting can be described as a process of disarming the Other, of warding off the menace that comes from the Other. The means of disarming the Other is the painted image, which may thus be described as a second-order gaze, an artificial eye, a fetish in the sense of an amulet or talisman that may ward off evil. However, in using this understanding of painting as a way to read Gallimard's transformation, we are immediately confronted by the fact that Gallimard is not only the painter, nor only both painter and image, but painter, image, and spectator, all three at once. This fact considerably complicates the combative relation between the painter and the gaze that Lacan sets forth. By painting himself as Madame Butterfly, is Gallimard simply making an image to fend off the gaze (in which case he would remain in the subjectivity of the painter)? Is he not also the painted image, and is he not, as he looks at himself in the mirror, also the spectator, the one to be tamed? As "Butterfly," Gallimard appears also as a clown—but is the clown mocking us or is she the object of our mockery, and for what reason? All in all, how are we to describe this ultimate act of Gallimard's *passion,* his *passage* from painter to image to spectator?[24]

This passion/passage that is painting, we might say, is a process of making visible that which could otherwise never be directly seen. Significantly, therefore, painting here rejoins the etymological meaning of the word "fantasy," which means, precisely, "to make visible."[25] But "making visible" at the end of *M. Butterfly* is no longer simply a making visible of the multiple positions available to the subject. Rather, it is a process of throwing off the colors that make up the "self," a process of stripping and denuding that is comparable with processes of change in the natural world: "If a bird were to paint," Lacan writes suggestively, "would it not be by letting fall its feathers? a snake by casting off its scales, a tree by letting fall its leaves?"[26]

As Gallimard looks at the "Butterfly" in the mirror, he is transformed into the spectator who is invited to lay down his own gaze. This laying down of the gaze is the laying down of the weapon, the protective shield that separates us from the Other. What Gallimard finally meets, in the painted picture of himself as Madame Butterfly, is that thing which, in its muteness and absoluteness, renders him—the man Gallimard—obsolete, inoperant, excluded.[27] If the gaze is that which is always somehow eluded in our relation to the world,[28] then what Gallimard meets, in his own Butterfly image, in a manner that can no longer be eluded, is the gaze as it has all along looked at him.

If this scene of transformation could indeed be seen as a performing of enlightenment—of Gallimard's discovery that Madame Butterfly is none other than he himself—it is also enlightenment-as-self-deconstruction. From the perspective of the man with desire, this enlightenment is not progress but a regression, a passage into inertia, into the thing he loves. With this passage and passion, which we call death, the illusory independence that one achieves through the primary narcissism of the "mirror stage," which shows one as "other" but gives one the illusion of a unified "I," disappears. Significantly, therefore, the instrument of death in the film is not simply the *seppuku* dagger in the opera *Madama Butterfly* or the knife in the play *M. Butterfly*, but a mirror—a mirror, moreover, which has lost its reflective function. Being no longer the usual means with which one says, "This is me, myself," the mirror now returns to its material being as a shard of glass with which to terminate life and pass into the inorganic. Gallimard's suicide completes and fulfills the fateful plot of *Madama Butterfly*, but instead of him performing "Butterfly," it is, strictly speaking, "Butterfly" which has been performing him. As the Frenchman "sacrifices" himself and passes into his beloved spectacle, the "Butterfly" that is the character, the story, and the music—in short, the gaze—lives on.[29]

Coda: New Questions for Cultural Difference and Identity

What I have attempted to show through a more or less Lacanian reading is the ineluctability of a serious consideration of fantasy—and with it, questions of cognition—in a story of exchange that is overtly "cross-cultural." What this reading makes explicit, I hope, is that fantasy is not something that can be simply dismissed as willful deception, as "false consciousness" to be remedied by explicit didactics. Once fantasy is understood as a problem structural to human cognition, all the "cross-cultural" analyses of ideology, misogyny, and racism that are rooted in a denigration of fantasy will need to be thoroughly reexamined.

If, in this fantasy, the orient is associated with femininity itself, then the problem of coming to terms with the orient is very much similar, structurally speaking, to the problem of coming to terms with woman in psychoanalysis—in that both the orient and woman have been functioning as the support for the white man's fantasy, as the representation of the white man's *jouissance*. However, what distinguishes Cronenberg's film from many examples of such representation—one thinks, for instance, of Bernardo Bertolucci's *The Last Emperor, The Sheltering Sky,* and *The Little Buddha*—is precisely the manner in which the lavish, visible painting of fantasy finally takes place not on the female, feminized body of the other but on the white male body, so that enlightenment coincides with suicide, while the woman, the other, escapes.[30]

What remains unknown, then, is the "supplementary" *jouissance* of woman (and, by implication, of the orient) as spoken of by Lacan, who, in an aptly deconstructionist manner, puts his emphasis on the word "supplementary."[31] What does woman want, and what does the orient want? At no moment in the film *M. Butterfly* does Song's subjectivity and desire become lucid to us—we never know whether she is "genuine" or masquerading, whether her emotions are "for real" or part of her superb playacting—until in the "showdown" scene in the police van. In that scene, we see for the first time that what she "wants" is a complete overturning of the laws of desire which have structured her relationship with Gallimard. In other words, in spite of her love for the Frenchman, what the "oriental woman" wants is nothing less than the liquidation of his entire sexual ontological being—his death.

Even though Song does not get what she wants directly, her wish is vindicated by the ending of the film. Gallimard's transformation into Madame Butterfly indicates that femininity and the "oriental woman" are the very truth of Western Man himself, and, because he is traditionally identified with power, he is so far removed from this truth that his self-awakening must be tragic. Gallimard's death shows that Western Man is himself no-thing more than a French penis dreaming of (being) an oriental butterfly.

By definition, the death of the white man signals the dawn of a fundamentally different way of coming to terms with the East. The film closes with "Butterfly" flying back to China. This "oriental woman" that existed as the white man's symptom—what will happen to her now that the white man is dead? That is the ultimate question with which we are left.

SIX

Women in the Holocene:
Ethnicity, Fantasy, and the Film
The Joy Luck Club

The Scar

IN THE EARLY scenes of *The Joy Luck Club* (directed by Wayne Wang, 1993), we notice a detail that does not at first seem significant. Auntie An-mei's neck looks somewhat unusual, and she seems always to wear clothes that hide it. Only much later—for An-mei's story is among the last ones to be told—do we find out that what we did not see very well earlier is a scar.[1] When An-mei was a little girl back in China, she was in the house of her grandparents one day, when a heart-rending scene of cursing and rejection took place. Her mother, who had been newly widowed, was being accused of having had sexual relations with another man. As a daughter she had thus brought shame to her family by her lack of the chastity befitting a widow. In spite of her mother's pleading, An-mei's grandparents did not want her back. In a moment of heated gesticulation, the adults caused a boiling pot of soup to spill on the young An-mei, scorching her neck with what was to remain a scar— a scar that, as she would tell us, was the only thing with which she had to remember her mother for a long time to come. Eventually, An-mei would see her mother again and discover the truth of her mother's so-called "lack of chastity." Her mother had been raped by a rich man, Wu Tsing, and had become pregnant. Since no one believed she had been raped, she had no choice but ask to be taken into his house as his fourth concubine. When she delivered her child, a baby boy, he was immediately taken to be raised as the son of the second wife. Living in a house full of suspicion, distrust, rivalry, and bad will, An-mei's mother had no sense of her own worth. Even though her untimely death from some pastries stuffed with opium was rumored to be an accident, An-mei knew it was suicide. At her mother's funeral, An-mei bravely demanded the repentance of all those who had caused her mother to die. Her mother killed her own weak spirit, she says, so that she could give An-mei a stronger one, and from that day on, An-mei learned how to shout.

In spite of its smallness, the scar is, in a number of ways, a crucial key to the narrative action of *The Joy Luck Club*. Structurally, it is a narrative hinge: it provides a means for An-mei's story to unfold and takes us back to a past that is otherwise unavailable to us. But it is not simply a narrative hinge in the abstract. As a mark, a closed-up wound left permanently on a female body, this scar is what links different generations of women together. If the daughter is scarred for life, it is because her mother was scarred for life: the daughter's body stands as a permanent witness, a testifying piece of evidence for the rejection, humiliation, and suffering of the mother. This piece of evidence, created by what happened to the mother but inscribed corporeally on the daughter, is the sign of an unforgettable relationship, in which the lonely and self-sacrificing mother is given companionship and comradeship.

Toward the end of this chapter I will come back to this scarring as the site of an ambiguous, ambivalent idealism in the age of "multiculturalism." Before doing that, I would like to discuss some of the problems inherent in the general reception of *The Joy Luck Club*.

"How Authentic Am I?": The "Ethnic Film" Reading

It would not be an exaggeration to say that the success of the film *The Joy Luck Club*, much like the success of the novel by Amy Tan, has largely been the result of a trendy enthusiasm for celebrating what are in the North American context called "minority cultures." In keeping with the major pedagogical tenets of cultural pluralism, which aim at (re)educating us about the existence of cultures "other" than the predominant WASP cultures of the West, an increasing number of representations of what are considered "minor" identities and ethnicities are found in our mainstream media.[2] Regardless of the contents of their works, "minority" authors are primarily identified as targets of "ethnic" information: we cannot mention Amy Tan or Maxine Hong Kingston without being reminded that their stories are about the "Asian American" or "Chinese American" experiences, the same way we cannot mention Toni Morrison, Alice Walker, or Spike Lee without being reminded that their works pertain to the "African American" heritage. In highlighting the process in which these "ethnic" authors are received, my point is not to question the Asian American or African American writers' rights to investigate their peoples' histories; rather, it is to challenge a fundamental difference between the treatment of such writers and that of mainstream cultures. My question is not exactly why "ethnic" writers are considered "ethnic," but: what politics is in play when we hear about the "Asian American," "Latin American," "African American" experiences without at the same time hearing about the ethnic origins and ethnic sensitivities of, say, Madonna, Arnold Schwarzenegger, Mickey Mouse, Bart Simpson, or H. Ross Perot?[3] What would happen if indeed we were to view these figures of mainstream cultural representation the same way we view the "Asian American" or "African American"?

With these questions in mind, it seems to me that there are two issues at stake in the reception of *The Joy Luck Club* as an "ethnic film." First, representations such as *The Joy Luck Club* are socially pre-scripted in a certain category, namely, as a representation of "people of color" and of "ethnicity"—while many of their contemporaries (such as Sally Potter's *Orlando*, Martin Scorcese's *The Age of Innocence*, Jane Campion's *The Piano*, or James Ivory's *The Remains of the Day*) are not. Second, to this categorical distinction of "ethnic film" is moreover attached a pedagogical function, namely, that these "others" are trying to rediscover their "origins," which are "Chinese," "Japanese," "African," "Latino," and so forth, and which are essentially different from the normative and well-understood baseline represented by the white man and the white woman. In terms of the conventions of representation, the West and its "others" are thus implicitly divided in the following manner: the West is the place for language games, aesthetic fantasies, and fragmented subjectivities; the West's others, instead, offer us "lessons" about history, reality, and wholesome collective consciousnesses. This division has much to tell us about the ways "ethnicity" functions to produce, organize, and cohere subjectivities in the "multicultural" age.

If we juxtapose against the multiculturalist narratives of "ethnicity" the work of Michel Foucault, we see that ethnicity is fast acquiring the kind of significance and signifying value that Foucault attributes to sexuality in the period since the seventeenth century.[4] One of the most well-known of Foucault's arguments is that sexuality is not natural but constructed, and that in the multiple processes of discursive constructions, sexuality has, however, always been produced as the hidden, truthful secret—that intimate something people take turns to discover and confess about themselves. The discursive, narrative character of the productions of sexuality means that even though our institutions, our media, and our cultural environment are saturated with sex and sexuality, we continue to believe that it is something which has been repressed and which must somehow be liberated. Foucault calls this

Women in the Holocene

"the repressive hypothesis," by which he refers to the restrictive economy that is incorporated into the politics of language and speech, and
that accompanies the social redistributions of sex. Foucault is clear on
the didactic and indeed religious implications of the repressive hypothesis:

> The essential thing is . . . the existence in our era of a discourse in
> which sex, the revelation of truth, the overturning of global laws, the
> proclamation of a new day to come, and the promise of a certain
> felicity are linked together. Today it is sex that serves as a support
> for the ancient form—so familiar and important in the West—
> of preaching.
>
> The statement of oppression and the form of the sermon refer back
> to one another; they are mutually reinforcing. To say that sex is not
> repressed . . . not only runs counter to a well-accepted argument, it
> goes against the whole economy and all the discursive "interests" that
> underlie this argument. (*History of Sexuality,* I, pp. 8 and 9)

In other words, the great progress of sexuality-as-signification in Western modernity has been going hand in hand with two tenacious, collective beliefs—first in repression, then in emancipation. For Foucault, the
question is thus not why we are repressed, but how we came to believe
we are: how do we, he asks, construct scenarios in which sexuality must
be "liberated"? One response is that the proliferation of discourses
concerned with sex would not be possible without the concurrent proliferation of fields of power:

> More important was the multiplication of discourses concerning sex
> in the field of exercise of power itself: an institutional incitement to
> speak about it, and to do so more and more; a determination on the
> part of the agencies of power to hear it spoken about, and to cause *it*
> to speak through explicit articulation and endlessly accumulated de-
> tail. (*History of Sexuality,* I, p. 18; emphasis in the original)

The discursive ferment and mechanisms that surround "ethnicity"
in our time share many similar features with the "repressive hypothesis" that Foucault attributes to the discourse of sexuality. Chief of all is
the belief in "ethnicity" as a kind of repressed truth that awaits liberation. In order to facilitate this liberation, it is not enough that we identify
the hidden motifs and inscriptions of ethnicity in all cultural representations; it is believed that we also need to engage in processes of confession, biography, autobiography, storytelling, and so forth, that actively
resuscitate, retrieve, and redeem that "ethnic" part of us which has not
been allowed to come to light.

Moreover, while ethnicity can no doubt hold a subversive, progressive value for individuals faced with institutions that are traditionally

blind and deaf to the inequities and iniquities created by ethnic difference, the institutions themselves are already busily incorporating within them various kinds of "ethnic consciousness." If, as Foucault tells us, schools, hospitals, bureaucracies, military camps, and other public establishments register "sex" even when they put on a sexually "neutral" front, then increasingly and transindividually, the same establishments are creating the information networks for the inscription, institutionalization, and active utilization of ethnicity as a form of practice that is steadily subjected to methodical systematic calculation. For instance, while giving "minority" candidates a better chance of being selected, "equal opportunity" and "affirmative action" employment policies also provide institutions the means of monitoring what are supposedly "private" and "personal" elements such as family history, "racial" heritage, sexual preference, and so forth. As E. San Juan, Jr. writes, in the United States

> "ethnicity" is the official rubric to designate the phenomenological plurality of peoples ranked in a hierarchy for the differential allocation and distribution of resources. This hierarchy in turn is guaranteed by the taken-for-granted doctrines of liberal democracy premised on individual competition, the right to acquire property and sell labor power, and so on.[5]

Whenever institutions mobilize themselves this way, we are in the realm, as Foucault's arguments show, not of personal liberation but rather of disciplinary subject formation. Would it be far-fetched to say that precisely those apparatuses that have been instituted for us to gain access to our "ethnicities" are at the same time accomplishing the goal of an ever-refined, ever-perfected, and ever-expanding system of visuality and visibility, of observation and surveillance, that is not unlike Bentham's Panopticon, the model of the ideal prison which Foucault uses to summarize the modern production of knowledge—a production that is inseparable from discipline and punishment, from the ubiquitous "economy" of sociopolitical control?[6] It is in the light of a generalized panopticism that William Spanos, for instance, discusses the pluralistic regimentation of humanistic inquiry in the modern Western university as the paradigm case of what Foucault means by the production of knowledge:

> However invisible and unthought by administrators, faculty, students, and historians, the polyvalent panoptic diagram thematized on the ontological level by Heidegger and on the sociopolitical level by Foucault traverses the heterogeneous structure of the modern "pluralist" university. It saturates the domain of higher education from the physical organization of institutional and classroom space to the

"spiritual" space of inquiry and knowledge transmission: the "author function," research, journals, learned societies, conferences, hiring, professional advancement, and both pedagogical theory and practice. The university as we know it has its historically specific origins in the Enlightenment and reflects and contributes to "the gradual extension" and "spread" of the mechanisms of discipline "throughout the whole social body."[7]

Panopticism is ultimately the extreme form of an efficient socializing gaze which oversees and conditions us even in our most "private" beliefs and "solitary" activities. The power of the Panopticon owes not so much to its existence as a tangible architectural structure monitoring our behavior from the outside, as to its capacity to be internalized by us as an ever-vigilant Other demanding from us our secrets, our histories, our collaboration. Implicit in the conception of the Panopticon was, as Foucault writes, the ideal of

> an architecture that is no longer built simply to be seen (as with the ostentation of palaces), or to observe the external space (cf. the geometry of fortresses), but to permit an internal, articulated and detailed control—to render visible those who are inside it; in more general terms, an architecture that would operate to transform individuals: to act on those it shelters, to provide a hold on their conduct, to carry the effects of power right to them, to make it possible to know them, to alter them. (*Discipline and Punish*, p. 172)

This power is evident as we think of the frequency with which, in the "multicultural" age, we answer the call and demand to narrate our "ethnic" pasts and lineages. The invisible interrogation behind the multiculturalist "ethnicity" apparatuses is: "How authentic are you?" —to which everyone voluntarily responds with self-conscious reflections, descriptions, and appellations. Once we respond, however, we are helping to complete the circuit set off by the panopticist interrogation process. The more detailed and earnest our research into our ethnic histories as such, the more successful the panopticist interrogation is in accomplishing its task.

It is not an accident, therefore, that this panopticist interrogation is usually most effective—i.e., that it exhibits its disciplinary "gaze" most luringly—when it is "investigating" those "others" who are supposedly far from what is held to be the cultural "norm." As in the cases of the clinic, the prison, the madhouse, and other such institutions for social outcasts, the systemic production of knowledge here is most efficient not only through the internalization of discipline by individuals—what Louis Althusser calls the "interpellation" of the subject[8]— but also through the active creation of what we might call the *National*

ETHICS AFTER IDEALISM

Geographics of the soul—the observation platforms and laboratories in which the "perverse" others—the "inmates"—can be displayed in their "non-conforming" and "abnormal" behavior, in their strangely coded practices and rituals. Such observation platforms and laboratories would include the confessional, autobiographical narratives told voluntarily by these "others" in their interaction with the panopticist gaze, which solicits from them not only their life stories but a sustained belief in the necessity of their confessions as arising from genuine "experience." In Joan Scott's terms, such "experience" is now given the value of a kind of foundationalism whose truth lies beyond the discursivity that is, in fact, its basis.[9] In an age when the sexual revolution is drawing to a close in part because of epidemics such as AIDS, the arena of panopticist interrogation that was previously monopolized by sexuality now gives way to experiences of "ethnicity," which in turn generate spectacular results.

This, then, is certainly one manner in which we can view *The Joy Luck Club*. If cinema, together with other types of technologized visuality, is one of the most effective apparatuses of subject-formation in our age, then *The Joy Luck Club* can certainly be described as playing up to the panopticist multiculturalist gaze in a number of ways. The film centers on life experiences that are revealed to us through autobiographical narratives. Each in her turn, the four mothers—Lindo, Ying Ying, An-mei, and Suyuan—reveal to us the historical layers of their subjectivities, each with a tale of the horrors and sufferings they had to go through as young women in another time and another land. Lindo lost her own mother and family when she entered the Wang family as a child bride, but she was eventually able, with courage and intelligence, to extricate herself from the sad fate that awaited her as an "infertile" daughter-in-law. Ying Ying fell in love with a playboy, who abandoned her for other women soon after they were married. In her resentment and anger, she drowned her own baby while bathing him. An-mei witnessed her mother's rejection by her own family and the humiliation she suffered in the Wu family. Suyuan, who had twins, had to abandon them during wartime, when she herself was so ill that she thought she was going to die. She never found out that the babies lived. (Suyuan's story came to us from her widower-husband.)

Even though the mothers' stories are not the only events that take place in the film, we feel that they are where the emotional densities of the film are most invested. These stories, (re)narrated with lush, sensuous colors, with characters and settings that stand in memorably bold contours, deliver into the contemporary English-speaking world of the daughters some kind of truth from a faraway past. At the same time, if the effect of these stories is one of liberation, it is also one of exoticism. Not only are the images of the past always given in aesthetically distinct frames that mark them off from the present, but even the mothers' idiosyncratic voices—their intonations, their exclamations, their stubbornness, their accents which are supposedly a mixture of English words and Chinese syntax—add to this aura of an otherness that is unknowable except through their acts of autobiographical narration. If these memories exist only in the mothers' minds, the film becomes in effect an opening, a disclosure of these minds, a rendering-in-visibility of the hidden dramatic forces that make up their magical, archaeological appeal.

In terms of the panopticist interrogation, *The Joy Luck Club* could thus be seen as an instance of the many current contributions toward the new discursive obsession called "ethnicity." Relying on some of the most used conventions of cinema—voice-over narration, sentimental music, melodramatic events, sensuous cinematography—the film generates a potentially endless process in which the past is "emancipated" for the present and the future. While we are given four sets of stories, the film could theoretically have included many more, with the same kind of emancipatory structure and utopian ending, whereby the dead and absent mother becomes precisely the point of narrative closure, of family reunion across continents, across vastly different cultural settings, and across time lost. As in Foucault's argument about sexuality, the repressive hypothesis—which in the present context amounts to the belief that the origins of Asian American cultural experiences have been forgotten, neglected, or silenced—goes hand in hand with the proliferation of dialogues, narratives, images, and details in such a way as to turn filmic representation itself into precisely the kind of "observation platform" in the terms described above. Ethnicity is here the "secret"—the truth of subjectivity—that must be released into the open in order for human social identity to be properly established. But as it is consciously dramatized, ethnicity also becomes a transparent sight/ site, enabling the emergence of a clear, legible subject and the rich but essentially family-oriented communication within the identified "ethnic" group. Thus the young Chinese American woman June, whose narrative voice organizes the entire filmscript, finally takes the place of her mother (Suyuan) and returns to the homeland, China, to meet her half-sisters and complete a journey that began decades ago.

If my reading were to stop at this point, then it could be summarized as a reading that basically understands the film as an instance of loyal service to the dominant American ideology of multiculturalism. A Foucauldian reading such as the one I have been following, with its tendencies to point to the institutional streamlining of subjectivities through the repressive hypothesis, would dovetail very well with a reading by way of Althusser's theory of ideology and Edward Said's *Orientalism*.[10] The criticism of an institutionally normalized subject who is effectively interpellated by society's practices of discipline and coercion in the name of "ethnicity" would, in this instance, accompany a criticism of *The Joy Luck Club* as a work of Orientalism that simply panders to the tastes for "ethnic diversity" among white readers and audiences alike.[11] In such a reading, all the signifiers of ethnicity, of "Chineseness," including the sceneries, costumes, mannerisms, verbalisms, acts of violence, and so forth, would have to be written off as a mythification, a degradation and distortion that has little to do with the "real" China and "real" Chinese people.[12]

Even though we cannot understand *The Joy Luck Club* without the insights of Foucault, Althusser, and Said—for those insights reveal in an indispensable manner the kinds of subjection and subjugation our technologies of representation entail, in ways that no individual human being can escape—it is my belief that a responsible reading of the film, precisely if it is sensitive and responsive to the issues of contemporary cultural politics, cannot stop at this point. While Foucault, Althusser, and Said would move our reading toward mechanisms of institutional control, networks of subjective manipulation, and other devices of the exercise of panopticist power, their insights must also be reciprocated by a form of reading that would (re)discover in the various systems of surveillance traces of resistance that survive in what Michel de Certeau calls a "proliferating illegitimacy."[13] We need, in other words, to supplement the overtly Foucauldian, anti-Orientalist reading with one that attends to some of the peculiarities of the film itself.

Legends of Fantasy: The Illegitimate Reading

To do this supplementary reading, we need to begin where the other type of reading tends to end—namely, the place of the stereotypes, the myths, the melodramatic details. We will go back to the scar on Auntie An-mei's neck.

In many ways the scar is a banal element. As I already mentioned, it is a means to indicate the bond between mother and daughter; it is a narrative hinge that allows us to return to the scene of the crime and explore the history of An-mei's mother and grandmother. In terms of narrative conventions, the scar is a stereotypical device for a return to the "origin." But precisely what does it tell us about "origins"?

Upon close reading, the scar reveals itself to be the place of a profound ambivalence. If it does serve the conventionalized turns of narrative, it also exists as a unique kind of mark—a physical *defect* at the juncture between the female body and the larger "lineage" of so-called "Chineseness" or "ethnicity." The significance of this defect is twofold: it displaces the patriarchal obsession with "origins" onto a bonding

among women; it highlights women's place in patriarchy as itself always already a dis-place-ment. On the scarred female body, the patriarchal idea and ideal of a continuous ethnic lineage are violently disrupted. The "origin" to which the scar leads back is not a plenitude but
a war zone; it is not about the joys of ethnicity but about sex, fertility,
marriage, widowhood, rape, concubinage, and other forms of oppression—all with the female body as its battleground. If ethnicity, like
sexuality, is ultimately about the management of human reproduction,
then what the bond/scar between mother and daughter demonstrates
instead is *sexuality and ethnicity as enslavement*, as something that they
have to resist together rather than help perpetuate. The scar signifies
not so much the continuity of ethnic "origin" as its seriality—rather
than being a definite beginning, the origin "exists" only insofar as it is
a series, a relation, a mark-made-on-the-other. Behind each mother is
thus always another mother. Mothers are, in other words, not a replace-
ment of "fathers" but their displacement; not simply another self-sufficient "origin" but always already a mark-on-the-other, a signifer for
another signifer, a metaphor. Most of all, "mothers" are legends: as
much as being popular "stories," they offer, in themselves, *ways of
reading*.

It is hence important that we wrest the "mothers" of this film from
the anthropomorphic or humanistic realism in which they are bound to
be lodged in most interpretations. Rather, I suggest reading these mothers as, first and foremost, metaphors and stereotypes. As much as their
stories, the mothers themselves, including the very physical details
about them, are part and parcel of a skillful use of metaphors and
stereotypes in the cinematic production of a new kind of fantasy. We
think here not only of An-mei's scar, but also of Suyuan's bad teeth and
bleeding hands (as she pushes the wheelbarrow with her babies in it
during wartime), the expressive looks of all the mothers' eyes, the
articulate tensions of their facial muscles, their tears, their smiles, their
strong and determined voices, and so forth. All in all, such physical
details constitute the mothers as encrypted texts, gestural archives, and
memory palaces.

But what is the point of showing that mothers are metaphors, stereotypes, larger-than-life figures? First, it is to break away from a connota-
tively negative reading of melodrama. The usual assumption about
melodrama, even for many who take serious interest in it, is that it is
about the polarization of good and evil, of black and white, and so
forth—in other words, melodrama has always been assumed to be the
opposite of subtle and nuanced representation.[14] My argument is rather
that melodrama, especially as it appears in film, offers a privileged view
of the basically machinic or technologized nature of what we call sentimental emotions. As filmic devices such as the close-up and the slow-

motion make visible previously unseen/undetected dimensions of human life, revealing therein what Walter Benjamin calls the "optical unconscious,"[15] so the figure of the mother, insofar as it is presented in affectively enlarged and amplified—that is, melodramatized—terms, reveals the gendered "unconscious" that is our "maternal linkage."[16] Enlargement and amplification: these are, concurrent with affect, terms of machinic magnification—of visual and aural intensification. We may thus say that, with the intensified focus on the mother, human emotions are magnified *technologically* the way pictures are "blown up." The resulting aesthetic effect is not one of identity with but one of a distant fascination for this awesome "animal" and "being" which strikes us as spectacle and drama, and in front of which we lose control of our bodies—we cry.

Second, by making a deliberate theoretical move away from the realistic "ethnic film" reading, my point is to situate *The Joy Luck Club* within our postmodern explorations of human origins *in general*. At this juncture, it would be useless to compare and contrast *The Joy Luck Club* with films such as *The Wedding Banquet* or *Farewell My Concubine*, since these films are also received in the same classification of "ethnic film." Instead, I think we need to juxtapose *The Joy Luck Club* with a film such as—of all the wild leaps of the imagination—*Jurassic Park* (directed by Stephen Spielberg, 1993). My purpose in making this conjunction is to problematize the politics behind the prevalent categorical difference of the "ethnic other," a politics which organizes and hierarchizes what are in fact contemporary representations.

What do *The Joy Luck Club* and *Jurassic Park* have in common? In order to put my argument across, let me be very schematic. First, both films are about ancestry; both are about a certain fascination with a type of being that precedes younger groups of people and to which/whom the younger generations owe their present condition. Second, both films set up fictive scenarios in which the fascination with this ancestral other—mothers in the one case and dinosaurs in the other—leads to the unfolding of historical life details. The crucial point is that our access to these ancestral others is inevitably *coded*. In *The Joy Luck Club*, the ancestral land—China—is reconstructed through narrative codes, through memories that unfold in the characters' new environment—America—and that are in turn made into film. In *Jurassic Park*, the extinct environment of the dinosaurs is reconstructed through "scientific" codes, which include DNA cloning and the innovative technology that goes into the making of Jurassic Park; this artificially "reproduced" dreamland with its gigantic animals is in turn simulated through computerized effects on the movie screen.

Third, in both films the relation between the ancestors and the descendants is not at all an easy one. Amid fascination are feelings of horror, danger, and repulsion, as well as a definite sense of the pastness of the world of these others. The fictional exploration of these other-worldly beings goes hand in hand with a knowledge of the chronologically and experientially alien nature of their existence. This alienness is conveyed through exotic details—in *The Joy Luck Club,* through the elements that compose the phantasmagoric visual present we see in flashbacks; in *Jurassic Park,* through the elements that compose the phantasmagoric spatial present, the make-believe setting of Jurassic Park. Fourth, in spite of the knowledge of their alienness, part of the fascination with these others lies in the feeling that the younger generations and the ancestral beings are deeply related, and that these others represent, whether in historical, ethnic, or biological terms, our predecessors, our previous life forms. In *The Joy Luck Club,* the mothers' narratives are merged into the daughters'; in *Jurassic Park,* returning from the fantasy land to the world of modern cities in a helicopter, the characters see below them against the surf a line of ungainly dinosaur-like pelicans.

A possible objection to my juxtaposition of the two films would perhaps stem from my apparent dismissal of the sacredness of the human stories. Am I not committing the enormity of virtually equating "ethnics" and ethnic (m)others with animals? I will respond to this type of question by saying, first of all, that the notion that humans, who are animals, are superior to "animals"—since such would be the assumption behind this type of question—is not one to which I subscribe. A detailed response to the question would necessitate a problematizing of the age-old philosophical, epistemological, and ethical constructions of such a notion of superiority, and it would take us far beyond the parameters of this chapter. But the question of whether humans are superior to animals, important though it is, is not really the main issue here.

The main issue is that the multiculturalist conceptions of "ethnicities," following the steady progress toward the disciplining and fragmentation of knowledge since the Enlightenment, are ultimately part and parcel of an ongoing systemic splintering of the whole notion of "humanity" into manageable units of information. In the age of cyberspace, hypertext, and virtual reality, "humanity" can no longer be conceived without numbers, statistics, computerized processes of digitization, documentation, and permutation. If the status of "humanity" is that of "the real," the real itself is, in this age of simulations, "produced from miniaturized units, from matrices, memory banks and command models."[17] And yet, if high-tech fragmentation of "humanity" as such is the *general* condition of life in a rationalistic, speed- and efficiency-driven world, the ideological burden of "humanity" lingers with weight when it comes to "ethnicity." Precisely when the surfacing of "ethnic others" and the production of "ethnicity" as knowledge should further break up the notion of "humanity" as it was tradition-ally conceived in white, European, masculinist terms, such a notion of "humanity"—of humans as "higher" animals, as "subjects" with "con-sciousnesses," as "voices" of truth awaiting emancipation—reemerges in "ethnic" forms.

In what amounts to the same argument from a different perspective: even while "humanity" is irreversibly exploded and imploded with scientific advances such as genetic engineering, in-vitro fertilization, test-tube babies, surrogate mothers, and so forth—advances of experi-mentation with biological (re)production which are inextricably part of the mise-en-scène of science fiction fantasies such as *Jurassic Park*—the same old myth of "humanity," complete with blood ties, kinship bonds, and tribal identity, is fabricated through the "others" in the name not of fantasy but of reality, history, and ethnicity. The politics of the division between "science fiction" and "ethnic film," insofar as it tends to disallow precisely the kind of allegorical juxtaposition of the two films I am suggesting, is very much a reconfirmation of the racist ideology which sees the world in terms of "West" and "East," "us" and "them," and which has been, since the heyday of European imperial-ism, the main epistemological support of an academic discipline such as anthropology.

Even though it is likely to be considered illegitimate, then, the juxta-position of *The Joy Luck Club* and *Jurassic Park* enables us to see precisely the process of the "delegitimation" of knowledge that Jean-François Lyotard describes as characteristic of the postmodern condition. Lyo-tard holds that the crisis of knowledge—which he defines in terms of the disappearance of what he calls metanarratives—occurs in both the speculative/philosophical and the political spheres. In the specula-tive/philosophical sphere, the crisis is caused by "an internal erosion of the legitimacy principle of knowledge" and can be summarized as "a process of delegitimation fueled by the demand for legitimation itself." The failure of speculative knowledge to sustain, from within its prin-cipled parameters, its claim to truth leads ultimately to the perspec-tivizing of "truth" itself. In the political sphere, there is an increasing discontinuity between truth and justice: while the emancipation appa-ratus derived from the Enlightenment "grounds the legitimation of science and truth in the autonomy of interlocutors involved in ethical, social, and political praxis," there is "nothing to prove that if a state-ment describing a real situation is true, it follows that a prescriptive statement based upon it (the effect of which will necessarily be a modi-fication of that reality) will be just."[18]

In our present context, the two films correspond to the two interre-lated aspects of this postmodern "delegitimation." On the one hand is the science fiction fantasy with its infinitely multiplying *perspectival* inquiries—multimedia, simulated, hyperreal—into the truthful origins of biological life forms such as birds. Such inquiries call into question the traditional boundaries between the various fields of knowledge, in particular the boundary between science and myth. On the other hand is the so-called "ethnic work of art" with its implicit *political* imperative of vindicating the neglected fate/history of an entire culture and people, an imperative whose claim to truth is, however, always mediated by narratives, institutions, and apparatuses of representation. These narratives, institutions, and apparatuses of representation give the "ethnic work" the value of equivalence with other similar works but little proof of justice: all such works are now seen to have equal claims to "truth" through their equally autonomous, but always local, "subjectivities." While I do not necessarily agree with Lyotard's conclusion that the world has therefore become a matter of "language games" since the grand narratives have lost their credibility, I think his explanation of the delegitimation of knowledge helps clarify the mutually implicated epistemological/discursive functions of the science fiction fantasy and the "ethnic film," and the way they participate *concurrently* in the critical condition he calls the postmodern.

I have therefore borrowed the title of my chapter from Max Frisch's novella *Man in the Holocene*,[19] to gesture toward the much larger implications of fantasy with which *The Joy Luck Club* should, I think, be seen.

The Joy Luck Club, for all its apparent historical elements, is ultimately a legend—and a legend of fantasy at that. The fantasmatic mother-daughter relationships could be seen not so much as corresponding faithfully to Chinese American "history" as a dramatization of its metaphoricity, its textuality and seriality, and its "reality" as a kind of continual storytelling.[20] However, precisely because it uses "local" signifiers which are non-white, the film will continue to be read as "ethnic" and always be recuperated into a Western notion of otherness, of us-versus-them. Between the film's material signification and its inevitable recuperation, there is no exteriority, no outside position. This in-betweenness—between fantasy and recuperation—is the very space in which the politics of representation will always be played out in the age of cultural pluralism.

Pedagogically, then, *The Joy Luck Club* can be seen as the kind of mainstream film that is valuable precisely because it is ambiguous. When we see the film not in terms of the realistic register of "ethnicity" in which it is inevitably cast by the forces of multiculturalism, but instead as a kind of idealism production through cinema, then it would be possible to locate it within a libidinal economy that will always imagine its "origins" in another time and another place. We would see that it is a con-temporary of other Hollywood monuments such as *Jurassic Park*, with which it shares a present of the imaginary, of fantasy.

For these reasons I will call the female characters of *The Joy Luck Club* women in the Holocene—as a way to emphasize that they are full members of a geological present that must be understood not as a separatist subculture but rather as our contemporary culture, with its continual, even if very old, attempts to (re)imagine, (re)make, and (re)-invent itself.

To return to the detail with which I began: the film is, ultimately, a kind of scar. It is a mark of the historical discrimination against peoples of color, a sign of the damage they have borne alongside their continual survival. The recuperation of this scar as an entertaining embellish-ment—as a new, exotic way to tell stories in postmodern America—will always be the function of the dominant technologies of power with their capacity for panopticist searches and invasions. But the scar is, as well, the mark of a representational ambivalence and inexhaustibility—in this case, the ambivalence and inexhaustibility of the so-called "eth-nic film," which participates in our cultural politics not simply as the other, the alien, but also as us, as part of our ongoing fantasy produc-tion. The film, in other words, is a scar blown up to the size of a motion picture, in which we see the veins, the tissues, the traces, and the move-ments of scar formation. It is a legend in which and with which we read—how the scar attempts to heal and how, despite the scarification, the skin has taken on new life.

SEVEN

We Endure, Therefore We Are: Survival, Governance, and Zhang Yimou's To Live

─────────

IF THERE IS A metanarrative that continues to thrive in these times of metanarrative bashing, it is that of "resistance." Seldom do we attend a conference or turn to an article in an academic journal of the humanities or the social sciences without encountering some call for "resistance" to some such metanarrativized power as "global capitalism," "Western imperialism," "patriarchy," "compulsory heterosexuality," and so forth. In many respects, "resistance" has become the rhetorical support of identitarian politics, the conceptualization that underwrites discourses of class, racial, and sexual identity.[1] As an imaginary appealing especially to intellectuals, "resistance" would have to come from somewhere. It follows that resistance is often lodged in something called "the people" or one of its variants, such as "the masses," "the folk," or, at times, "the subalterns." What is implicitly set up, then, is a dichotomy between the pernicious power on top and the innocent, suffering masses at the bottom, whose voices await being heard in what is imagined as a corrective to the abuses of political power.

What is often missing in such an imaginary of popular resistance is the crucial notion of a mediating apparatus, a specifically defined public space, that would serve to regulate the relationship between those who have political power and those who do not. The *absence* of such a mediating apparatus has vast implications for the conceptualization of political governance. In this chapter, I would like to explore some of these implications by discussing aspects of the ideological conditions in contemporary China, particularly as such conditions appear in Zhang

Yimou's 1994 film *Huozhe* (*To Live*, Century Communications Ltd.; distributed in the United States by the Samuel Goldwyn Company).

"The People"

In twentieth-century China, the figure of "the people" has likewise been invested with the value of political resistance.[2] The overthrow of the ancient, monarchical form of political power in 1911 was accompanied by theorizations of *min*—"the people"—and it was on the basis of three principles—the people's race/ethnicity, livelihood, and sovereignty—that they were henceforth to be governed. "The people" as such was figured in the naming of the new political order founded in 1912 by Sun Yat-sen—*Zhonghua minguo*, literally, "the Chinese people's state." Even though the English translation of this name, "The Republic of China," does contain the idea of governance by the populace through the etymology of the word "republic," it does not highlight "the people" as literally and prominently as the Chinese phrase. (*Zhonghua minguo* is the name that continues to be used by the Taiwan government today.) In the decades subsequent to 1912, as the Chinese Communists gained control over the nation, the idea of "the people" was further defined in terms of the oppressed classes, in particular the rural peasants and the urban proletariat. Overturning the Confucian class hierarchy that had placed peasants and workers below scholars, the Chinese Communist conceptualization of society would put such subaltern classes at the very top, as the core of the new nation. In the era after 1949, when China proudly reestablished its status among the nations of the world, the collective rhetoric employed both inside and outside China was that the new China was a modern, *because* class-conscious, political state, a state founded on *popular resistance* to the feudalist corruption of the former elite classes of ancient China as well as to the imperialism and capitalism represented by the United States and Western Europe. The construction of national identity under communism, then, was firmly girded by "the people" and their "resistance," as the new nation's name, *Zhonghua renmin gongheguo*—"The People's Republic of China" —emphatically declared. As a means not of reflecting but of producing reality, the practice of naming extended far beyond the title of the new nation. As slogans such as *geming wuzui, zaofan youli* ("it is not criminal to make revolutions, it is right to rebel") became part of the everyday vocabulary during the frenzy of revolution, and as streets, hotels, hospitals, restaurants, department stores, and other public places acquired new appellations such as "Revolution," "People," "Friendship," "Struggle," "Proletariat," and their like, human relations, too, were being reformed through renaming. Titles based on the traditional kinship system (with its complex hierarchical differentiations) gave way to the nondifferentiating "comrade," a form of address that announced the egalitarian basis of Chinese social relations.

Since the Cultural Revolution (mid-1960s to mid-1970s), the ideals of the Communist Revolution have been challenged and, in many cases, abandoned.[3] However, even as Chinese intellectuals have come to realize, in disillusionment, that revolution and dictatorship are part of the same power structure, they have nonetheless continued to be fascinated by that entity called "the people." In the writings and films of the post–Cultural Revolution period, "the people" have once again become a site of utopian interest, a site to which writers and filmmakers repeatedly turn for inspiration. We think of the stories of Bai Hua, Mo Yan, Su Tong, Ah Cheng, Han Shaogong, Gao Xiaosheng, and Chen Zhongshi, among other authors, while contemporary films with rural, folkish, and popular themes by such directors as Wu Tianming, Chen Kaige, Tian Zhuangzhuang, Zhang Nuanxin, Xie Jin, and Xie Fei are known even to audiences who are not otherwise acquainted with contemporary China.[4]

In many of the fictional representations by these writers and filmmakers, the turn to "the people" is accompanied by the portrayal of suffering. Following their literary and filmic predecessors in their frequent recourse to melodrama and sentimentalism, contemporary Chinese writers and filmmakers explore suffering as an alternative political language, thus giving their works the appearance of affirming "individual rights and freedoms against totalitarianism."[5] But if this apparent interest in individual rights and freedoms is future-oriented and forward-looking, it is also nostalgic. As Immanuel Wallerstein writes:

> The temporal dimension of *pastness* is central to and inherent in the concept of peoplehood. . . . Pastness is a central element in the socialization of individuals, in the maintenance of group solidarity, in the establishment of or challenge to legitimation. Pastness therefore is preeminently a moral phenomenon, therefore a political phenomenon, always a contemporary phenomenon.[6]

In their discontent with current circumstances, Chinese intellectuals seem to be seeking in the "ordinary folk" a source of *past* knowledge that has remained uncorrupted by the lies and errors perpetrated in the decades of bureaucratized revolution. Inscribed in representations of China's remote areas and often illiterate populations, the search for such uncorrupted knowledge stems from a wish, in the post–Cultural Revolution period, for enlightenment through what is considered "primitive" and "originary." In terms of a shared political culture, therefore, this unmistakable nostalgia is not simply nostalgia for "the people" as such; it is also nostalgia for the *ideals* of popular resistance that once inspired political revolution. The continued fascination with "the people" suggests an attempt to cling to the beliefs that lay at the foundation of modern Chinese national identity. Yet precisely because the turn to "the people" is nostalgic as much as utopic—a desire for home as much as for change—it inevitably reencounters all the problems that are fundamental to that turn.

For instance, the invocation of "the people" has often gone hand in hand with another invocation—"the West."[7] During the Great Leap Forward, the rhetoric of *chao ying gan mei* (literally, overtaking England and catching up with the United States) was used to mobilize the entire country to labor hard for national self-strengthening.[8] Specifically, England and the United States stood for technological advancement, an area in which China needed to improve. Acknowledging the necessity of "Western technology," however, undermined belief in "the Chinese people" as the ultimate source of national empowerment in a fundamental way. For if China did in fact need *external* input in order to attain the status of a world-class nation, then what did that make "the people," the supposed mainstay of national identity? To solve the problem raised by this inconsistency, the Chinese Communists resorted—in spite of their claims of overthrowing tradition—to a formulation that has been used by Chinese politicians since the nineteenth century: "Let us adopt science and technology from the West, but let us preserve Chinese culture"; "let us modernize, but let us modernize with Chinese characteristics"; "let us adopt capitalism, but we will call it Chinese socialist capitalism." Such variations on the nineteenth-century dictum *zhong xue wei ti, xi xue wei yong* (Chinese learning for fundamental principle, Western learning for practical use) point to an ambivalence that structures the conceptualizing of a political culture based on an unmediated notion of popular resistance.

In such conceptualizing, "the people" become a fantastical stand-in for national specificity—in this case, for what is "Chinese." On the one hand, this thing that is "the Chinese"—their people, their culture, their value—is thought to be unique and self-sufficient; on the other hand, it is in need of preservation and protection from outside forces. "The Chinese"—people/culture/value—is what makes China China—that is, what no one can change or take away; at the same time, "the Chinese" is what "the West" can endanger—that is, what someone *can* change and take away. Caught between cultural pride and cultural necessity, the investment in national and cultural specificity as the basis of political identity is marked by an impossible rift from the beginning. To patch over this rift, a particular kind of essentialism has to be introduced, one which often takes stunningly provocative forms, demonstrating the logic of a well-lived, though tattered, ideology.

Consider the People's Republic's notorious manner of handling human rights. Here, China's foremost problem of governance, overpopulation, is approached not as a problem that can and should be solved gradually, but rather as an immutable fact—an immutable fact that is, moreover, cast in the form of an *essential lack*, the (potential) lack of food. Such, then, is the attitude of the Chinese authorities: it is inconceivable that the West tell China what to do on the issue of human rights because *human rights in China* simply means having enough to eat. Since the People's Republic has done more than any previous Chinese government to feed the Chinese people, it is already honoring human rights *in the Chinese way.* Human rights as insisted upon by Westerners—in the form of, say, freedom of speech and trial by law—amount to foreign interference in Chinese *internal* affairs. China—in the position of a victim—must resist such imposition, invasion, and so forth.

Instead of being used as an occasion to rethink the fraught relationship between the governing and the governed, the problem of overpopulation becomes a justification for the abuse of political power, an excuse to stop, rather than to begin, any consideration of alternative forms of governance. What is interesting is that such a justification for the abuse of political power must be aimed at an external target. In the world of postcolonial awareness, the intransigent attitude of the Chinese gerontocracy toward political governance conveniently finds its guise in the form of national self-determination against "the West."

A number of important implications are revealed in this process, all following from the fantastical construct of a "self-sufficient" China/ Chineseness that can and must govern itself. First, this need for self-governance is defined, paradoxically, by way of an essential lack—the lack of food—and thus as a matter of biological survival: the need for self-sustenance. Although China's long periods of starvation in the past might have had much to do with government policy and with the unequal distribution of food among different classes, history is bypassed in favor of an essentialist survivalism. Second, as the reduction of human rights to a matter of having enough to eat indicates, issues of political representation can be likewise reduced to—and abstracted as—something potentially lacking/missing. Accordingly, while it is this potentially lacking/missing thing that defines China's uniqueness, that makes China China, "the people" are in effect just a bunch of gaping mouths and, as such, are precluded from having political representation. In the vicious circle of "political rights"-cum-biological-needs, "the people" are literally held hostage by themselves—by their "essential need" to survive. Instead of being recognized as something done to or against "the people," the denial of political rights will thus always be *condoned* in their best interests. Third, the continual abuse of power, secured as it is by the structure of this vicious circle, can legitimate and perpetuate itself on the grounds of "Chinese" internal affairs.

Cultural and national identity, which is the crux of the relationship between the governing and the governed, is then simply a matter of cumulation, compounded by acts of essentializing, acts of absorbing and assimilating every problem inward—into the entrails of the physical body, into the interior of the nation, into the systemic propriety of the culture—and redefining it as "Chinese."

The Story of *To Live*

The people, popular resistance, and the relationship between such resistance and political governance are among the issues Zhang Yimou examines in his film *To Live*. Based loosely on the novella of the same title by the contemporary mainland author Yu Hua, *To Live* is, on first reading and viewing, very much a story of its time.[9] Like many examples of fiction and film produced since the mid-1970s, *To Live* looks *back* to events of the past through a look *at* some ordinary people—the Xu family—whose saga runs from the late 1940s to the 1970s (the period after the peak of the Cultural Revolution).

The film begins in a gambling house. Xu Fugui, the only son of a well-off family, is already heavily in debt, as recorded in a log kept by the dealers. Refusing to pay heed to the advice of his parents and his pregnant wife, Fugui squanders the family fortune, including the ancestral home which is sheltering them. Having thus lost his house, his father (who dies after signing the house away), and his wife (Jiazhen, in despair, has left with their daughter and gone to her own family), Fugui is reduced to making ends meet by selling the few possessions he still owns. Many months pass before Jiazhen returns with their daughter, Fengxia, and a newborn son, Youqing. With the help of Long'er, the man who took over his ancestral home, Fugui begins a new career as a singer and player in a shadow-puppet theater, making his living by performing with a troupe. He and Jiazhen go through a series of epochal events—the Civil War between the Nationalists and the Communists, the Communist Liberation of China, the Great Leap Forward, the Cultural Revolution—and lose both their children in the process. At the end, four members of the family survive—Fugui, Jiazhen, their son-in-law (Wan Erxi), and their grandson (Mantou/Little Bun).[10] By this point, conditions in China are seemingly improving.

At one level, the ability "to live" can undoubtedly be understood as the basic resistance of the common people to the random disasters befalling them under a political system that has failed in its mission. However modest, the plea for the condition of "living" serves in this instance as a metacriticism, a critique of the critical imperatives of the political regime, which was itself founded on the ideas and ideals of resistance and struggle. Because this political regime has resorted time and again to violence and murder in order to realize its dreams, and has replicated the authoritarianism it once sought to resist, the film's sympathetic portrayal of "living" is made in the spirit of a resistance to bureaucratized resistance, a struggle against the state-sponsored struggle of official rhetoric. To be able to live through—and *in spite of*—disasters should in this light be seen as a "back to basics" approach in what I have elsewhere called the post-catastrophic discourse of contemporary China.[11] After the grandiose messages of revolution, for which millions of lives have been lost in the name of salvation, it is as if the sheer possibility of simply living has become cause enough for celebration and respect. The commonplace "to live," then, has the same nostalgic function as the figure of "the people" in that it, too, asserts the value of a return to something fundamental. Having lived through years of war, poverty, separation, illness, fatal accidents, and the loss of loved ones, ordinary people now prefer to occupy themselves with the mundane and the banal—such as eating, for instance. The film concludes with the survivors of the family's three generations gathering for yet another meal.

The Food That Does Not Go In

As in Zhang's other films, the shift in the medium of representation—from literary writing to film—offers a significant clue to his reading of the "original" subject matter. The major change introduced by Zhang is, notably, the elimination of Yu Hua's first-person narration.[12] Hence, while our understanding of the events in the novella relies on Fugui's memory and narration, in the film Fugui becomes simply one among many characters. From the perspective of reception, the effect is that of a shift from a single voice which predominates and guides (the reading) to multiple characters, events, and discourses. This shift, though perhaps a technicality, is crucial nonetheless because it introduces a departure from the ideological implications of the novella. Yu Hua's literary style, which uses simple, matter-of-fact prose, presents the past in the form of what is already past. With Fugui as the only survivor in (and of) his own tale, the feeling of closure, of a story and a history having been completed and come to an end, is put across with the certainty of a retrospective—"it all happened this way." Zhang's film, by contrast, forsakes the relative stability of a kind of writing based on the remembrance of things past. By abandoning the nostalgic perspective of a sole surviving narrator, Zhang opens up the narrative in terms of temporality—"it is still going on, it is to be continued." What is perhaps foreclosed in the retrospective narration of Yu Hua's novella is conversely supplemented by the story's unfolding on the screen, the presentness of which transforms the significations of "living," of what it means "to live."

Moreover, by eliminating the story's monological narration, the film enables the interactions among the characters to surface much more readily, and it is through such interactions, which can no longer be attributed or confined to the understanding of a single character, that a very different kind of narrating unravels alongside the realistic one. To be sure, Zhang, like all good popular artists who understand the importance of popular appeal, does make ample use of the current interest in the lives of "common people" to tell a moving and entertaining story on the screen with the full coherence of illusionism.[13] But he has also done something more: by taking seriously the Chinese Communist dictum of paying attention to "the people," Zhang has produced a film which literally takes a long, hard look at "the people," one that reveals them as sentimental, loving, and filial, but also as petty, small-minded, and, above all, *ready to sacrifice others in order to protect themselves*. Unlike the Party officials and the many Chinese intellectuals who continue to idealize "the people" by invoking them poetically as the bearers of revolution, resistance, and hope, Zhang gives us an unglorified portrait of the people—not exactly as the embodiment of evil but, more disturbingly, as a host for the problems that have beset China's construction of its "national" identity through political governance. If Zhang's film is a critique of the ideology of the Chinese regime, as I believe it is, it is a critique that materializes by reinforcing the critical terms legitimized by that regime—"the people" and their "resistance"—to the hilt.

In a cultural context in which food occupies such a central physical and imaginary place, what better way is there to look hard at "the people" than through the event of eating, an event which is fully resonant with the theme "to live"? Zhang's handling of eating is, as I will argue, nothing less than extraordinary. In Yu Hua's novella, food is central to the narrative action in that it serves to propel the plot, deepen characterization, and intensify conflicts. Among the novella's most memorable scenes are those depicting starvation and the search for edible things in the countryside.[14] In Zhang's film, however, food takes on a drastically different set of connotations. While he never neglects the physical appeal of food—as what fills the stomach—Zhang also *desentimentalizes* the representation of food as a fundamental lack. Instead of using food—or its absence—as a means of mobilizing the narrative action, Zhang represents it as an indigestible detail—as what does not quite go "in," what does not get eaten with satisfaction. Remaining thus in a relation of *exteriority* to the human bodies that are supposedly its "end," food is decoupled from the essentialist survivalism to which it has always been attached and becomes an occasion for the staging of another kind of consumption—the consumption of political oppression. In the following three examples, food assumes not so much the form of a substance to be ingested as the form of the leftover, the absurd, or the weapon.

Jiaozi (Meat-Filled Dumplings). One morning, Youqing is abruptly wakened from a deep sleep and forced to go to school—his classmates have come by on their way to remind his parents that all students are expected to show up early to learn about steel-smelting. Having just brought home their family's share of *jiaozi* from the town as a reward for their hard work, Jiazhen proceeds to prepare a lunchbox for her son, making sure that he has plenty of the mouth-watering dumplings. That same day, Youqing is killed in an accident. Still tired, he has fallen asleep against a wall; when a vehicle crashes into the other side of the wall, it collapses on the little boy. Youqing never has a chance to open his lunchbox. When we see the *jiaozi* again, they have been left cold and untouched, their culinary appeal completely superseded by the grief at Youqing's graveside, a place where food is traditionally displayed as a way of paying respects to the dead.

Mantou (Steamed Wheat Buns). Fengxia gives birth to her son in a hospital, the management of which has been assumed by the youthful Red Guards, who are as contemptuous of the older and more experienced medical doctors, whom they consider "reactionaries," as they are complacent about their own ability to handle medical emergencies. Such attitudes quickly change when Fengxia begins postpartum hemorrhaging. Earlier, hoping to ensure a safe delivery, the Xu family had gone against hospital rules and brought in a top gynecologist, Professor Wang, pulling him from a procession in which he and other intellectuals were being paraded as symbols of "feudalist corruption." But Professor Wang has not eaten for three days. When he is offered some *mantou*, he gorges himself so hastily that he becomes almost comatose— a condition aggravated by the water he is then given by those who are trying to help. In the absence of any medical intervention, Fengxia bleeds to death.

Already, in these two brief examples, the handling of food suggests that eating is something other than "filling the stomach." What is normally welcome is in both cases associated with the sacrifice of innocent children. Would Youqing have died if his parents had not forced him to go to school early in conformity with others? The meat-filled dumplings, a rare treat during the days of the Great Leap Forward, become in the end *leftovers*—the waste of ideological abuse, undoubtedly prepared with parental love and patriotic loyalty, which find their ultimate victim in the young child. The most familiar and familial items of consumption—*jiaozi* being best when homemade and always served during festivities—here take on a defamiliarized and defamiliarizing relation to what they normally signify. Rather than being eaten and absorbed, the lumps of dough and meat now stand as reminders of a life that has been irrecuperably wasted.

Similarly, would Fengxia have died if intellectuals and skilled professionals such as Professor Wang had not been mindlessly abused during the madness of the Cultural Revolution? The *mantou*, meant to ease Professor Wang's hunger so that he can assist in the childbirth, rehydrate and expand within his starvation-shrunken stomach. Failing thus to be properly incorporated, the *mantou* indirectly kill Fengxia. However well-intentioned, "filling the stomach" in this case leads to death, with food emphatically marked by the errors and terrors of history. Toward the end of the film, as the Xu family visit the graves of both children, Fugui reflects on the past, lamenting the fact that he had given Professor Wang too many *mantou*—otherwise, he says, the professor could have saved Fengxia's life. Or else, he adds, it was the water that they should not have given him. Fugui even supplies a mathematical elaboration: "People say that once you drink water, one *mantou* in the stomach turns into seven. Professor Wang ate seven *mantou*. Seven times seven is forty-nine. That'd knock anyone out of action!" When they learn that Professor Wang has since then avoided anything made from wheat, eating instead only rice, which is more expensive, Jiazhen exclaims—in what comes across as an utterly bizarre conclusion to this tale of epochal crisis and sorrow—"What a food bill he must have every month!"

Statements such as Fugui's and Jiazhen's seem absurd not because they reduce "great" suffering to mathematics and economics, but because such reductions confront us with a stark discontinuity in emotional experience. From anticipating the birth of a grandchild with both anxiety and hope, to witnessing the death of one's child, then mourning, followed by a return to "normal" life, and finally the ritualized family visit to and conversation at the grave, the changes and reversals of emotional intensity that occur around food play off one another in such a way as to reveal what—for the lack of a better term—must be called a dialectic, whereby moments of poignancy swing between a tone of sentimental vulnerability, on the one hand, and of absurdist irony, on the other. There is no tragic moment, as a result, that does not simultaneously border on the comic and the ridiculous, or vice versa.

Noodles. Of all the moments related to eating, the most compelling one is a scene which features Youqing during the Great Leap Forward period. Fengxia, as we learn earlier in the film, became deaf and mute after a childhood fever. She is the object of ridicule among the town schoolboys, who mock her with malicious tricks such as shooting at her behind with a slingshot and then waiting in hiding for her response. Incensed by such abusive behavior, little Youqing has attempted to protect his older sister. One day when the families in the town gather for a meal in the communal dining hall, Youqing gets himself a big bowl of noodles laced with hot chili sauce and walks up to the boy who leads his gang in abusing Fengxia. Climbing up on a chair behind the boy, who is busily eating, Youqing raises the bowl and, in a gesture that resembles the offering of a sacrament, pours the noodles and sauce over his enemy's head. Outraged, the boy bursts into tears, while his father quickly calls the crowd's attention to the Xu family. Fugui, greatly embarrassed by Youqing's incomprehensible behavior, scolds his son, demanding that he apologize. When Youqing refuses, Fugui grabs him, spanking him until Jiazhen and others separate them. Only later, when they are alone at home and Jiazhen has explained the background to Youqing's act, does Fugui realize that he has wronged his son.

This scene of collective food-sharing comments provocatively on two distinct forms of *political* behavior. What is the difference, it asks, between Youqing's act and Fugui's act? One is an attempt, albeit child-ish, to demand social justice for a person who cannot speak for herself. The other is a public punishment of a child by an adult who succumbs to crowd pressure. Because solidarity between father and son would threaten the father's status, he must distance himself from his son by punishing him. At the same time, though, this face-saving act of dis-tancing also reestablishes and reaffirms the father's linkage with—his possession of and authority over—his child. In terms of food, we could say that whereas Youqing gives up eating his food in order to use it as a weapon of "disorderly conduct," Fugui attempts to restore order so that the group, including himself and his family, can resume eating.

Implicitly patriarchal, Fugui's act is typical of a certain attitude to-ward the community. The fear of ostracization means that the process of socialization—of learning to live with others—is one of punishment and discipline, and such punishment and discipline invariably entails sacrificing the minor, the innocent, the oppressed. The more unreason-able the community, the more relentless it will be in sacrificing such underclasses. Hence, the measures taken by Fugui against Youqing are intended less to discipline the child than to identify with the commu-nity—to demonstrate Fugui's own worth within the community. Sacri-ficing the minor, the innocent, or the oppressed in exchange for the acceptance of the community ultimately constitutes an act of *self*-em-powerment and *self*-governance.

The Space of "the Public"

The close links between sacrifice and socialization raise questions about the way "the public" is conceived and accordingly, the way governance is practiced and mobilized. Like "the people," "the public" is, theoretically, an empty space, a space to be manipulated. In the political culture of a nation such as China, which is governed by "strong men" rather than through the mediation of law, and where, as one critic puts it, the political machine "serves at the same time as a judicial apparatus," "the public" becomes simply a space for the use of those who hold political power.[15] For the ordinary person afraid for his own life, then, "the public" functions much more as a space in which to submit to authority and to hide oneself than as an arena in which to speak out against injustice and to propose political alternatives. As modern Chinese history has demonstrated time and time again, those who dare to tell the truth are more often than not sacrificed.[16] The vigilance of "the public" is wholly aimed at *conformity and invisibility*, not dissent and intervention.

This requisite conformity and invisibility has prevailed to such an extent that even an event as revolutionary as the appearance of the Red Guards in the "public space" during the 1960s amounted to just another version of the oppression and persecution of the innocent. Conceived of as a groundbreaking intervention in China's tradition, the Red Guards were supposedly the opposite of the patriarchal social order. Behind their mobilization was an uncompromised idealism: let our children, our oppressed classes speak up; let them overthrow corrupt forms of power; let them tell us what to do; let them create a new social space! And yet at the same time, the fundamental conceptualization of "the public" went unchallenged, so the fervor of the Red Guards simply degenerated into the very same self-righteous abuse of political power that had characterized their elders.

This conception of "the public" as a space in which to conform with the powerful is recognizably different from that to which those living in the West are accustomed. In the West, the public is arguably also a space of governance—but with a significant difference. With the mediation of law, "the public" functions in the latter context as a constraint on those who exercise power, subjecting them to scrutiny and holding them accountable. What this means is that the space of the public is no longer at the disposal of only those with political power; it is also where multiple discourses, reflecting vastly divergent, at times opposing, perspectives, achieve legitimacy solely through a continual competition for power. Any attempt to manipulate the public space in an authoritarian fashion will simply have too many hurdles to overcome and will thus be much less likely to achieve any extended dominance.[17]

Time and again, the West's habituation to this legally bound "public" has blinded it to China's alternative conception. During the Tiananmen Massacre of June 1989, for instance, even as the West was imagining that its intense gaze would check the Chinese authorities' display of authoritarianism, these authorities were reacting in exactly the opposite manner. They reacted as if they had been provoked into action in a public space where their authority had been challenged and needed to be reestablished. Thus it was precisely the West's attention, aimed at discouraging militaristic violence, that helped to generate this violence. The Chinese authorities had to prove that they, proprietors of their own political power, were in control of the public space, and they did so by slaughtering their own "children."[18]

In this regard, the scene in which the father publicly punishes the son in *To Live* can be read as a miniaturized rerendering of that dramatic punishing scene watched by the entire world in June 1989. In both situations, demands for social justice lead to protests and demonstrations, which in turn catch the attention of a crowd. Like Fugui under the pressure of public attention, the Chinese authorities reacted by striking out at the children who had embarrassed them—crushing them with tanks and gunfire. To this day, these acts of violence continue to be justified in terms of sustaining peace and prosperity—that is, of restoring "social" order.

These conflicting views of "the public" and of governance are replayed every time an outspoken person emerges to criticize the political regime in Beijing. Fang Lizhi, Wei Jingsheng, Martin Lee, Szeto Wah, Christine Loh, Emily Lau, and Harry Wu are just a few who come to mind.[19] In order to do what they seek to do, which is to bring about democracy in territories under (or soon to be under) Chinese rule, these radicals must act as though they were ignorant of the concept of "the public" that is implicit in that rule. In doing so, they have again and again provoked the Chinese authorities' profound anger. What is maddening to these authorities is not merely what the radicals say in their speeches and writings about China's various acts of social injustice, but also the defiant, "uncouth" manner in which they voice their criticisms in public. When that public is international, their "misbehavior" becomes unpardonable. In keeping with the circular reasoning of their essentialist governing ideology, the Chinese authorities typically handle such defiance by turning the radicals into outcasts, through criminalization and imprisonment or through deportation and ostracization. Often, such "outcasting" is put in explicitly nationalistic and ethnic terms, with trouble-makers accordingly labeled "traitors" who have betrayed China to the "foreigners," the "Western imperialists."[20]

With its overtones of absurdity and sentimentalism, the scene in which Fugui spanks his son in submission to the pressuring public gaze is hence emblematic of the predicament of governance in Chinese political culture. Such governance is driven by a public sphere that, unable to serve as the site for a potentially autonomous opposition, readily collapses into a mechanism for coercion by brute force. Without the effective intervention of a restraining legal apparatus, this public space requires the individual to assume a subordinate position vis-à-vis "public opinion," a position enforced by discipline and punishment. The patriarchal implications of such subordination include the fact that its enforcement will always be aimed at the powerless, who must always be disciplined and punished regardless of the grounds on which their discontent is voiced. The governing-governed relationship in this context becomes tripartite: governance is enforced not only by soliciting the governed to serve the arbitrary and brutal interests of "the public," but also by specifically manipulating them into willingly sacrificing those who are disadvantaged—in the name of the *public good.* In turn, these disadvantaged members of the public may internalize such governance as *self*-governance—by either becoming as violent as their governors (if they succeed in procuring power for themselves) or submissively enduring violence to themselves (if they remain "ordinary citizens"). Since the majority of society must remain "ordinary citizens," governance means, ultimately, the dissemination of a political culture in which people are always prepared to tolerate violence and to accommodate further violence. It is under such patterns of governance and self-governance that "endurance" excels as the foremost moral virtue in the struggle "to live." Perhaps nowhere is the violence that goes into the making of this moral virtue more evident than in the Chinese character for "endurance"—*ren*—which is composed of a "knife" above the "heart."

We Endure, Therefore We Are

Technically, how can a critique of an abstract quality such as "endurance" be made on the movie screen? With his usual penchant for understanding what works in the medium of film, Zhang added a series of events which are not found in Yu Hua's novella. This "supplement" not only contributes to the spectacular cinematic visuality that is a hallmark of all of Zhang's films, but also exemplarily allegorizes the contradictions inherent to the people's "survival."

Near the beginning of the film, after Fugui has reduced his family to poverty, he goes to Long'er for help. Having won the Xu family's ancestral home that Fugui gambled away, Long'er refuses to lend him any money, but instead offers him the loan of a box containing some bric-a-brac from the past—a set of shadow-puppets.[21] From then on, Fugui, who, in an earlier scene, showed off his singing talent in the gambling house, will make his living by singing with a traveling troupe of puppeteers.

During one performance near the end of the Civil War, Fugui and his fellow performers are conscripted into the Nationalist Army by force. Because the puppets are on loan from Long'er, Fugui insists on lugging them along in their heavy box. When the Nationalists are defeated by the Communists, Fugui, like many others, becomes a prisoner of war, only to discover that his burdensome puppets have suddenly become a treasure: accidentally picked up by the bayonet of a Communist soldier, the figures dazzling against the sun provide a means of entertainment for the troops. In performing for the soldiers and giving them some relief from the dull wartime conditions, Fugui becomes a minor hero and is awarded a certificate for having served the People's Liberation Army. When he is finally able to return home, this certificate provides proof that he and his family are "exemplary" citizens at a time when others, especially landowners, are being hounded. (Long'er, for instance, is dragged off to be executed before Fugui's eyes.)

Then, during the Great Leap Forward, when every household's iron is confiscated for smelting as part of the national self-strengthening effort, Fugui's puppets are, once again, threatened. But just as they are about to be confiscated, Jiazhen makes a suggestion to the town chief: Why not use the puppets to entertain the workers? Fugui's livelihood is thus salvaged a second time. Finally, during the Cultural Revolution, when relics of the past become dangerous to own because of their association with a "corrupt" ideology, Fugui is advised to burn his puppets before they are discovered. Even then, the wooden box in which the puppets had been stored is transformed into something useful: a nest for the chicks to be raised by Fugui's grandson. As he had once told Youqing, Fugui now tells Mantou: when the chicks grow big, they will turn into geese; when the geese get big enough, they will turn into sheep; when the sheep have grown, they will turn into oxen. . . . As life gets better and better, the little boy will no longer ride on the back of an ox but on trains and airplanes.[22]

As a means of making a living, the shadow-puppets are richly suggestive of the complex significance of "the people" and "popular resistance." The puppet theater is, first and foremost, a practice of the past —an art form associated with premodern China. Yet in spite of its anachronicity, the puppet theater is a resilient cultural mode that continues to be performed in various regions where it is associated with local folk traditions. In terms of the pedagogical mission of the political regime, it is precisely such relics as the shadow-puppet theater that interest Chinese Communist historians, for they are part of the "popular material culture" that constitutes the new conceptualization of a revolutionary China. Furthermore, as a symbol of the people's tradition, the puppets in *To Live* endure, surviving one disaster after another. Even after they are finally destroyed, the box which once held them survives and nurtures new life. Are these puppets not the best testament to the common people's will to live? Instead of merely affirming this, Zhang's film makes us reflect on the nature of "endurance" itself: what precisely is endurance, and what does it tell us about the way China is governed?

Like the puppets, the characters in the film show a remarkable ability to persist through trying circumstances. Not only do they adapt to the physical hardships of life, but they seem equally capable of accommodating themselves to the ideological manipulations of the state. Once wealthy landowners, the Xu family adjusts to the low status of "poor townsfolk," settling in and deliberately conforming with every move they make. In an early episode, for instance, Fugui and Jiazhen learn from the town chief that Long'er, the new owner of their ancestral home, refused to surrender the house to the authorities and burned it down instead in an act of "counterrevolutionary sabotage." Fugui's first reaction is one of shock at the destruction—after all, all that "sturdy timber" used to belong to the Xus. But, remembering that he is in public, he quickly adds that it is not their timber but "counterrevolutionary timber." Jiazhen gets the message immediately: "Yes," she echoes, "it's counterrevolutionary timber." In another episode, as the family sits down for a meal, Erxi, the son-in-law, mentions that their old friend Chunsheng, who had been an important cadre member, has been arrested and is in the process of being purged, so they should keep their distance (*hua qing jie xian*—literally, "draw a clear line") from him. Once again, Fugui readily acquiesces, glancing anxiously at the picture of Chairman Mao that was Chunsheng's wedding present to his daughter.

Such small incidents, comments, and details, which pass almost unnoticed because they are such a "natural" part of the story, cumulatively amount to an alternative reading of "the common people." This reading does not celebrate the common people's ability to live— to adapt to and endure harsh circumstances—as an unequivocal virtue; rather, it problematizes it as China's most enduring ideology.[23] In Zhang's film, the conventional notion of endurance as a strength is not simply reproduced but consciously staged, and it is through such staging, such dramatization or melodramatization, that a crucial fantasy which props up "China"—whether as a culture, a nation, a family, or a common person—is revealed. "We, the Chinese, are the oldest culture, the oldest people in the world," this fantasy says. "The trick of our success is the ability to stick it out—to absorb every external difficulty into ourselves, to incorporate even our enemies into our culture. We endure, therefore we are."

Like the structure of all powerful ideologies, endurance-cum-identity works tautologically: the ability to endure is what enables one to live, but in order to endure, one must stay alive. "To endure" and "to live" thus become two points of a circular pattern of thinking which reinforce each other by serving as each other's condition of possibility. In accordance with this circular, tautological reasoning, the imperative "to live" through endurance becomes what *essentially* defines and perpetuates "China." As such, it operates as a shield in two senses: "living" protects China from destruction at the same time that it prevents China from coming to terms with reality. That is, China—preoccupied exclusively with its own survival—is *in reality* its own worst enemy because that preoccupation is precisely what has led China's political history, with all its catastrophes, to be repeated ad infinitum.

The best demonstration of this self-perpetuating ideology of endurance and survival in *To Live* is none other than the shadow-puppets, whose capacity for survival becomes most evident, ironically, in their own destruction. For if, as the town chief points out, the stories performed by the puppet theater are all "classic feudal types"—all about *dihuang jiangxiang, caizi jiaren* ("emperors, kings, generals, ministers, scholars, and beauties")—and that is why the puppets must be burned, then isn't the fascination with such stories reproduced in the very act of burning, which is, after all, an act performed in filial worship of Mao Zedong as an emperor, and in mindless obedience to the Party and the Revolution? Although the puppets are destroyed on account of their feudalist ideological import, *feudalist ideology itself is kept alive in the very event that seeks to extinguish it.* Moreover, tradition, now an empty box, continues "to live" nonetheless by supporting new life—both the grandson and his chicks. And this new life is imagined in the form of a fantastic, progressive *telos*—from chickens to geese, to sheep, to oxen, to trains and airplanes—of a life that keeps getting "better and better" without ever getting any better at all.[24]

By abandoning the singular perspective of one character and by foregrounding interactions among different characters over such additional, apparently "technical" elements as the shadow-puppet theater, Zhang enables a radically nonconforming view of endurance and survival to emerge. His approach is, strictly speaking, an *ethical* one insofar as it is an approach to the *ethos*—the way of life—of a group of people, in this case "the Chinese." Ethics in this sense is not the abstract moral/ philosophical sphere of Western modernity but the structure, dynamics, and values of social life in a specific community.[25] More than any of Zhang's other films, *To Live* focuses on practices in the context of the Chinese ethos, elaborating—as it exposes—China's "national" ideology. Through this most accessible, chronological narrative of the lives of "common people," Zhang raises the most profound political question: how is China governed, managed, and fantasized as a collective? The answer proposed by his film is equally profound, and remarkable: China is governed, managed, and fantasized as a collective by the self-fulfilling, self-perpetuating ideology of endurance and survival—by an ethical insistence on accommodating, on staying alive at all costs. And yet, such an insistence, despite its nobility, is not *ethical* enough, for it can be and frequently has been co-opted by precisely the forces it seeks to resist. The ideology of endurance and survival has been so thoroughly and "spontaneously" incorporated into "the imaginary relation" between the Chinese and their real living conditions[26] that the government can blatantly disregard human rights in the name of human rights, since, after all, "human rights" means "having enough to eat," and China's food supply is an essentially "internal affair." When any intervention in China's handling of this crucial issue can be successfully dismissed as "Western imperialism"—yet another external threat to be endured and survived by the Chinese—a time-honored form of governance remains in full force.

Refusing to Live: The Glimpse of an Alternative Political Culture

If my reading of this fundamental critique of Chinese society in Zhang's film is at all tenable, then it should not be surprising that a saga of so many heart-rending episodes would also have many funny and farcical, indeed absurd, moments. If a film can be said to have an affect, that of *To Live* can only be described as the affect of excess. This excess stems from the crisscrossing of various modes of emotional intensity: melodrama and sentimentalism (with many tear-jerking interludes), comedy (with belly laughs at unexpected moments), and scenes that provoke other strong feelings (such as those generated by the wonderfully performed intimate relations among the various family members). But the affect of excess also points to the presence of an otherness, a chord of emotional dissonance struck from within the realistic narrative that neither tragedy, farce, nor familial bonding manages to muffle.

This emotional dissonance is the result of a narrative structure that alludes to the possibility of an alternative reading as it unfolds, so that the experience of "seeing" the film becomes one of virtually looking at a hologram. While there is undoubtedly a cohesive frame of reference, which allows us to follow the story, there is at the same time another configuration that is equally present on the surface, waiting to be seen. What is crucial is that the recognition of this other configuration inevitably disrupts, destabilizes, and distorts the more obvious one, although we can choose to "see" only that one and to ignore the other. Coming from a director who has lived for decades in a totalitarian state where the authorities continue to obstruct his work,[27] this holographic mode of storytelling is, we may surmise, a tactic of smuggling subversive messages past censors. As I have already mentioned, such subversive smuggling is often achieved by means of passing incidents, comments, and details. As well, it is achieved by means of minor characters.

For instance, little Youqing, who disappears halfway through the film, subverts the predominant message of survivalist endurance more than once. After being wrongly punished in the communal dining hall, Youqing decides to play a practical joke on his father at the suggestion of his mother. During one of Fugui's performances, Youqing serves his father a bowl of tea—laced with large amounts of vinegar and chili sauce. Drinking the tea unawares, Fugui chokes and spits it out, splashing the puppet theater screen and making everyone laugh. In a scene that is filled with the most infectious feelings of warmth and fun, thus, the son's mischievous act—another spin-off of the idea of unincorporated food—provokes his father into a momentary "revolt." A person who usually "swallows" everything, Fugui finally acts in a way that is, in terms of the ideological structure of the story, the opposite of endurance.

The other character in Zhang's film besides Youqing who represents the possibility of an alternative behavioral code is Chunsheng. As Fugui's sidekick in the gambling house and the traveling puppeteer troupe, then during the Civil War, Chunsheng is throughout the film kept in the role of a character on the side, a character who, unlike Fugui, is not central to the story. He sometimes strikes us as a bit crazy, such as when he claims—on a battlefield covered with corpses—that he wants to drive a car so much that he would gladly die for that experience. Years later, Chunsheng unexpectedly reappears as the district chief who has accidentally killed Youqing, and whom the Xu family (Jiazhen in particular) refuses to forgive. As a result, Chunsheng is relegated to the position of a suspect outsider. On important occasions, such as Fengxia's wedding, he is neither formally invited to join the celebration nor served tea as a guest in the house.

During the Cultural Revolution, like many officials of standing, Chunsheng is tried and persecuted as a "capitalist" running dog. One night, after his wife has apparently committed suicide, he comes to see Fugui and confesses in despair, "I don't want to live any more!" As Chunsheng bids him farewell, Fugui urges him to be strong and to go on living. For the first time since Youqing's death, Jiazhen softens and asks Chunsheng to come into the house. She reminds him that he owes their family a life, a debt that endows his own life with value. Chunsheng, however, neither agrees nor disagrees. Although we hear the admonition "to live" loud and clear, Zhang's film leaves it unclear as to whether Chunsheng will accede to this imperative. His disappearance into the dim light at the end of the street, an image of melancholic uncertainty, marks a departure from coerced survival at all costs.

ETHICS AFTER IDEALISM

As someone who even considers refusing to endure, "to live," Chunsheng can be linked to some of Zhang's most defiant characters, such as the peasant woman, Judou, in *Judou* and the maid Yan'er in *Raise the Red Lantern*. In terms of the ideological structure of *To Live*, Chunsheng's walking away introduces a distance, a chasm, within the picture of a continuous collective "living" and offers a glimpse of the possibility of an alternative mode of self-governance and political culture. It is, however, no more than a glimpse. The working out of the implications of this barely glimpsed alternative would have to be a long-term intellectual, political, and ethical project.

EIGHT

A Souvenir of Love

We don't know what love is. Sometimes people
even think it is a "local custom."

—Lee Bik-wa/Li Bihua, Yinji kau/Yanzhi kou

ANY VISIT TO Hong Kong in recent years tells one that strong feelings
of nostalgia are at work in the general consumer culture. As *wai gau/
huaijiu*[1]—the most commonly used Chinese term for nostalgia—becomes a trend, the city culture of Hong Kong takes on the appeal of an
ethnographic field. Architectural landmarks such as the Repulse Bay
Hotel, the Peak Restaurant, and the Western Market have been rebuilt
or renovated in such ways as to resurrect their former colonial "flavor."
Exhibitions were held in 1992 of the postcards of Hong Kong from the
late nineteenth to the early twentieth century, of Hong Kong film posters dating back to the 1950s, of Hong Kong cigarette and groceries
posters dating back to the 1930s, as well as of various kinds of mass
culture publications and daily wares from the 1950s and 1960s. Furniture, music, clothes, shoes, and cosmetics of the past decades are being
revived, and it has become fashionable to collect "antiques" such as
pocket and mechanical watches, records, old newspapers, old magazines, old photographs, old comic strips, and so forth, in addition to
the more traditional collector's items such as coins, stamps, snuff bot-
tles, utensils, paintings, calligraphy, and carpets. The nostalgic hold
on history, tradition, and culture has made way for the endless production of commodities.

As a Hong Kong journalist writes, "For the nostalgic class and its
rapidly expanding club membership, what is beautiful has to be in the
past tense; to appreciate the beautiful is like entering a time tunnel in

order to reach for hidden secrets."[2] Is the upsurge of nostalgia in Hong Kong "the flight of the owl of Minerva," a desperate reaction to the approach of 1997, when Hong Kong returns to China and thus, for many, loses its identity? Is it not also because Hong Kong, as one of the last outposts of European territorial colonialism, merely shares the ongoing worldwide trend of simultaneously raiding and idealizing the past—a trend that has long been present in both elite and mass culture, in the form of art and ethnographic museums, auctions, films, music, retro-dressing, and much more?[3] If one of the strategies of colonialism and Orientalism has been that of nativism—of conferring upon colonized peoples the status of local natives with local histories and customs, in contrast to the universalized, "cosmopolitan" status of "first world" colonial powers—then it seems that the recent waves of nostalgia in Hong Kong constitute a cultural politics of *self*-nativizing that is as complex and as deserving of attention as critiques of colonialism and Orientalism themselves.

A full discussion of this cultural politics will obviously require much more than the space of one chapter. My reading of the film *Rouge (Yanzhi kou,* Golden Way Films Ltd., 1987) will, I hope, offer some useful starting points. Several questions inform this reading: (1) the relationship between nostalgia and one of the most widely accessible instruments of mass communication and entertainment, the filmic image; (2) the mutual implication between romantic love and ethnography; (3) the agency of chance; and (4) the force of nostalgia as an alternative temporality for fantasizing a "community" amid the identity-in-crisis of contemporary Hong Kong.

The Nostalgic Filmic Image

What is nostalgia? It is commonly understood to be a longing for the past, or, etymologically, a homesickness. The Chinese *huaijiu* literally means "missing or reminiscing the old." Nostalgia is often assumed to be a movement backward in time: the past happened, time passed, we look back to the past from the present, we feel that the past is more beautiful but we can no longer return to it; in this longing for the past, we become "nostalgic." As Caryl Flinn writes in regard to nostalgic trends in American pop culture: "Classical and contemporary accounts alike riddle their conceptions of the present with lacks and deficiencies, obliging the past to function as a site of comparative cohesion, authority, and the hope . . . of 'something better.'"[4]

In classical Chinese poetry (*shi* and *ci*), the convention for expressing nostalgia was often that of a lack/loss projected onto physical space.

Poets lamented that while the seasons, scenery, architecture, and household objects remained unchanged, the loved ones who once shared this space with them were no longer around. Idioms such as *taohua yijiu, renmian quanfei*—"the peach blossoms are there as always, but the human faces have completely changed"—summarize the feeling of lack/loss peculiar to this kind of nostalgia by contrasting the stability of the environment with the changefulness of human lives.

For Hong Kong people, as for people elsewhere in the "developing" world, the main problem with nostalgia defined in the classical poetic way is the constant disruption of their physical and architectural environments, and thus of their sense of the stability of place. (In *Rouge*, the protagonist's first major shock is precisely the disappearance of her original surroundings.) In the 1980s and 1990s, the omnipresence of real estate speculation means not only that "original" historic places are being demolished regularly, but also that the new constructions that replace them often do not stand long enough—to acquire the feeling of permanence that in turn gives way to nostalgia—before they too are demolished. In the midst of a chimerical concrete jungle, where one's senses are forever jolted by the noise of wrecking balls, bulldozers, pile drivers, air hammers, and power drills, how does one begin to be nostalgic? If the expedience of technology means that human separation itself need no longer be mournful because of diminished travel distances, it also means that our relations to the past are drastically altered because of the unprecedented disintegration of stationary places. Nostalgia now appears differently, working by a manipulation of temporality rather than by a simple projection of lack/loss onto space. If and when the past is to be (re)collected, it is (re)collected in compressed forms, forms that are fantasies of time.

Two sets of questions, then: first, instead of thinking that nostalgia is a feeling triggered by an object lost in the past (a mode of thinking that remains linear and teleological in orientation), could we attempt the reverse? Perhaps nostalgia is a feeling looking for an object? If so, how does it catch its object? Could the movement of nostalgia be a loop, a throw, a network of chance, rather than a straight line? Second, how can nostalgia be "represented" in film? What is the relation between nostalgia and the filmic image? I will approach the second set of questions as a way to return to the first. This requires an examination of the status of images that are the most explicit "sites" of nostalgia in *Rouge*—the *recollections*.

In the novella *Yanzhi kou*, the story is narrated by Yuen Wing-ding/Yuan Yongding, the journalist. It begins when Yue Fa/Ruhua, the female ghost, appears in Yongding's office asking to place a personal ad in the newspaper. The use of Yongding as the narrator helps anchor the narrative firmly in the contemporary time frame; following Yongding, we read "about" Ruhua as a character described and recorded by him. In *Rouge*, however, the more stable narrative perspective of Yongding is abandoned. In a way that is more appropriate for the film medium, the text of the film progresses with a double narrative, with scenes from the contemporary time interspersed with scenes from the past.

In *Rouge*, we begin, in fact, with Ruhua's story, but only later do we know that it is *her* story, recounted from *her* point of view. The opening shots show Ruhua, dressed in an old-style *kei po/qipao* with a high, round collar, in the process of putting on makeup. Instead of using a lipstick, she uses a piece of red dye-paper that women used in the olden days. This small gesture alone becomes the definitive mark of a different time, opening onto several scenes in a *jau ga/jiujia*,[5] or restaurant, frequented by prostitutes and their patrons. The time is about 1934; the place, Shek Tong Tsui/Shitangzui, a Chinese "red light district" of Hong Kong during the 1920s and 1930s. Henceforth alternating between the past and the present, the film juxtaposes the two temporalities without offering us the stable anchorage in the present that is offered in the novella. The past—that is, Ruhua's story—is given to us in beautiful golden colors that contrast sharply with the mundane documentary tones of the present. The extravagantly sensuous images of the 1930s demonstrate the logic of the flashback, which Gilles Deleuze describes as "an inexplicable secret, a fragmentation of all linearity, perpetual forks like so many breaks in causality."[6]

By moving Ruhua to the place of a narrator rather than letting her remain a character within Yongding's narration, director Stanley Kwan (Kwan Gum-pang/Guan Jinpeng) makes maximum use of the effects of the cinematic image as a type of "free indirect discourse." As Pier Paolo Pasolini argues in his classic essay "The Cinema of Poetry," the free indirect discourse, used frequently in modernist literature to present a character's inner thoughts and feelings as if they are there without the author's mediation, can also be applied to the understanding of film, in which images are used to signify particular characters' perspectives.[7] In *Rouge*, the past is beautiful and romantic because it is remembered by Ruhua as such. Whereas in the novella Yongding has to deduce or interpret from Ruhua's tone of voice or facial expression the kind of emotion she attaches to the past she is narrating, in the film Ruhua's "narration" *is* the images in front of us. (The ingenuity of the film script lies in the fact that there is no voice-over.) As Pasolini writes, the free indirect discourse is most effective when the character whose "view" we see is an abnormal one. It is thus by using Ruhua, a ghost and an insanely passionate woman, that Kwan intensifies the perspectival and idiosyncratic but enchanted quality of the images of the past.

However, these "recollection" images or flashbacks are not simply subjective and private. If they constitute the story as told by Ruhua the narrator, they do not *only* present her as narrator. On the screen, Ruhua is present not as the voice/gaze of an invisible storyteller but as an image. She is a character in the story *supposedly told by herself.* Because she appears as a character, we are watching these images as if they were told from the viewpoint of a narrator who is not Ruhua. Strictly speaking, therefore, the status of these recollection images is neither completely subjective (belonging to one character, Ruhua) nor completely objective (belonging to no one and thus to everyone). At once private and public, the recollection images occupy a peculiar space between the character and the author, between a single consciousness and an omniscient one. While Ruhua is their "subject," she is also present as one of their objects. The best parallel to this is the dream in which one *sees oneself* as a persona, in which one is both the dreamer and the dream(ed).

Memory and dream are precisely the analogies Pasolini draws with cinematic images. In a way that differs sharply from great structuralist film theorists such as Christian Metz, Pasolini thinks that if one is to speak of a "language" of cinema, that language is not a "grammar" (as proposed by Metz and others) but an inscription of an irrational kind. The cinematic language, Pasolini writes, is oneiric and concrete at once.[8] Unlike written texts, cinema constructs its materials not from verbal language but from images; such materials, which Pasolini calls prelinguistic or pregrammatical, are "brute." And yet, in their bruteness and physicality, images nonetheless have a long and intense history that is derived from the "habitual and consequently unconscious observation of environment, gestures, memory, dreams."[9]

The most interesting aspect of Pasolini's essay concerns the relation between images understood this way and the possibility of the free indirect discourse in film. As I already mentioned, in literature, free indirect discourse is usually produced by the author's adopting the "psychology" of a particular character and presenting events in that character's language without quotation marks. The abstract nature of language makes it quite possible for it to capture the specificity of a character without losing track of the author's voice. This is why, for instance, Mikhail Bakhtin could theorize the novelistic discourse of Dostoyevsky in terms of what he calls the "struggle" between the author and character.[10] The abstractness of language means that the boundary between the "inside" and "outside" of any perspective—and hence between author and character—is blurry and potent grounds for contention. In cinema, Pasolini argues, the implications of the free indirect discourse are quite different. While directors do, as we see in *Rouge,* adopt the "voices" or "gazes" of particular characters, the abstract effect achievable in a written text is not possible on the screen because of the concreteness of the filmic image. Thus, when a director creates a particular vocabulary for a particular character, Pasolini writes, "even this particular vocabulary ends up a universal language; for everybody has eyes."[11] Through a comparison between verbal and imagistic free indirect discourse, thus, Pasolini highlights the physicality and palpability of the cinematic image as qualities that are especially adept for the metaphoric expression of the unconsciously remembered relations we have with reality.

We are now able to define the relation between nostalgia and the filmic image in *Rouge*. Like directors mentioned by Pasolini such as Antonioni and Bertolucci, Kwan here adopts the perspective of an "abnormal" character in the creation of his film's images. This "abnormality" allows him a certain liberty. The images from Ruhua's memory are intoxicating because of their absorbed, obsessive, narcissistic quality. But precisely because of the physical and palpable nature of these images, the emotion that accompanies them—nostalgia—becomes collective as well as completely private. In those scenes from the past, the full gestural, physiognomical, and thus societal nature of the image is deployed: apart from the colors, architecture, costumes, interior decor, there are all the bodily movements, the facial expressions, the eye-to-eye exchanges between the lovers that strike us as at once familiar and exotic, at once belonging to the present (the moment we are watching) and the past (the time of Ruhua's story). As Pasolini would say, such images constitute a reality in which objects are "charged with meanings and . . . utter a brute 'speech' by their very presence."[12] That brute speech would be the prelinguistic "long and intense history"—the unconsciously remembered relations with "reality" that are shared and dreamed collectively by a community.

If Ruhua's imagistic recollections are the "sites" of nostalgia, then what can we say about nostalgia? Nostalgia is not simply a reaching toward the definite past from a definite present, but a subjective state that seeks to express itself in pictures imbued with particular memories of a certain pastness. *In film,* these subjectively pictorialized memories are there for everyone to see: nostalgia thus has a public life as much as a purely private one. The cinematic image, because of its visible nature, becomes a wonderfully appropriate embodiment of nostalgia's ambivalence between dream and reality, of nostalgia's insistence on seeing "concrete" things in fantasy and memory. One could perhaps go as far as saying that Ruhua's recollections are not simply images of nostalgia; rather they contain a theory of the *filmic-image-as-nostalgia*. It is against this theoretical understanding of the filmic-image-as-nostalgia that the two predominant components of *Rouge,* the love story and the sociology of prostitution, come together. I will now turn to these components.

A *Souvenir of Love*

Love, a Local Custom

As pointed out by some critics, the love story in *Rouge* is a traditional and hackneyed one.[13] Its narrative turns, its fascination with the amorous relationship between a virtuous prostitute and a romantic youth, its assignment of the fateful burden of love to femininity, and its sorrowful ending remind us of typical features of the Mandarin Duck and Butterfly novels of the early twentieth century. A brief summary of its story goes as follows. In the 1930s, when prostitution was still legal in Hong Kong, Ruhua was one of the most famous prostitutes in the Shitangzui district. She met Chan Chun-bong/Chen Zhenbang, a young man from a wealthy family who was known to his friends by his familial title of Sup Yee Siu/Shier Shao (twelfth young master). Ruhua and Shier Shao fell madly in love, but Shier Shao's family objected to their marriage because of Ruhua's background; they also wanted him to marry his cousin. Ruhua and Shier Shao made a brief attempt at living on their own, with he becoming an apprentice to a Cantonese opera master, while she tried to make as much as possible by "bleeding" rich clients.[14] Angered by the sight of their son in the socially despised role of a minor stage performer, Shier Shao's parents interceded and demanded that he return home. Realizing that there was no escape from family pressure, the two lovers decided to commit suicide together by swallowing opium. At 11:00 P.M. on March 8, the hour at which they were supposed to make their exit together from this world, Ruhua asked Shier Shao to remember "3811" as their secret signal of communication in the life to come. Ruhua died and has been waiting for fifty-three years for her lover to show up in the underworld, but Shier Shao has not appeared. It is now 1987 and Ruhua is tired of waiting. She traded some of the years of her future life (one year for each day spent in the living world) and came back to look for him, hoping that he would respond to her newspaper ad indicating the meeting time of 3811 "at the same old place."[15]

Clearly, Ruhua is an interesting character because of her *chi qing*, her excessive capacity for being faithful in love. During the flashback that shows Ruhua and Shier Shao making love for the first time, we hear Shier Shao describe her: "You are very *yum/yin*"—the Chinese term for the quality of excessiveness that has, in common parlance, become the word for "lewd" or "lascivious." *Yin*, however, is precisely the rare quality that was used to describe a lover like Jia Baoyü in *The Dream of the Red Chamber*. As used in the context of *Rouge*, it is meant to signify Ruhua's essential difference from other people.

The love story from the 1930s is consciously juxtaposed with the relationship between Yongding and his girlfriend, Ling Chor Guen/Ling Chujuan, a tabloid reporter. Instead of a tenacious love like that once shared by Ruhua and Shier Shao, the contemporary lovers strike us as having a relationship of convenience, in which they are not eager to form a permanent union, and in which even the expression of affection and intimacy can be disrupted by professional duties. (Near the beginning of the film, for instance, Yongding gives Chujuan a surprise present of a pair of shoes, but she is too much in a hurry to do her tabloid assignment to appreciate his thoughtfulness.) In contrast to Ruhua, Chujuan seems boisterous, self-centered, and inattentive to her loved one.

Throughout the film, Ruhua alludes to her past and future as if the meaning of her life, rather than beginning and ending at any one point, were repeating and recurring continually. A feeling of cyclical time, in which the past and the present intermingle as if in a dream, in which the debts of the past may be paid in the present, and in which unfinished events of the present may be completed in the future, accompanies Ruhua's endeavor of returning from the dead. By contrast, Yongding and Chujuan are much more bound to their time. Being journalists by profession, the contemporary lovers are acutely conscious of time as a limit. As Ruhua's first encounter with Yongding shows, an ad in the newspaper costs so much, takes so much time to be placed, will appear for so much time, and so forth. The contemporary, mediatized world is one in which time is measured and evaluated accordingly. Time is money. Time is also the linear movement of speed, the unidirectional, irreversible movement of modernity that goes forward incessantly. This is the time of progress—of fast food, brief sex, and short-lived romances.

After the initial feelings of fear, anger, and suspicion, Yongding and Chujuan are eventually so moved by Ruhua's love story that they decide to help her find Shier Shao. As they become drawn into the details of Ruhua's life, they also become aware of their own ordinariness. In the film, there are these dialogues between them:

> Chujuan: Would you fall in love with Ruhua?
> Yongding: Her emotions are too strong; I would not be able to take it.
>
> * * *
>
> Chujuan: Would you kill yourself for me?
> Yongding: How could we be so romantic?
> Chujuan: Just say yes or no!
> Yongding: No. How about you?
> Chujuan: No.
>
> * * *
>
> Chujuan: Nowadays, who would be as faithful as Ruhua? It's difficult being a woman; even when you try your hardest you don't know

what it's all for. I am jealous of Ruhua, she has really won me over. What she dared to do, I won't dare for the life of me—I haven't even thought of it.

Yongding: Yes. We are ordinary people. We just need to feel good when we are together. For us there is no such thing as killing oneself for love; there is no such grand plan as risking lives. . . .

Like a number of other characters created by Li Bihua, such as the immortal terra cotta warrior in *Chun yung/Qin yong* [Terra cotta warrior] and the Peking opera actor Ching Dip-yee/Cheng Dieyi in *Ba wong bit gei/Bawang bie ji* [Farewell my concubine], Ruhua not only embodies a different time and value, but also represents an otherness that is absolute. Her *chi qing* makes her a peculiar object of the past which is no longer available. This, then, is the additional meaning of her "timelessness"—Ruhua is timeless not only in the sense of a time that is repetitive and cyclical, but also a time that has stood still or evaporated. This is why Ruhua is so "well preserved." As Yongding comments:

> She is forty-eight years older than me. Forty-eight years—that's a whole lifetime for many people. If Ruhua had been merely living, she would now have become a frail old woman, her skin all wrinkled, her eyes without lustre. If she had been reincarnated, she would still have been over forty—the embarrassing age that is neither "middle" nor old. And yet, she is standing beside me in her lovely youthful beauty, simply because she is stubbornly faithful in love. . . .[16]

Rouge is, in this regard, not only the story of a ghost talking nostalgically about a past romance, but is itself a romance with Ruhua, a romance that is nostalgic for superhuman lovers like her.

Whereas the Mandarin Duck and Butterfly novelists of the 1910s and 1920s would have moralized didactically and warned us against the destructive nature of Ruhua's love as such, Li Bihua finds in it the occasion for a different kind of project. For Li Bihua, Ruhua's *chi qing* is interesting in ways that exceed purely romantic and literary reasons. Ruhua is an anthropological type that has become extinct. In the novella, thus, we find this observation by Yongding: "We don't know what love is. Sometimes people even think it is a 'local custom.'" This short remark revealingly brings together the romantic and the sociological strands of *Yanzhi kou*.

For readers and viewers of the late 1980s, this Mandarin-Duck-and-Butterfly-style story is intriguing not least because of its social setting. Li Bihua had clearly done a great deal of historical research for the writing of her text, which contains all kinds of interesting details about prostitution as a profession in early twentieth-century Hong Kong. *Yanzhi kou* can, among other things, be read as a recreation of a particular historical period through its practices, mannerisms, linguistic uses, costumes, architecture, and peculiar brand of human relations based on the commodification of sex. To its own success, the film makes ample use of these historical details. Among the gifts sent by Shier Shao to seduce Ruhua, for instance, are a pair of scroll-like tablets decorated with fresh flowers—what was called a *fa pai/huapai*—on which is written a couplet beginning and ending respectively with the two characters in Ruhua's name, and an imported brass bed, indicating his exclusive rights to her. As audiences, we watch with voyeuristic pleasure the enticing scenes of Shier Shao removing Ruhua's layers of clothing when making love to her and of the lovers "chasing the dragon" in bed together. The hairdo, makeup, clothing, and shoes worn by men and women of the 1920s and 1930s, together with their etiquette, vocabulary, and body gestures are attractively displayed on the screen.

The social details from the past constitute a kind of ethnography, a culture-writing. In the process of conjuring up a different time, the details become native witnesses and aboriginal evidences that fascinate and persuade the contemporary viewer. But most interesting of all is the type of enclave Li Bihua chooses for her culture-writing. Of all possible sites of production, it is a brothel which becomes the locational evidence of the past; of all possible culture workers, it is a prostitute who becomes that past's witness, with an obstinate faithfulness in love that is exemplary of a kind of heroism. If the Confucian ancients taught us the "great" virtue of *she sheng qü yi*—a readiness to give one's life for justice—Ruhua teaches us the "small" virtue of a readiness to give one's life for love. While other Chinese directors conceptualize the past more "properly," then, the conceptualization of the past in *Rouge* is an improper one. While others use emperors, empresses, and major eunuchs (e.g., Li Hanxiang, Tian Zhuangzhuang); sympathetic poor peasants in the countryside (e.g., Xie Jin, Chen Kaige, Zhang Yimou, Xie Fei, and other mainland Chinese directors); or smart, frustrated adolescents (e.g., Hou Hsiao-hsien, Edward Yang, and Wong Ka-wai), Li Bihua and Stanley Kwan use socially despised workers in a socially despised occupation to produce a past that is at once glamorous and trivial, earthshaking and inconsequential.

Notably, therefore, in spite of the abundance of the kinds of ethnographic details that could have filled the pages of the traditional *difang zhi*, the local gazetteers, what distinguishes *Yanzhi kou* from a conventional writing of history is precisely Li Bihua's refusal to downplay its fictional component, the component of love. Instead, both the novella and the film suggest that conventional ethnography needs to be supplemented by fiction, for it is fiction which provides the most intriguing "historical" or "ethnographic" material. More so than all the arcane objects on display, it is the love embodied by Ruhua that makes this particular ethnographic account memorable. The thing that is no longer comprehensible to contemporary men and women, the exotic ethnographic object par excellence, is Ruhua's *chi qing* per se.

Once we see this mutual implication between ethnography and fiction, the many "clichéd" features typical of the love story—the initial encounter, the mutual attraction, the repartees, the tactics of romantic conquest, the obstacles created by familial objection, and finally the suicide—take on the significance of inevitable but irretrievable customs and rituals. Conversely, the notion of ethnography as a scientific and objective account of a "primitive" society is now deconstructed as lacking in any consideration of fiction and fantasy. The effect of the signification of nostalgia in *Yanzhi kou* and *Rouge* is that neither fiction (love) nor ethnography (history) can be understood without the other. The degree of our "historical" interest in the world of the 1930s is in many ways in direct proportion to the degree of our "irrational" mes-merization by a passion we feel is foreign to our time. Ruhua is, on the one hand, a "native" long thought to have gone extinct, who suddenly turns up in the modern metropolis and who insists on reliving the practices of her society. On the other hand, she is also the romantic ethnographer, intent on a certain belief in the past, only to discover that the native object she vows to find is irredeemably lost.

Upon seeing that the man in her dream has vanished precisely be-cause he is still alive, Ruhua returns to him a locket of rouge.[17] Shier Shao had given this pendant to her at the climax of their relationship, when they knew that they were about to be forced apart. Like all souvenirs of love, the locket was intended for promise and trust. But like all allegories of times past, the souvenir is also emblematic of the death of what it commemorates. Ruhua the lover and ethnographer returns to her "field" only to discover that it has long dissolved, and that the souvenir she has been wearing for fifty-three years is . . . a corpse of love. As she "wakes up," she disappears into the haze of darkness and from our sight.

Chance Encounters

Whose fault is the truth? Who or what is the agent for the revelation of the pathetic sight of a senile Shier Shao, an opium addict working as a mere extra, pissing and smoking in the dark, deserted corner of a movie studio? This is one of the multiple-layered questions that the rich, inexhaustible text of *Rouge* asks us. If love is indeed a promise, an infinitely reciprocal exchange of faith, who has broken the terms of the promise? Shier Shao, obviously, because he did not die. But is Ruhua herself not also a culprit, because she came back to look for him? Within the terms of trust, her return amounts to *dis*trust, a refusal to wait forever and unconditionally. It is also a transgression of the taboo implied in any memory of a beautiful experience, the taboo against turning back. Her "discovery," then, is a kind of punishment: because she returns, because she looks twice, she loses what (she has hitherto thought) she has. It is important to note that Ruhua's distrust does not begin now, fifty-three years later, but was already present at the time of the lovers' suicide. Ruhua's love did not blind her to her lover's cowardice. In the film we are told that before they committed suicide together, Ruhua, out of fear that Shier Shao would be too timid to swallow the opium, had secretly put an overdose of sleeping pills in the wine he drank. Her logic was that if he should back down from the opium, he would still have died from the sleeping pills, but if he took the opium and died, then the pills would not have mattered. This way, she made sure that he would be (dead) with her forever.[18] (On first discovering Ruhua's murderous act, Chujuan was scandalized; only later does the younger woman accept that even this act was one of love.)

However, if we accept that Ruhua is punished, it is not possible to say who is punishing her. The only agency indicated by *Rouge* is fate or chance, the mysterious network of coincidences that in due course bear pertinent meanings. Hence, if Ruhua's separation from Shier Shao in 1934 was caused by his family's chance rescue of him that she could not have planned, her way back to Shier Shao in 1987 is led by an equally unpredictable coincidence. In an age when everyone has countless numbered documents and possessions, how could Shier Shao be located simply with "3811"? After ruling out identity cards, phone numbers, driver's licenses, and other possibilities, Yongding and Chujuan finally wonder: "What about beepers?"[19] Using the code 3811, they are eventually connected, as if by miracle, to Shier Shao's son, who tells them his father's whereabouts. (After being rescued in 1934, Shier Shao married his cousin and, well before the birth of his son, had squandered his family's fortune. His wife is long dead and his son has nothing but contempt for him.) Do we call this "reunion" of Ruhua and Shier Shao "chance" in the sense of a purely arbitrary happening, possible only "in fiction"? And yet, does chance not strike us precisely when what it brings bears an uncanny recognizability and an uncanny accuracy in hitting home? What is "home"? To be nostalgic, we remember, is to be homesick . . .

There is a way in which the truth-yielding work of chance has announced itself long before Ruhua sees the truth. This work is not metaphysical but literary, textual, and mediatized.

Consider, once again, the beginning of the film. As I already mentioned, the film differs from the novella by beginning with Ruhua's story rather than Yongding's. The visual staging of Ruhua and Shier Shao's first encounter emphasizes chance as the most active agent in the events of this tragic story. As we go back to the 1930s, we see Ruhua dressed as a man performing a song in front of her patrons. Against the noisy, lively background of the restaurant, the young Shier Shao appears. He ascends the stairs, exchanging interested glances with passing prostitutes. He is captivated by the music. As he enters the room where his friends and their prostitute companions are drinking, the music stops: Ruhua and he discover each other. As she resumes singing with the line "Look at the pair of swallows against the setting sun," the world has changed for him. The song is a well-known "southern tune" (*nam yum/nanyin*) sung in Cantonese, "Hak to chau hun"/"Ke tu qiu hen" [A melancholy autumn away from home].[20] In retrospect, it was as if the song was flowing down the stairs looking for an object, and it found Shier Shao.

The words of "Ke tu qiu hen" tell of the love of a scholar and a courtesan-songstress. Alone under the cool autumn moon, the scholar sings nostalgically of his lover's beauty and talent, of the memorable times they spent together, and of his worries about the dangers that presently surround her. Despite her loved one's poverty, this woman, unlike the mercenary members of her occupation, chose to remain absolutely faithful to him. Is this old love story not like the tune itself, a "chance" *and* prescripted happening that catches not only Shier Shao but also Ruhua the singer/seducer? For audiences who do not recognize the tune, this opening scene is by itself a beautiful capturing of the elusive romantic encounter of a prostitute and a dandy; but for those who do, the preordained *and thus* nostalgic nature of the encounter is remarkable. This encounter signifies how the "spontaneous" love between the Ruhua and Shier Shao—the "original" story from the 1930s—is itself already a modern (re)enactment, a nostalgic (re)play of older tales, legends, and romances. Behind one encounter is another encounter: as they sing and listen while exchanging fateful glances with each other, Ruhua and Shier Shao are also being sung by the song and its literary romance, which, we might say, has been waiting to meet them. If romance is a matter of "being caught" unexpectedly, what we have here is not only the romance of the two lovers catching each other, but also the romance of the past catching human beings unawares. In their encounter with the text that is the past, the lovers become, as it were, that text's actualization and self-fulfillment.

This encounter between the past (fiction?) and the present (reality?) is demonstrated in other scenes of the film. Toward the end, when Ruhua and the contemporary lovers have almost despaired of finding Shier Shao, we find Ruhua watching a Cantonese opera song being performed on the street. The camera indicates that although the actor on the stage is a stranger, Ruhua sees him as her lover. This dreamlike identification of her lover takes place once again against the background of a story of love—the song being performed this time is "San bak lum chung"/"Shanbo lin zhong" [Shanbo on the eve of his death], the last words supposedly sung by the faithful poor scholar Leung San-bak/Liang Shanbo, mourning his love affair with Chuk Ying-toi/Zhu Yingtai, who has been forced to marry someone else. And finally, where would the lovers from the 1930s meet again but in a movie studio, where Ruhua in her lovely youthful self appears as surreal as the actress in the background, who is flying about in a kung-fu movie being shot on the set? In a way that is characteristic of many unexpectedly funny moments in the film (most of which are lost in the Mandarin and English translations), the actress is instructed by the director: "You are both a female knight-errant and a female ghost. You must act both awesome and spooky!" Is this "real" movie a replay of or a play on the movie we have been watching, or vice versa?

The predominant feeling that our time in this world is but a matter of stumbling upon things and events long inscribed in an unconscious ancient memory distinguishes Li Bihua's sense of nostalgia from that of other contemporary Chinese writers. Unlike many who seek the past in terms of *xiangtu*, the idealized and often "earthy" homeland in the countryside, Li Bihua's writings are always characterized by a fascination with the materials of past *literature*—with words, phrases, idioms, legends, and history books.[21] In Li's writings, what is perceived to be lost is never rural, "innocent," or even "original." Basing her narratives on urban, literate culture (and often the culture of Hong Kong), Li constructs loss as something that is not specifiable and yet traceable in the intertextual relations between the past and the present. This traceability owes itself to the alluring work of chance, the agent that is the equivalent of "God." "God" is now a labyrinth.

Nostalgia, an Alternative Temporality for a Community?

If cinema is an index to our contemporary culture at large, then the nostalgia we see in Chinese cinema may well be the episteme of Chinese cultural production in the 1980s and 1990s. Nostalgia links together the otherwise diverse intellectual and artistic undertakings of the mainland, Taiwan, and Hong Kong. In mainland Chinese films and writings since the early 1980s, nostalgia often takes the form of a contemplative inquiry about China's rural, mythic origins, as well as a renewed interest in the China of pre-Communist days. In Taiwan, nostalgia expresses itself in the massive concern about the suppressed wounds of Taiwan's local history.[22] In Hong Kong, apart from protean appearances in the plenitude of commodity culture, nostalgia often becomes, as in the case of *Rouge*, an aesthetic emotion in which the idealization of the past functions side by side with a submission to chance, fate, physiognomy, *feng shui* (geomancy), and other varieties of *shushu* (techniques of calculating the unknown).

And yet, if its romance with the past seems to offer a way of imagining identity that is alternative to the one imposed by the rationalistic, consumerist, high-tech world, nostalgia is nonetheless most acutely felt not as an attempt to return to the past as such, but as an effect of temporal dislocation—of something having been displaced in time. Nostalgia is first and foremost a register of the movements of temporality. This is why the narrative structure of *Rouge,* like many films made in Hong Kong in the 1980s and 1990s, is itself nostalgic. These films are not, despite their often explicit subject matter, nostalgic *for* the past as it was; rather they are, simply by their sensitivity to the movements of temporality, nostalgic *in tendency.* Their affect is tenacious precisely because we cannot know the object of such affect for sure. Only the sense of loss it projects is definite.

Apart from being seen on its own terms, then, *Rouge* should also be seen in conjunction with a host of contemporary Hong Kong films, such as *Ying hung boon sik/Yingxiong bensi* (*A Better Tomorrow*) I, II, III; *Choi suk/Cai su* (*The Raid*); *Hak to chau hun/Ke tu qiu hen* (*Song of Exile*); *Sheung hoi ga kei/Shanghai jiaqi* (*My American Grandson*); *Bai Ho/Po Hao* (*To Be Number One*); *A fei ching chun/A fei zhengzhuan* (*Days of Being Wild*); *Gup dong kei hup/Ji dong qi xia* (*The Iceman Cometh*); *Yun Ling-yuk/Ruan Lingyü* (*Centre Stage*); and many others. Representing a range of genres and made by directors as different as Tsui Hak, Ann Hui, Poon Man-kit, Wong Ka-wai, and Mak Dong-hung, as well as Stanley Kwan, these films collectively exhibit a nostalgic tendency in their explorations of alternative times and alternative values. What they have in common is an attempt to fantasize the past, which is usually embodied in some character who, like Ruhua, is a larger-than-life "other" with strong, insistent moral beliefs that are out of sync with those of current times. In the comical *The Iceman Cometh,* for instance, the past and the present meet when two soldiers who have been frozen in ice in a fight since the Ming Dynasty are defrosted in contemporary Hong Kong. After completing his duty of killing his enemy, the good iceman returns to the Ming by a reincarnation machine. Like Ruhua, this righteous iceman brings with him a nostalgic romance with the past; like Ruhua's loyalty to her lover, the iceman's loyalty to his emperor makes him an irreproducible curio in the age of mechanical human relations.

The ways of looking at the world unique to such characters—their "gazes," as it were—are arguably the most important objects of fascination presented by these films. As Slavoj Žižek writes in a different context: "In nostalgic, retrofilms, . . . the logic of the gaze *qua* object appears as such. The real object of fascination is not the displayed scene but the gaze of the naïve 'other' absorbed, enchanted by it."[23] What we really see when we watch these nostalgic films is "the gaze of . . . the one who was 'still able to take it seriously,' in other words, the one who 'believes in it' for us, in place of us."[24] Ultimately, therefore, "[t]he innocent, naïve gaze of the other that fascinates us in nostalgia is . . . always the gaze of the child."[25] Li Bihua, described by one critic as the writer who set the entire nostalgic trend in Hong Kong,[26] has herself authored many stories experimenting with the idea of reincarnation, in which memorable characters with childlike credulity appear. For instance, there are the aforementioned *Qin yong* and *Bawang bie ji*, as well as *Ching se/Qing she* [Green snake], *Poon Gum-lin ji chin sai gum seng/Pan jinlian zhi qianshi jinsheng* [The past and present lives of Pan Jinlian], *Moon chau gwok yiu yim: Chundo fongji/Manzhouguo yaoyan: Chuandao fangzi* [Femme fatale from Manchukuo, Kawashima Yoshiko],[27] and others. Like chance, the credulous, stubborn, childlike "gaze" signifies a temporality that is irrational, repetitive, mischievous. Like chance also, the child can be a tyrant who loves to play hide-and-seek and who demands absolute submission. If nostalgia may be considered an alternative way of conjuring up a "community" amid the ruthless fragmentations of postcoloniality, the community being conjured up is a mythic one. The love of love, of fate and chance, and of the childlike gaze are some of its dimensions.

Like any elaborate form of emotion, nostalgia as presented in *Rouge* and other recent Hong Kong films is the product of a materially well-endowed world. That is why, perhaps, it finds its expression so appropriately in the cinematic image, the technical convention that requires for its continual existence the supply of enormous wealth. (The leading characters in *Rouge* were played by Anita Mui Yim-fong/Mei Yanfang and Leslie Cheung Gwok-wing/Zhang Guorong, two of the most highly priced showbiz figures of Hong Kong.) In the nostalgic filmic image, the entire world turns into a sadly beautiful souvenir. But if its compressed images always convey a sense of loss and melancholy, nostalgia also works by concealing and excluding the dirty and unpleasant elements of social hardships. The degenerate, seductive, and tortuous forms of nostalgia's labor are things with which any critique of the "identity crisis" in a postcolonial space such as Hong Kong must come to terms. The point of this chapter has been to provide a beginning for such a critique.[28]

NINE

Between Colonizers: Hong Kong's Postcolonial Self-Writing in the 1990s

Hong Kong: An Anomaly in Postcoloniality?

MOST DEBATES on postcolonial politics center on issues that are by now familiar to those working in cultural studies. There are, first, the disputes and conflicts concerning the ownership of particular geographical areas, an ownership the ramifications of which go beyond geography to include political representation as well as sovereignty over ethnic and cultural history. Though these "postcolonial" disputes and conflicts date back to the days of territorial colonialism, they remain the reality of daily life in places such as South Africa, Israel, Lebanon, and Jordan. Second, there are the debates around reclaiming native cultural traditions that were systematically distorted by the colonial powers in the process of exploitation. In the case of India, for instance, historians argue for the need to wrest India's past from colonialist historiography—that is, from the ways in which India was ideologically as well as economically and territorially dominated by the British.[1] In other words, even though India has been territorially independent since 1947, the Indian people's "postcolonial" struggle against British colonialism remains an urgent cultural task. Third, there is the question of neocolonialism in countries that were once European colonies and that, after national independence, have been targeted for aggression and exploitation by the United States during its period of global power. We think here especially of the United States' "client states" in Central and Latin America, and the Middle East.

Although it shares similar problems of postcoloniality, East Asia does not fit neatly into any of the above categories, which is probably why many of our foremost critics of colonialism have remained silent on this topic. East Asia—China, Japan, Korea, and Taiwan—is difficult to generalize about for several reasons. With the exception of Taiwan, which was occupied by the Dutch and the Japanese, and which is currently under Nationalist Chinese rule, none of the East Asian countries was territorially occupied by the old European colonial powers for a long time. (In this respect, they are different from their neighbors in South and Southeast Asia—India, Bangladesh, Sri Lanka, Vietnam, Cambodia [Kampuchea], Laos, Thailand, Burma [Myanmar], Indonesia, Malaysia, Singapore, Brunei, and the Philippines—which were under British, French, Dutch, Spanish, or U.S. domination at one time.) Even when they were occupied, most East Asian countries retained primary use of their own languages, which continue to serve purposes of writing and historiography and thus of preserving their cultural traditions in forms that are not easily supplanted by the West. The rapid economic development in some of these countries—notably South Korea, Taiwan, Hong Kong, and Singapore—over the past two decades makes it impossible to assign to them the "third world" status of disadvantaged African countries.

Moreover, the record of official communism in China and Korea, as well as in Vietnam, has been quite embarrassing to those who mobilize the traditional arguments of Marxism, which has been the ideological perspective from which most criticisms of colonialism and neocolonialism are made in the liberal West. To complicate things further, there is the imperialism practiced by East Asian cultures themselves: the territorial and economic aggression of Japan before and after the Second World War, and the imperialist policies practiced on Mongolia, Taiwan, Tibet, and Xinjiang by China, itself once the leader of the "third world," render the typical "East versus West," "colonized versus colonizer" dichotomy facile and useless. Then there are Hong Kong and Macau, the British and Portuguese colonies that are (before 1997) the last remaining outposts from Europe's heyday of territorial imperialism. These two areas, of course, are too small to merit attention and are usually entirely omitted in most debates on postcoloniality.[2]

Theoretically, it is around the prefix "post" in the word "postcolonial" that most interpretative confusion occurs. "Post" is usually interpreted in two ways, both of which, far from being mutually exclusive, have to do with temporality. These two ways are "having gone through" and "after." From them a host of questions arise: if a culture is "postcolonial" in the sense of having gone through colonialism, does that mean colonialism is no longer a part of its life? If we are referring strictly to the completion of territorial colonialism, now presumably a thing of the past, how do we talk about the ideological legacies, the cultural effects of colonialism? Is the "post" in "postcolonial" simply a matter of chronological time, or does it not include a notion of time that is not linear but constant, marked by events that may be technically finished but that can be fully understood only with consideration of the devastation they left behind?[3]

In this chapter, I address these problems by discussing the work of Luo Dayou, a popular songwriter who has worked both in Taiwan and in the British Crown Colony of Hong Kong. My goal is to argue that the problems faced by Hong Kong, though little known beyond its community, are entirely relevant to current debates on postcoloniality. The most critical of these problems is that Hong Kong will not gain territorial independence at the end of British colonialism. This is due to the fact that a large part of Hong Kong (the Kowloon Peninsula and the New Territories) has been "on lease" from China to Britain since the mid-nineteenth century, and, when the 99-year lease expires in 1997, Hong Kong will be "returned" to China. Thus, while Hong Kong's predicament as a colony may be similar to that of other previous colonies, it does not have the privilege of an independence to which it can look forward. Between Britain and China, Hong Kong's postcoloniality is marked by a double impossibility—it will be as impossible to submit to Chinese nationalist/nativist repossession as it has been impossible to submit to British colonialism.

As such, Hong Kong's "postcolonial" reality expunges all illusions of the possibility of reclaiming a "native" culture, illusions that have remained the strongest grounds for anticolonial resistance among previously colonized countries around the world. Instead, Hong Kong confronts us with a question that is yet unheard of in colonial history: *how do we talk about a postcoloniality that is a forced return (without the consent of the colony's residents) to a "mother country," itself as imperialistic as the previous colonizer?* Is Hong Kong then simply an anomaly in the history of colonialism? Or does it not, in its obligatory "restoration" to China, in fact crystallize and highlight the problem of "origins" that has often been suppressed in other postcolonial cultures because of ethnic pride?

Postcolonial Self-Writing: Nativism or Postmodernism?

Characteristically, the problems of postcoloniality bear upon cultural production, especially the production of popular cultural forms. Like their counterparts in Eastern Europe and elsewhere, the rock-and-roll and other types of popular music produced in Hong Kong, Taiwan, and mainland China are increasingly attracting the attention of cultural theorists. While many critics have pointed out the potentially conservative nature of popular music, rarely do they stop to elaborate on the purposes to which such conservatism can be put. For Chinese communities in East Asia, pop music has played a significant role in organizing patriotic feelings in mass events such as the Tiananmen demonstrations of 1989 and the many subsequent protests (in Hong Kong, Taiwan, and elsewhere) against the violence of the Beijing government. Among the most often played and heard songs in the post-1989 period are, for instance, "Long de chuan ren" [Descendants of the dragon] and "Xie ran de fengcai" [Blood-stained spirit].[4] A distinct characteristic of many examples of contemporary Chinese pop music is the nostalgic quality of its lyrics. Although many pop songs are produced in urban centers for the consumption of audiences who have access to electronic equipment such as cassette and compact disc players, Walkmans, Discmans, and karaoke machines, these songs themselves nonetheless allude melodically to the *rural* and *mythic* origins of Chinese culture, with titles such as "Huangtu gaopo" [Yellow earth high slope], "Huanghe yuan" [A wish for the Yellow River], "Baba de cao xie" [Father's grass shoes], "Changcheng yao" [Ballad of the Great Wall], and the like. At a time when Chinese urban culture, like urban culture elsewhere in the non-Western world, involves tension and conflict between "traditional" and "Western" values, and when areas such as Tibet, Taiwan, and Hong Kong are demanding their rights to a governance based on their own histories and the nature of their communities rather than submitting to the authorities in Beijing, the abundance of rural and mythic images in Chinese pop music, like the same images in contemporary Chinese films, serves to perpetuate the illusion of a "folk" whose "continuous" heritage is five thousand years old.[5] The evocation of heritage as such commands solemn reverence to antiquity. No matter how much violence is inflicted on the Chinese people, it is believed, the notion of the folk as heard in songs such as "Wo shi zhongguo ren" [I am Chinese] and "Zhonghua minzu" [The Chinese nation/race/people] supposedly unites the people and gives them hope for the future.[6]

This, then, is the first of the postcolonial dilemmas faced by peoples of the non-Western world—the inevitable tendency toward nativism as a form of resistance against the dominance of Western colonial culture. In *An Indian Historiography of India*, for instance, Ranajit Guha movingly argues the need for Indians to reclaim the right to the writing of their own history, so as to remove the habits of India-writing so deeply entrenched in British colonialism. The restoration of what we might thus call a colonized culture's agency for self-writing remains a primary and ineluctable task in the postcolonial aftermath. And yet, writing about Hong Kong, I find it impossible to follow Guha's ideas to their logical conclusion. While combating British imperialism may be a goal shared by India and Hong Kong, this self-writing—"Indian historiography of India" in Guha's title—is fraught with difficulties and contradictions in the latter. Indeed, if self-writing is a kind of empowerment in which the telos consists in the repossession of what was stolen, the decolonization of Hong Kong is part of *China*'s self-writing. From the perspective of those living in Hong Kong, however, the reverse is not true: what is self-writing for China is definitely not self-writing for Hong Kong; the restoration of China's territorial propriety in/ through Hong Kong does not amount to Hong Kong's repossession of its own cultural agency. Take the question of language for instance: what would it mean for Hong Kong to write itself in its own language? If that language is not English, it is not standard Chinese (Mandarin/ Putonghua) either. It would be the "vulgar" language in practical daily use—a combination of Cantonese, broken English, and written Chinese—a language that is often enunciated with jovial irony and cynicism. The difficulties and contradictions involved in Hong Kong's self-writing are aptly summed up by the renowned Hong Kong author and critic Leung Ping-kwan:

> The identity of Hong Kong is more complex than that of any other place. . . . Vis-à-vis foreigners, Hong Kong people are of course Chinese, but vis-à-vis the Chinese from the mainland or Taiwan, they seem to have the imprints of the West. A Hong Kong person who came from China after 1949 is obviously an "outsider" or "someone coming south"; but to those who "came south" during the 1970s and 1980s, such a person is already a "local." A Hong Kong person may speak English or Putonghua, but it is not the language with which he is familiar since childhood; and yet what he knows best, Cantonese, is not convenient for writing. He recites the Chinese classics while at school, but in his eventual employment he would have to acquaint himself with forms of commercial correspondence or the brief and cute wordings of advertising. Such linguistic impurities are also a reflection of the impurities of Hong Kong's cultural identity.[7]

Hong Kong thus presents a problem that is crucial but rarely discussed in postcolonial debates, namely, the struggle between the dominant and subdominant within the "native" culture itself. To argue for the autonomy of a historiography by the "natives" themselves, so that the past that has been usurped from them can become available and accessible once again in the "native" language, we would need at the same time to acknowledge (1) the impurity of that "past" and (2) the

vicissitudes of the "native" language, which is also impure and multiple because it is in constant practical use not only by the educated but
also by the illiterate; not only by the culturally centered but also by the
culturally marginalized. With due respect for Guha's work, I suggest
that his advocacy of a postcolonial native historiography has been
developed in strict accordance with the historical presence of the British
as an *outside* colonizer in India. The presence of the British means that
the epistemological clarity between the inside and outside can be maintained and that the argument for the native-culture-as-resistance can be
made unproblematically. As such, however, what is often sacrificed is
the history of struggles within India among the various ethnic languages and cultures.[8] Dipesh Chakrabarty draws attention precisely to
this problem when he writes that "the project of provincializing 'Europe'"—a project that is essential to deconstructing European history's
hegemony over other ethnic histories—"cannot be a nationalist, nativist, or atavistic project. . . . *[O]ne cannot but problematize 'India' at the same
time as one dismantles 'Europe.'*"[9] Chakrabarty's insight is echoed by
Partha Chatterjee in the latter's careful observation of the problems
inherent to the idea of the singularity of national history, the idea that
national history has a single source in a particular ethnic group (such as
the Hindus in the case of India) or a particular region. Chatterjee writes:

> It might be speculated that if there were many such alternative histo-
> ries for the different regions of India, then the center of Indian history
> would not need to remain confined to Aryavarta or, more specifically,
> to the "throne of Delhi." Indeed, the very centrality of Indian history
> would then become largely uncertain. The question would no longer
> be one of "national" and "regional" histories: the very relation be-
> tween parts and the whole would be open for negotiation. . . . But we
> do not yet have the wherewithal to write these other histories. Until
> such time that we accept that it is the very singularity of the idea of a
> national history of India which divides Indians from one another, we
> will not create the conditions for writing these alternative histories.[10]

Similarly, in the context of a "postcolonial" Hong Kong, I would argue
that one cannot but problematize "China"—the "throne of Beijing"—
at the same time as one dismantles "Britain."

In other words, Hong Kong, even though it shares with India the
historical predicament of British domination, is in a position to realize
acutely that it cannot assert its autonomy by way of the national/
native—that is, Chinese—culture without compromising its own history. Conversely, Hong Kong culture has always been dismissed by the
mainland Chinese as too Westernized and thus inauthentic. To write
itself, Hong Kong must move beyond not only British but also Chinese

habits of historiography, and thus beyond the simplicity of the paradigm "foreign colonizer versus native colonized." The first thing Hong Kong needs to combat from the inside is the totalizing nativist vision of the Chinese folk.

The idea of a folk, as we know, is always the instrument of the dominant culture, which has a vested interest in ensuring that the powerless remain powerless by justifying and legitimating its rule. In the twentieth century the political effectiveness of the rhetoric of the folk was demonstrated by nazism and fascism.[11] Inextricable from this rhetoric is a nostalgia for ever-receding origins. Those who do not share this nostalgia are "traitors." This is how Hong Kong is often "written" by the mainland. If Hong Kong's postcoloniality means both a kind of freedom (from the restrictions of "national" culture) and a kind of danger (anything is possible), it is also the reason Hong Kong is usually viewed with disdain by most mainland Chinese as a symbol of decadence, artificiality, and contamination, while "proper" Chinese cities such as Beijing and Nanjing are viewed with a reverent sense of their centrality in Chinese history. Once culture is thought of in terms of the center versus the periphery, mainstream interpretations move in ways that are familiar to all of us: as the upholding of the center becomes the primary task, it is seldom possible to depart from the practice of centrism and its concomitant feelings of loss, grief, xenophobia, and hope of *national* self-strengthening. Precisely because the center is a fragile construct, any form of culture that does not conform with such centrism is decried as a threat and a menace.

And yet—and here we come to the other dilemma faced by postcolonial peoples today—the necessary critique of nativist centrism does not mean a happy endorsement of the "postmodern" by way of many recently popularized concepts such as "hybridity," "diversity," and "pluralism," which are usually invoked as a liberatory alternative to cultural phenomena that are held up as monolithically dominant and prohibitive. (One can add to this list of popularized concepts many others, such as "heteroglossia," "dialogism," "heterogeneity," "multiplicity," etc.) Like the advocates of nativism, advocates of postmodern hybridity (I will henceforth refer to them as "postmodern hybridites") typically obliterate significant portions of the reality of a colonized culture. While nativists suppress the fundamental impurity of native origins, postmodern hybridites tend to downplay the legacy of colonialism *understood from the viewpoint of the colonized* and ignore the experiences of poverty, dependency, and subalternity that persist well beyond the achievement of national independence.[12] For the postmodern hybridite, the word "postcolonial" does not differ in essence from "cosmopolitan" or "international." One such critic I know once said that the whole world is postcolonial today because, he explained, every country has gone through the experience of either being colonized, having been a colonizer, or having been colonized. The violence of this kind of thinking lies in the smoothness of its "either/or," as if it were a matter of choice between being a colonizer and being colonized, and as if the difference is merely relative. For the postmodern hybridite, Britain, Canada, and Australia would be no different from Bangladesh, Hong Kong, and Vietnam. The enormous seductiveness of the postmodern hybridite's discourse lies, of course, in its invitation to join the power of global capitalism by flattening out past injustices. Because we are already, whether or not we choose it, in the grips of that power, and because that power works efficiently (for such is the meaning of power), the recitation of past injustices seems tedious and unnecessary. Instead of emphasizing "colonial" in the word "postcolonial," the postmodern hybridite's emphasis falls on "post" in the strict sense of "after" and "over with," and, since all "posts" are considered the same, "postcolonial" is easily construed as synonymous with "postmodern." In a space such as that of Hong Kong, the postmodern hybridite would criticize not British colonialism (read: "international openness") but Chinese nationalism (read: "native conservatism"), thus obliterating or blurring the complex history of the rise of modern Chinese nationalism as an overdetermined response to Western imperialism of the past few centuries.[13]

The coercive naïveté of the postmodern hybridite can be exposed by a simple anecdote. I was riding on the city bus in Minneapolis one day in June 1992, when I witnessed a teenager of Indian origin, a friend of mine, being maligned by an old Englishman: "Are you from India, or Pakistan? You speak such good English—for a colonial!" This incident of colonialist harassment was then exacerbated by the bus driver, who cautioned the teenager against "being difficult with the elderly" and threatened to refuse to allow the teenager to ride that bus should she repeat such untoward behavior. The atrocity of this encounter did not lie only in the Englishman's oblivion to historical facts. It was also racism. Would it have been conceivable for this old man to have attacked a Canadian or an Australian, or for that matter, a U.S. teenager with the same "compliment"? White ex-colonials don't count as "colonials": the old man approached the teenager entirely on the grounds of skin color, so as to patronize her. And, the place being nice white Minneapolis, the bus driver was of course oblivious to this racist attack and was able to hear only a youth displaying anger toward an elder. Reflection on this incident should wake up anyone still mired in the idea that we are all "postcolonial" in the same way.

In recent years, cultural workers in Hong Kong (writers, columnists, singers, dramatists, designers, etc.) have become more and more interested in representing the history that is unique to their experience. What is unique to Hong Kong, however, is precisely an in-betweenness and an awareness of impure origins, of origins as impure. A postcoloniality that marks at once the untenability of nativism *and* postmodernism distinguishes Hong Kong's "Chinese" self-consciousness and differentiates it from other "Chinese" cities. Because a colonized city is, in the politics of its daily formation, "corrupted," it does not offer the illusion of a cultural virginity nor thus the excitement of its possible rehabilitation. The postcolonial city knows itself as a bastard and orphan who, as Luo Dayou writes, "grew up in the state of being abandoned, struggling for a compromised survival in the gap between East and West."[14] Instead of priding itself on the purity of culture in the form of a continuous folk, Hong Kong's cultural productions are thus often characterized by a particular kind of negotiation. This is a negotiation in which it must play two aggressors, Britain and China, against each other, carving out a space where it is neither simply the puppet of British colonialism nor of Chinese authoritarianism.[15]

My point in using Hong Kong to talk about the postcolonial city is hence to argue for a third space between the colonizer and the dominant native culture, a space that cannot simply be collapsed into the latter even as resistance to the former remains foremost. Crucial to the understanding of this third space are two questions. First, in being a colony, is Hong Kong not in fact a paradigm of Chinese urban life in the future? If we accept that it is in postcoloniality that the modernity of Chinese cities, like the modernity of other non-Western cities, is most clearly defined, then Hong Kong has for the past 150 years lived in the forefront of "Chinese" consciousness of "Chinese" modernity, while the reality of modernity-as-postcoloniality has been repressed in mainland China precisely by the illusion of the "native land" and the folk itself. As an exception to the rule, Hong Kong serves as the model of postcolonial awareness with all its ambiguities, an awareness that is only now surfacing among mainland Chinese intellectuals (at home and abroad) and in the more developed mainland Chinese cities, most of which still retain a naïve fascination with "the West" as such. As Leung Ping-kwan says, "The problems currently faced by mainland China were the problems faced by Hong Kong in the 1950s."[16] Second, while the development of urban culture in mainland China may be experiencing a retreat of the state, Hong Kong is experiencing an encroachment of this very same state.[17] What this means is that Hong Kong must articulate a concept of autonomy and community that would help maintain its prosperity. Such a concept, I propose, can be found in Luo Dayou's music. Instead of turning submissively to the mainland government with its fascist manipulation of the idea of the folk, Luo's work makes audible a set of social and political concerns the urgency of which exceeds national boundaries.

The Songs of Luo Dayou

In the following, I analyze Luo Dayou's music from a perspective that is consciously opposed to the rhetoric of the Chinese folk and that, however, resists the naïveté of the postmodern hybridite.[18] The issues I want to address include the following: How does postcoloniality structure the modernity of urban life? How do we come to terms with the junk aesthetics of pop music? What kinds of alternative or oppositional notions of community can be gathered from such junk?

Luo Dayou's songs are often about cities. At the most explicit level, there are sarcastic allusions to pollution, crime, and traffic congestion—things that are true of all cities even though specific names like "Taipei," "Gaoxiong," "Hong Kong," and "Beijing" are invoked. But Luo's songs are interesting not only because of their content. Instead, an awareness of the city emerges in the special forms that characterize all his songs: the pastiche, the fragment, and the broken text, all of which recall previous forms of culture and displace them at the same time. My favorite example is "Zhi fu zhe ye," an entirely untranslatable song that is not ostensibly about cities. For those who do not know Chinese, this song can be nothing more than a catchy tune with a catchy refrain. For those who use the Chinese language, however, this song rings familiar because its whole "rationale" is based on one of the most idiomatic expressions alluding to the teaching of the ancients. *Zhi, fu, zhe*, and *ye* are four of the most commonly used words in classical Chinese prose. While their individual meanings depend on the context, together they have become a standard phrase signifying "classics" or the "teachings of the Confucian masters." Relying on the popular knowledge of this phrase, Luo uses it in an ingenious way: he breaks up the phrase into its four component words again, but this time, each of these four words becomes a way to organize a line, a unit of apparent meaning. With *zhi, fu, zhe, ye* structuring the content or serving as refrain, the composition of the entire song materializes between a kind of sense and nonsense in a manner that is guaranteed to make the custodians of the classics shake their heads in disapproval.

Playing with the language of the ancients, Luo shares the rebellious spirit of many in Hong Kong, Taiwan, and China. But what distinguishes him from, for instance, the mainland Chinese singer Cui Jian, is the way words in his songs perform at a level that is more than a signification by way of sound. Cui Jian's lyrics more often than not are mere "pretexts" for music; his tunes are as lively as his words are ungrammatical and nonsensical. For Cui, whose criticism of mainland official culture retains many of the iconoclastic feelings of Chinese youth since the May Fourth period, it is as if "meaning" were dead. Before new meanings arise, signification becomes sheer physical productivity or productivity of the physical, in the form of noise, beat, husky voice, and heavy electronics. The flip side of this productivity is total despair—not only at mainstream culture but also at the futility of the endless reforms and revolutions characteristic of modern China.

Luo's use of music is very different. Words are still useful. In his lyrics we find the residues of an old book culture, which, even in fragmentary form, continues to signify a certain literacy derived from words alone. If the city is, traditionally, the center of literate culture, then Luo Dayou's songs are innovative because he keeps foregrounding that relation between the city and literacy. It is difficult to imagine him as an artist without/outside the city. If the relation to literate/textual culture is being sabotaged in the rock-and-roll of China, we do not find the same kind of explosion in the songs of Luo. While the post–Cultural Revolution frustration of mainland Chinese cultural productions expresses itself in forms that often ridicule and belittle verbal culture (and hence, we might say, the privilege and propriety traditionally enjoyed by the written word with its monopolistic grip on Chinese culture in general), in Luo Dayou we find an attempt to re-create a form of literacy, a form of intelligence and intelligibility that is still embedded in verbal culture but that meanwhile has been modernized and technologized. If the old Chinese book culture appears in postcoloniality in the form of ruin, it also appears in the form of a rune, as something to read, as a new and enigmatic composition that demands a new kind of attention. Luo's lyrics can be written only by someone who has been deeply immersed in the classics but who decides not to destroy but to reassemble and recompose them.[19] Consider some of the verbally packed lines of "Xianxiang qishier bian" [the seventy-two transformations of reality]:

> There were 72 martyrs at Huanghuagang;
> Confucius had 72 disciples;
> The Monkey King's magic involved 72 transformations
> We have arrived at the 72nd year of the Chinese Republic . . .
>
> High-rises are rising higher and higher,
> But the quality of human relationships is sinking lower and lower.
> Friends are more and more polite to one another,
> As they see one another less and less.
> The price of apples is not as high as before—
> Perhaps they don't taste that good anymore.

Color TV is getting more and more fabulous,
But those who know black from white are fewer and fewer.

An explosion very different from the masculinist destructionism of
Jian's music is at work here. The song moves across genres and disciplines, from chronicled mainstream history (the 72 Huanghuagang
martyrs who shed their blood for the eventually successful Chinese
Revolution of 1911), to the disciples of Confucius, to the legend of the
monkey king, to technology and sociology (the cars and high buildings
of the modern metropolis), to philosophy (the observation of how impersonal urban human relationships are). What is explosive is not the
narrated contents but the movement of the composition itself. In a
matter of seconds, we witness the surprising juxtaposition of the most
unrelated things. This juxtaposition at a breakneck pace invents new
relations among familiar forms of knowledge and demands a hitherto
unattempted deciphering of modernity.

In *Marxism and Literature,* Raymond Williams offers a theory of culture in terms of what he calls the "dominant, residual, and the emergent." While both the residual and the emergent contain elements that
can be fully incorporated within the dominant, Williams's main argument is that they also signify experiences and practices that have an
alternative and/or oppositional relation to the dominant culture. The
residual thus refers to meanings and values that were "effectively
formed in the past" but that are "still active in the cultural process . . .
as an effective element of the present." The emergent, which Williams
distinguishes from both the dominant and the residual, "is never only
a matter of immediate practice; indeed it depends crucially on finding
new forms or adaptations of form."[20] Insofar as Luo's songs make use
of classical texts, idioms, poetry, folk songs, and popularized romantic
themes,[21] they partake of the ongoing "residues" of a familiar native
culture with which every cultural worker has to come to terms. Whether
we like it or not, his lyrics say, this familiar native culture is there, like
an oft-played tune whose refrain structures our consciousness before
we are aware of it. At the same time, as he gathers these residues in bits
and pieces, Luo does not so much "restore" as rearrange. An outstanding example is the old Xinjiang folk song "Qingqun wuqü" [Dance song
of youth], which Luo has rearranged in at least two different versions,
each time adapting it for a different social inquiry.[22] In the sense that
they make composing and decomposing the primary event in the encounter between "folk" tunes and "high tech" electronics, between
Chinese materials and Western instrumentalizations, Luo's songs powerfully demonstrate the cultural practice that Williams calls emergent.

What is emergent is not simply a "local" ethnic history to be re-
claimed in postcoloniality, but also a conscious bracketing of precisely

the traditional concepts, themselves ideological leftovers of imperialism, of "national culture" and its "local" variants. Given the circumstances under which Luo works, his occasional tactical surrender to these traditional concepts is understandable. Precisely because the notion of a Chinese folk is not only residual but also dominant and hegemonic, it is extremely difficult for such emergent work as Luo's to be recognized and affirmed. As Williams writes, "Again and again what we have to observe is in effect a *pre-emergence,* active and pressing but not yet fully articulated, rather than the evident emergence which could be more confidently named."[23] What we have to observe is the compelling way in which Luo's emergent compositions *enact* the impurity of the postcolonial city's origins.

Luo's lyrics are a kind of signification that is as verbal as it is musical. This is why he can be read as well as heard, and why his songs require more than musical interpretation. This does not mean that he privileges the verbal above the musical, but rather that his work is intersemiotic— between sign systems, between verbal and musical notations, between reading and listening. Whereas one can argue that Cui Jian crosses over from words to music and thus abandons linguistic sense for the more "pure" sense of musical sound, the quality of Luo's work is best described by its full deployment of the intersemiotic reality of late twentieth-century Hong Kong city life.

This is a city life in which all productions—industrial, commercial, and economic—are dominated by another—the production of signs. The production of signs is at once superficial and abstract, in that it triggers meanings rather than concretizing them. For instance, the brevity, brokenness, and mutability of many Hong Kong verbal expressions become codes with which to read the past (the Chinese language) or the foreign (the English language), but at the same time we can also say that the past and the foreign, temporal and spatial "others," are now abbreviated in the form of codes: millennia of native histories and plenitudes of foreign language usages now appear as playful, secretive, allegorical signs, in the form of familiar phrases that are never more than phrases, that no longer belong to completely coherent syntaxes or contexts, and whose entire function now is to *conjure* the past, the serious, the foreign, the trendy, the "cool." The specificity of Luo's compositions consists in this conjuring. His cryptic words and phrases often serve as nothing more than signals, leaving the listeners to respond in any way they choose.

As signs and codes, the lyrics are intersemiotic with other signs such as those of fast food, mass communication, pocket novels, videos, karaoke, and so forth, in the sense that all such signs share a relation to postcolonial city culture, a relation that is legible only in its intersemioticity. In other words, Luo's songs do not make sense without, say, the culture in which reading has become a matter of scanning through pocket novels and listening has become coextensive with the auto-performance that is typified by the karaoke machine. This kind of intersemiotic production of meaning constitutes the form as well as substance of contemporary city life in East Asia, and Hong Kong, along with Tokyo, Taipei, and Singapore, is in the vanguard.

Neither Roots nor Hybrids: The Emergent Community

The intersemioticity of Luo's work is refreshing at a time when most interpretations of Asian and non-Western cultures still linger around the themes of tradition versus modernity, and ethnicity versus internationalism. Such interpretations have the tendency to cast "local" cultural activities ultimately in a nostalgic mode, as a quest for identity. Going backward is also going downward: accompanying the metaphor of "quest" is the metaphor of "roots," the meaning of which is assumed to be self-evident. Thus even though much pop music is written for urban audiences, these audiences are often reminded that their "roots" are far away in the rural past. To this extent, even the so-called "counter-cultural" mainland Chinese productions such as *He shang* ("The River Elegy") are nostalgic root-searching; their "critical" mode of understanding modern China is bound, by melancholia, to what modern China is not and never was—a timeless land and a unified folk.

In an international setting, root-searching assumes guises that may at first seem contradictory. For instance, despite its Westernized instrumentalizations, many Asian listeners I know find Luo's music to be "Chinese"- or "Oriental"-sounding. This response contrasts remarkably with that of some Western listeners, who tell me that Luo's music sounds "familiar" to their Western ears—that is, that it does not sound "Chinese" or "Oriental" enough. If the first response is nativist, the second is Orientalist. Behind both responses is the same essentialist wishful thinking typical of root-searching—the thinking that, in spite of the history of Western colonialism, non-Western cultural productions should remain pure, original, truly indigenous, and truly other-"sounding." For root-searchers, the task of interpreting culture is tied to the establishment of identity rather than being seen as a process in which differences constantly erupt and demand a new conception of the "whole." These conservative interpreters of culture find the metaphor of "roots" congenial because "roots" signify a return to the past so that the multiplicity of the present is reducible to a long-lost origin. But as Gayatri Spivak puts it, "[A]nyone who can conceive of looking for roots, should . . . be growing rutabagas."[24] Insofar as it problematizes the purity of ethnic origins and stages the impossibility for a colonized culture such as that of Hong Kong to remain immune to the forces of Western industrialization, commodification, and cultural imperialism, Luo's music foresees both the nativist and Orientalist "responses" and already contains, in its very intersemiotic modes, a critique of their wishful thinking.

Were we indeed to follow the "quest" and "root" motifs, no "Chinese" city would have greater reason for existentialist angst than Hong Kong. Being in the south, having been colonized by the British, having been occupied by Japan during the Second World War, having become Westernized and commercial, and now being "returned" to China, the history of modern Hong Kong could always be written as some form of quest for a "Chinese" identity that was preempted and made impossible from the beginning, and most significantly by its inerasable colonial "taint." Hong Kong's quest for China, then, would be judged in accordance to its fundamental futility: the more Hong Kong tries, the more it reveals its "lack" of "Chineseness" and the more it is a deviation from the norm of the folk. The past would follow Hong Kong like an unshakable curse of inferiority.

The quest for roots, however, is merely one type of signification among many in Luo Dayou's music. More interesting and pressing is how, at the same time that it renders the quest for a Chinese identity an unnecessary illusion, the intersemioticity of Luo's compositions makes room for a different kind of critical activity. This is the negotiation for a democracy that exceeds nativist and national bonds/bounds, but that does not obliterate the facts of colonial history in the postmodern hybridite's mode. The combination of these two negativities, "neither roots nor hybrids"—what I earlier called a double impossibility—constitutes the articulation of an alternative community.

One major feature of this articulation is Luo's repeated demonstration of the social problems that Hong Kong shares with other cities of the world. His conception of his own company, the "Music Factory," is thus along the lines of global ecology: "This factory is the only one that insists on manufacturing sounds as a way to beautify a small climate and protect the environment" (Luo, Production Notes). Similarly, two of his songs address the problem of children—be they the "masters of our future" or the "orphans of Asia"—as one for which we are all responsible. I translate them in their entirety here, with the view of giving the reader a sense of the composite or intersemiotic makeup of the new literacy that, as I have been arguing, Luo's songs generally put forward:

> You walk through the concrete jungle and its crowds,
> Looking at the neon lights floating in the modernized city.
> Suddenly you think of the distant past and its unrealized dreams,

ETHICS AFTER IDEALISM

Remembering what people once told you, that you were the master
of the future.

Every pedestrian waits faithfully at the crowded cross-walk;
Everyone is looking at those traffic lights that symbolize fate.
In this red-orange-yellow-green world, you, master of the future,
Keep looking into every strange face for the glory of your
childhood.

Every baby that arrives in the world today
Opens its eyes looking for genuine concern.
Every life that arrives in the world waits with hope,
Because the world we transform will be their future.
Don't think that our children are too small to understand
anything—
I hear the silent protests in their quiet dreams:
We don't want a sky polluted by the games of science!
We don't want to be turned into computer-creatures by your
inventions!

One day our children will tell their younger generation:
You must discipline yourselves.
This motto is flying about in the wind like kites.
When the future world is filled with strange melodies,
Perhaps you will remember this old song—
Flying about . . .

We don't want a sky polluted by the games of science!
We don't want a time and space taken over by practical life!
We don't want a horizon that is more and more blurry!
We don't want a Spring that is more and more silent!
We don't want to be turned into computer-creatures by your
inventions!
We don't want to be turned into mechanical children by your
forgetfulness!

We want sunshine, green grass, the earth, the wide blue sky;
We don't want red nightmares made from red dirty soil . . .

"Weilai de zhurenweng"
[Masters of the future]

*   *   *

The orphans of Asia are crying in the wind—
Their yellow faces smeared with red dirt,
Their black eyes filled with white fear.
The West wind is singing sad songs in the East.

The orphans of Asia are crying in the wind—
No one wants to play games of equality with you;

Everyone wants your favorite toys.
Dear children, why are you crying?

So many look in vain for answers to those unanswerable questions;
So many sigh helplessly in the deep of the night;
So many wipe their tears in silence.
Dear mothers, why is this so?

"Yaxiya de guer"
[The orphans of Asia]

Apart from voicing social problems that Hong Kong shares with all other cities, another major feature of Luo's articulation of an alternative community lies in his firm commitment to Hong Kong's history and difference, on which a responsible way of handling its future is to be based. As he writes in the prologue to the disc collection, "Gaobie de niandai" [The era of saying goodbyes]:

I am watching this city.

I am astonished by her maturation. No matter how much her journey is filled with frustration, sorrow, resentment, anger, and contradictory feelings of love and hate, an unrelenting sense of mission, which I have not felt for years, rushes up in me as I look back upon those countless pictures put together by blood and tears.

I know we are all carrying a heavy burden—the burden of returning to her a romance which originally belongs to her, which she deserves, and which we have destroyed or cast into negligence.[25]

This sense of mission toward Hong Kong, shared by many of Hong Kong's younger artists today,[26] is perhaps most clearly expressed in the song of Luo's that is the most well known, "Queen's Road East," sung originally in Cantonese. A main thoroughfare that dates back to the old colonial times (the times of Queen Victoria) and that runs through a good part of the Hong Kong Island, "Queen's Road" is an emblem of a bygone era, a passage, and a transition. Its spatial presence stands as a tangible record of the many modes of temporality Hong Kong has been forced to go through, only to arrive at its current crisis. Hong Kong's imminent transferral from its current colonizer to its future colonizer is an event whose potential terror all of its citizens dread but which only the privileged have means of escaping. Between "the Queen" (now Elizabeth II) and "the Comrade" is the unknown future of a city whose inhabitants are brokers who are effecting the biggest deal in history:[27]

A noble friend is on the back of my coin—
She is always young and her name is "Queen."

> She accompanies me in all my exchanges.
> Though expressionless, she is the converging point of all
>   achievements.
>
> My dearest friends leave this city with a "bye bye."
> We now depend on the great comrades for new developments—
> Real estate speculations can take place everywhere as usual,
> But the name of "Mongkok"[28] may have to change.
>
> This virtuous friend/comrade looks familiar and friendly;
> That's why horse-races will continue twice a week.
> The people here too must race toward the final destination—
> To become citizens of powerful countries, all you need is money . . .
>
> "Huanghou da dao dong"
> [Queen's Road East]

These few lines give us a glimpse of the social and political density of the song in spite of its clichéd and comic makeup. "Queen's Road East" speaks ironically of Hong Kong's volatile economic realities: horse-racing, a long-term colonial gambling institution that the Chinese authorities have promised to allow to continue after 1997, co-exists with monetary ventures such as real estate speculations, but also with the crisis of the rapid emigration from Hong Kong of those who are professionally or financially able.

More than the urban cultural productions of mainland China and Taiwan, both of which still hold claims to being representative of a nationalistic Chinese identity (even though Taiwanese nativist sentiments against Han and mainland Chinese hegemony are increasingly strong),[29] the Hong Kong in Luo's music speaks of a kind of lack of nationality, a nationlessness, that is at once the city's past coloniality, present uncertainty, and (one hopes) future openness. Hong Kong's claim to the homeland of China is a sentimental and residual one, and, as such, a sign perhaps of the most artificial kind. Instead of invoking a longing for the motherland, Luo's lyrics refer us to a forcefully different notion of community—of community as what is based on cultural work and social responsibility rather than on the realpolitik coercions of blood, race, and soil. The remembrance of and insistence on such a community, to quote Williams once again, make up the "structures of feeling"[30] in Luo Dayou's music. I conclude with the lyrics of a love song, "Dongfang zhi zhu" [Pearl of the Orient]:

> A small meandering stream flows toward the south—
> It flows into the fragrant river, to see if
> You, Pearl of the Orient, my love,
> Are still as romantic in spirit as ever.

Between Colonizers

A crescent moon shines over the harbor,
The night is deep and lights are shimmering bright.
The Pearl of the Orient is sleepless through the night,
Keeping the promise of change-as-eternity.

You have let the sea winds blow for five thousand years,
Every tear seems to tell of your dignity.
Let the sea accompany me in blessing you—
Please don't forget my face, yellow and always loyal.

Boats are meandering into the harbor—
Looking back at the boundless sea.
Pearl of the Orient, embrace me,
And let me warm your disconsolate breast.

TEN

Things, Common/Places, Passages of the Port City: On Hong Kong and Hong Kong Author Leung Ping-kwan

"WHAT IS GOING to happen to Hong Kong after 1997?" In the past few years, as Hong Kong's peculiar colonial fate gains international attention, this is the question I often encounter in conversations. The point of this last chapter is not to attempt an answer but to argue, through a discussion of Hong Kong and Hong Kong author Leung Ping-kwan/ Liang Bingjun (pen name Ya See/Ye Si),[1] a way of reading coloniality and colonial literature that is alternative to the perspectives that are currently available. Even though 1997 is the event that crystallizes all the crises that constitute Hong Kong as a "borrowed place, borrowed time,"[2] it is a background but not the focus here. My interest in Hong Kong, a city in which I grew up, is that it is a particular kind of passageway, which was created by the accident of history but which nonetheless persists from the nineteenth century to the present with a uniqueness and resilience that is unknown in world history.[3]

Considerations of cities always seem to put their emphases on space and place. Geography, architecture, landscape, urban planning, physical remains, and topographical details occupy the students of city life. When writers look at Hong Kong spatially, they often find it unremarkable. Indeed, geographical and spatial considerations of Hong Kong have little choice other than to emphasize the smallness and insignificance of the city. Hong Kong is a barren rock at the southern tip of

China; Hong Kong is overcrowded, smelly, dirty, unbearably hot and humid in the summer, and aesthetically devoid of ancient landmarks of world renown. Even those who admire the brilliance of the "Pearl of the Orient" at night have to admit that Hong Kong is lacking when it comes to the grandeur of stupendous natural landscape, and that the postmodern concrete jungles that make up its city space are not exactly comparable to the historic sites that they can see across the border in the People's Republic of China.

If land and space are what inspire visions of greatness and give rise to a heroic sense of history, land and space mean very different things in Hong Kong. With a large part of its useable space built from filling the sea, Hong Kong totals only slightly over 400 square miles, which has to hold a population of over six million people. Land is not some beloved "native soil" but is first and foremost a commodity. From "Crown land," the land owned by the colonial government; to land owned by big transnational consortiums for industrial and commercial purposes; to the living space available to the ordinary citizen, land, that seemingly ultimate because immovable signified, is always a priced signifier and an ingenious invention that rises higher and higher in the air. The general scarcity of space means that what is commonly taken for granted in Western Europe and North America—quotidian living space—is so expensive that few people can afford much of it. In the early 1990s, the average price of residential space is approximately Hong Kong $4,000 (approximately U.S. $500) per square foot, which means that a miniscule residential flat of about 500 square feet in a multistoried highrise would cost about Hong Kong $2 million (somewhat over U.S. $250,000). To rent the same amount of space, if it is in a relatively convenient location, one would need to pay about U.S. $1,200 a month.

As in the case of thriving cities, the scarcity of space has not meant that Hong Kong is shunned by those who *can* afford space at exorbitant prices. On the contrary, Hong Kong is home to some of the wealthiest people in the world, from Chinese tycoons to British colonial bureaucrats to business people of every breed and nationality. The lifestyles of these people make one realize that it is money, rather than land, which creates vision in Hong Kong. When one is rich enough to afford a luxurious flat in one of the extravagant highrises at the midlevels or on the peak, one commands a "view" that is, quite simply, breathtaking. By contrast, if one is poor, one feels more or less like a "cageman," which is the title of one of Hong Kong's most acclaimed films in recent years.[4] As this title suggests, the prototypical human being here is the person locked inside the space of half a bunk bed, in conditions that few in the West can imagine. Even though the film does not go beyond the realistic depiction of lower-class life in Hong Kong, its images and events refer compellingly to the general scarcity of space and land, the brunt of which is borne by the underprivileged.

These brief allusions to space, while marking the absolute disparity between the rich and the poor—a feature Hong Kong shares with all major world cities—at the same time highlight Hong Kong's economic success and its enviable status as one of the most financially prosperous places even at times of worldwide economic recession. (In the 1990s, for instance, the Hong Kong government had annual budgets that cut taxes and increased spending.) As the title of a popular music collection, *Capital*,[5] suggests, the secret of this colonial "capital" is its capital.[6] However, what I want to point out is not so much Hong Kong's economic success as the fact that this success has always been interpreted more or less as the *compensation for a fundamental lack*, as the sign of something gone wrong. Typically, this kind of interpretation goes as follows: Hong Kong thrives economically *only* because it is lacking in political autonomy and self-determination. For instance, Lau Siu-kai expresses it this way:

> The closing of the political path naturally leads to whole-hearted devotion of efforts to economic pursuits, opportunities for which are plentiful. The rise of apolitical materialism is a logical response of the Hong Kong Chinese to the unequal availability of political and economic opportunities in the unique setting which they find themselves.[7]

While Lau's comments are still largely descriptive, a sense of contempt for Hong Kong's "economism" and "materialism" is much clearer in the following passage by Ackbar Abbas, largely because of the author's wit:

> One of the effects of a very efficient colonial administration is that it provides almost no outlet for political idealism (until perhaps quite recently); as a result, most of the energy is directed towards the economic sphere. Historical imagination, the citizens' belief that they might have a hand in shaping their own history—this gets replaced by speculation on the property or stock markets, or by an obsession with fashion and consumerism. If you cannot choose your political leaders, you can at least choose your own clothes. We find therefore not an atmosphere of doom and gloom, but the more paradoxical phenomenon of *doom and boom:* the more frustrated or blocked the aspirations to "democracy" are, the more the market booms.[8]

There is no description of economics which is not at the same time a moral judgment. The above readings of Hong Kong's economic development are in keeping with an age-old understanding of libidinal economies based on a binary opposition between lack and compensation. For these authors, it is because the people in Hong Kong are lacking in something essential—political power—that they have to turn their energies elsewhere, economics. And yet this elsewhere, this *other* development, which is assumed in an a priori manner as compensatory in function, is then judged to be superficial, excessive, and pathological. As Abbas's clever rhyme of "gloom-doom-boom" suggests, the more Hong Kong excels in its materialistic accomplishments, the more this excellence must be taken to be a sign of its deficiency, degeneracy, abnormality, and hence basic inferiority. To expose the untenability of this type of argument, we can ask a simple question: if Hong Kong's materialism is "compensatory," then how should we understand the materialism of, say, the United States, where people do have political self-determination? Would such a materialism be more "natural"?

Reading as a feminist, I suggest that this kind of discriminatory judgment about Hong Kong's materialism, even though it does not seem at first sight to have anything to do with women, can be juxtaposed with Freud's writings on femininity. Like "Hong Kong" for many an interested observer, female sexuality for Freud (especially in his later years) was an enigmatic libidinal economy to be interpreted. And yet this fascination, which establishes a discourse for femininity to be examined closely, ironically also dismisses femininity as pathological. In Freud's readings, as is well known, femininity is a sexuality that must make up for its lack of the penis in order to *be*. Because this lack is viewed by Freud (rather than by women) as so very basic (since the penis is, for Freud, indispensable), femininity becomes—except in the case of motherhood in which the production of a son equals a woman's possession of a penis at long last—a tragedy, an unpleasant fate to which women's libidinal precociousness and inflexibility, which stand in contrast to men's youthfulness and spontaneity, testify. Everything women do and excel in—Freud's example is specifically the technique of plaiting and weaving—becomes simply a concealment of their fundamental lack. The better women do, then, the more they prove their shame about not having "the real thing."[9]

The juxtaposition of Freud's reading of femininity and the prevalent reading of Hong Kong's materialism reveals much more than the traditional negative equation of femininity and the city. Rather, it shows how both kinds of readings, which emerge from very different cultural contexts, nonetheless share a common premise—namely, the identification (which takes place at the invisible/inarticulate part of discourse) with established, "proper" realms of power; an identification that must, in the course of asserting itself, denigrate the nonestablished and the "improper." In Freud's case, the patriarchal nature of such an identification is made clear (conveniently) by the explicit content of his discourse—sexuality. However, if it is the identification with power, rather than simply the discourse about sexuality, that is symptomatic of a certain kind of masculinism, then what the juxtaposition with Freud clarifies is that in the typical dismissal of Hong Kong's materialism as disease and compensation, a dismissal that does not apparently concern sexuality or women, the forces in play are, in fact, also masculinist and misogynistic.

The analogy between Hong Kong and feminine sexuality would seem even less fortuitous once we turn to the conceptions of Hong Kong by some of the most well-known mainland Chinese writers. From the perspective of the mainland Chinese, Hong Kong's "lack" has to do with its coloniality, a coloniality which, in the language of sexuality, is equated with Hong Kong's loss of her sexual integrity. Consider these lines from the writer Ai Wu at the point of his departure from Hong Kong:

> When the ship had travelled a good distance, there seemed to be a low, plaintive call coming from the direction of the Colony. "Will those who love me please forgive me? I'm being raped by the British imperialists!"[10]

And this poem, "Hong Kong," by the poet Wen Yiduo:

> Like the yellow panther guarding the gates of the imperial palace
> Oh, Mother! my post is a strategic one, yet my status so humble.
> The ferocious Sea Lion presses upon my body,
> Devouring my flesh and bones and warming itself on my blood.
> Oh, Mother! I wail and cry, yet you hear me not.
> Oh, Mother! quick! let me hide in your embrace!
> Mother! I want to come back, Mother![11]

While the male writers from contemporary Hong Kong see Hong Kong's economic success as a compensation for the basic lack of the real thing, political power, the mainland male writers focus on Hong Kong's status as a colony. Once again, Hong Kong's condition is analogized to certain pejorative notions of femininity. Ai Wu sees Hong Kong as a woman who has been sexually violated; Wen Yiduo sees Hong Kong as a child in need of Mom. For them, Hong Kong's "lack" becomes the occasion for Chinese political idealism. This political idealism, moreover, takes a particular form—the form of rescue. Hong Kong is, in the eyes of these passionate literary men, the maiden who cannot defend herself against the dragon, the imperialist, and must therefore be delivered from her plight by the rescue operation of a Saint George. Alternatively, Hong Kong is *in need* of a mother: she is longing to be reunited with China; her "real" source of identification is mainland China, and so forth.

The moral righteousness of these masculinist interpretations shows us how, as a modern city, Hong Kong cannot be considered apart from the two dominant historical issues of its "economism" and its "coloniality." Given that these are the facts of Hong Kong's origins (on which I will elaborate in a moment), the question I want to raise is: is there a way of thinking and writing about Hong Kong without repeating the compensatory logic and salvational motives of these familiar interpretations? Without attributing to Hong Kong the derogatory sense of lack nor thus the need of a savior, how might we go about describing its uniqueness and its difference—how might we go about thinking of it as a city? Instead of asking how Hong Kong falls short of other major cities, what does Hong Kong tell us about our assumptions about cities in general? What is it about Hong Kong as a city that offers us new insights into the conceptualizations of modern city culture?

If, for the time being, we stay with the analogies of "rape" and "need for a mother," we realize that the "rescuer" of Hong Kong, the "mother" that Wen Yiduo assumed to be China proper, is itself not innocent of the crime of rape. For Ai Wu and Wen Yiduo, who were writing in the pre–Second World War period, anti-imperialism from a Chinese perspective was in many ways a justifiable cause because of European and Japanese territorial aggression against China. In the 1980s and 1990s, however, anti-imperialist claims from the People's Republic become in the main a way to mask Chinese imperialism, an imperialism that is well known and very visible in areas such as Tibet and, increasingly, Hong Kong. By pointing fingers at "Western" imperialists, China veils its own violence against its people and its colonized territories. As is the case of Chinese politics after the Tiananmen Massacre of 1989, the history of "Western imperialism" and "Western colonialism" is recalled strategically as a means to gain allegiance from the people and thus make them forget China's own far from innocuous complicities. By making "the West" and "Western imperialists" their overt enemy, the People's Republic thus allows itself *to hold on to the status of a victim* (whose people and land are being appropriated from her) *while it openly acts as a militaristic empire.*

This is the reason why a contemporary Hong Kong essayist, Ha Gong, attributes the act of raping Hong Kong to China as well as Britain, revealing thus the complicity and collaboration between colonizer and "rescuer" rather than their opposition. Referring to the talks conducted since 1984 between China and Britain over Hong Kong's fate after 1997, Ha Gong offers an image that sums up Hong Kong's predicament:

> The Sino-British talks closely resemble two men gang-raping Hong Kong, with the victim being denied the right to scream or protest. After the event, a member of a certain legislative body appeared on the scene and demanded a detailed enquiry into the background of

the rape. But a number of staunch supporters of rapists' rights stood up and called for the legalization of rape, shouting at the victims that they were entirely without shame.[12]

The perfect example of this "gang-rape" of Hong Kong by both the colonizer and the "rescuer" was the construction in Daya Bay, which is in close proximity to Hong Kong, of China's first nuclear plant. This project proceeded in spite of the fact that, unlike other cities near nuclear plant sites, Hong Kong is unevacuable in the case of an emergency. Writing in a deliberately ironic mode, another Hong Kong essayist, Wong Ting-jee/Wang Tingzhi, describes the situation this way, thus giving us a very different picture of the "motherland":

> All Wang Tingzhi's readers should . . . show their utmost support [for the construction of the nuclear plant]. The reasons are as follows: Daya Bay nuclear power plant is a very sizeable commercial transaction between Britain and China. If it doesn't get built, Britain loses that much business. Thus, to oppose the plant is to ruin someone else's livelihood; immoral actions of this sort are wrong. Daya Bay nuclear power plant is moreover one part of the Great Socialist Motherland's Great Socialist Construction and it's a "virgin factory", a first for China. That its chosen site should be Daya Bay, right next to Hong Kong, is to the greater glory of the Hong Kong people, who later, using its electricity every day, will feel the warmth of the Motherland's tender embrace. Those who oppose the construction of the plant are simply showing themselves to be unworthy of the Motherland's generosity.[13]

Once it is clear that the motherland itself too is a "rapist" driven by its own unscrupulous self-interest, it becomes necessary to wrest Hong Kong from the sentimental metaphors of ethnic bonding and point to the exploitative realities involved in Hong Kong's "return" to China. My point is, of course, not a defense of British colonialism, but rather that we need to dispel as well the myth of a Chinese nationalism masquerading as savior and possessor of a community that has, in fact, very little in common with the People's Republic at this point. And this, I think, is the most unique feature of Hong Kong's postcoloniality: the end of British colonialism will be followed by a new colonialism, that of its "motherland." If Hong Kong has been a "borrowed place, borrowed time," then its current predicament is, paradoxically, that it is "suddenly faced with a future."[14] Hong Kong's imminent colonization by the People's Republic in the name of a reunion and repatriation violates the telos of the conventional thinking about coloniality, in which coloniality is followed by emancipation. Hong Kong's return to China forces us to ask: what happens when colonialism is not a past but a future, when colonialism has not yet left all its tracks but is looming in the time we normally associate with hope, change, and freedom?

It is here—at the limits of land, space, political power, self-determi-nation, and future emancipation, all of which Hong Kong supposedly "lacks"—that I would plot my reading of Leung. In this reading, iden-tifying what Hong Kong does not have does not mean seeing what *it has* in terms of compensation, since to do so would be to follow the type of interpretative move which, however well intentioned, continues to valorize and privilege what is believed to be "lacking." Instead, I would suggest that cultural workers such as Leung can be seen as actively producing and remaking the very origins of Hong Kong's coloniality in their "representations." These representations do not seek the impos-sible task of overturning those origins, nor do they assume the mode of a *ressentiment* that envies what Hong Kong never had in the first place. Rather, these representations accept these origins as Hong Kong's fateful difference—its own libidinal economy—and invent their own survival space therein. What results is neither a compensatory tran-scendence of these origins nor a negative aesthetics antithetically posed toward its society, but modes of writing that become themselves a special form of passageway—*a material working through* the most diffi-cult of times.

Before I go into Leung's poems, a few words about Hong Kong's "origins."

The Port City, the Common/Place

Hong Kong, like most colonial cities,[15] has always been a port. The history of Hong Kong as a city is relatively short, dating back to the mid-nineteenth century when it was ceded by China to Britain as a result of the Opium war of 1839–42. Before then Hong Kong was a fishing village with a population of about 7,000. As a city, therefore, Hong Kong did not evolve into its modern form of a commercial center from a long history of internal culture-accumulation; it does not possess the typical symbols of long civilizations—national treasures and precious monu-ments—that make up the appeal of ancient cities. Far away from Lon-don and Beijing, Hong Kong has always thrived on its local cultural practices, customs, and rituals. This is one reason why, for a long time, it was dismissed as a "cultural desert." Hong Kong's city*ness*—that is, its international or cosmopolitan status—is indistinguishable from the violence that established it as such, namely, British mercantile imperial-ism. As pointed out by some scholars, Britain's acquisition of Hong Kong was much less motivated by territorial gain than by the wish to have a point of entry into the "Far East." In acquiring Hong Kong,

> what was sought was a commercial and not a territorial empire, and
> the island was taken over reluctantly, primarily for the purpose of

establishing the necessary organs of law and order and administration, free from Chinese intervention or control. . . . The Colony was not thought of in terms of territorial gain, but as the minimum space required for what were thought to be the necessary British institutions. Its function was to be the headquarters of British trade, administration and general influence in the Far East.[16]

Together with its coloniality, then, economics and commerce *are* Hong Kong's "origins": there has never been any alternative social framework in the territory in modern times. When critics lament and disapprove of Hong Kong's mercenary degeneracy, they are ignoring and forgetting these origins. What they need to come to terms with, I suggest, is not the extent of this degeneracy, but the ways Hong Kong has carved out its own space in the past century and a half within the environment permitted by this originary violence—not, in other words, how Hong Kong makes up for its lack, but what it has made of this lack, this original exploitation, which is its only condition of possibility.

Etymologically, the word "port" illuminates all the aspects of Hong Kong's "origins" that are suppressed in the eventual interpretations of the city. "Port" refers, of course, to Hong Kong's status as an *entrepôt*, an entrance point or *port*al to China and Asia. It also refers to Hong Kong's amazing economic development—to Hong Kong's status as a vast em*por*ium with a plenitude of ex*port*s and im*port*s. More significantly, though, it alludes to the trans*port*ing function that is part and parcel of Hong Kong's intended role as a carrier of valuables and values between cultures. In performing this function to its utmost capacity, Hong Kong has fully established itself as a land of op*port*unities. If Hong Kong remains in the avant-garde of world city culture, it is because it makes *port*ability, including the portability of postmodern cultural identities, a fact of life.

Some might say that this port status of Hong Kong—as the convergence point between East and West—is a cliché, a commonplace that has been repeated over and over again. My point is exactly that we need to think more closely about the implications of the commonplace. Why is the commonplace always the sign of inferiority? Why is it always repressed—brought up in interpretations only to be quickly sidestepped, dismissed as insignificant?

The commonplace might be seen as occupying the same kind of status as the "center" in Jacques Derrida's early writings. Like the center, the commonplace is the place of value, the place where evaluation "takes place."[17] However, despite their similar function, the commonplace and the center have entirely different destinies. The center is always viewed as some metaphysical bestower of value. Even after the lesson of deconstruction, after it has been put "under erasure"—which means that we recognize its necessity without endorsing it as a virtue—

the center continues to function as *central*. The commonplace, even though it is as indispensable as the center, occupies instead the place of the *debased*.

What does this mean in the culture of modern cities? If the center is the value that transcends its local, material body to become the "general equivalent," the commonplace is the value that, in spite of its general use, remains confined to the local and the material. Paris and London, capitals of imperialism, remain to this day "centers" of world civilization despite their bloody histories; Manila, Saigon, Calcutta, and Hong Kong, even though they have partaken of the same histories, are consigned to the margins. The European capitals persist as "origins" from which universal value rises and flows; the (post)colonial port cities, imagined as mere recipients of such value, live the lives of the forever "local" and negligible.

To underline Hong Kong's port status is thus to think about the significance of the commonplace the way deconstruction has taught us to think about the center—with a different emphasis. For deconstruction, the center is a necessity, but it cannot be endorsed as a virtue. The commonplace, we might say, may be unvirtuous, but it is always necessary. In particular, we need to think about what may be called the commonplace of the commonplace—the "money" of Hong Kong. As I already mentioned, Hong Kong's economism and materialism have always been viewed pejoratively as a kind of disease, even in readings which recognize the central nature of Hong Kong's economic reality. My proposal is that it is only when we take the "diseased," excessive nature of Hong Kong's "economism" and "materialism" seriously that we would be able to see the inextricable mutuality between center and commonplace, and to return to the commonplace the function it shares with the center—namely, that for all its dirty, smelly, unpleasant reality, it is the origin of value, the place which everyone, regardless of identification and social status, passes through.

As a manner of interpretation, this would mean reading even Hong Kong's creative and artistic cultures in terms of, rather than in opposition to, its material reality. Rather than locating the point of Hong Kong's "creative culture" away from its material bases, away from the commonplace of its "economism," how might we go about reading this culture as intrinsic to the *port-ing* of value? And, once we have done this, how might we use the commonplace to read the center? What might Hong Kong tell us about London and Beijing, rather than vice versa?

In the following, I read the poetry of Leung, one of Hong Kong's leading writers (who also writes novels, short stories, critical essays, and film scripts), not by opposing him to the material economic culture of Hong Kong, but by showing how he makes the "origins" of Hong Kong—origins that are economic and colonial—part of the process of his writing. Leung himself has described his poetry as "homeless." As he tells us in an essay, in order to write as a poet in Hong Kong, he must be "accommodating" and be willing to exchange his role with more marketable ones.[18] Even so, as a poet, Leung does not hold himself aloof from the material reality around him in a superior manner; rather, he is so thoroughly immersed in the materialisms and infatuations of his society that he does not write without at the same time showing us how that society works, without at the same time taking us through the passages that constitute "Hong Kong."

The Poems of Leung Ping-kwan[19]

The first feature about Leung's poems that needs to be mentioned is that they are meant to be read in Cantonese, the language used by most of the inhabitants of Hong Kong. While Cantonese can be written in the same Han characters of standard Chinese (Mandarin/Putong-hua), which have been unified since the Qin dynasty (221–206 B.C.), the language has its own grammar, syntax, expressions, and set of tones. Writing "Chinese" for people whose mother tongue is Cantonese is therefore already learning to use a different language the preeminence of which comes primarily from its long status as *script*. In Hong Kong especially, this has always meant negotiating between the "standard" that is Mandarin/Putonghua and the colloquial daily usages of Cantonese that one actually speaks and hears, suppressing the latter's "local" features, and translating such features into "readable" Chinese, which exists as a kind of common, viable "currency." On the other side, meanwhile, has always been the currency of English, which is the "general equivalent" toward which all non-Western cultures are obliged to move in the postcolonial world. Like standard Chinese, English is not just a means of communication; rather it is a usurper of linguistic and cultural space, a usurper which itself has become the standard of evaluation. As Leung writes:

> I think various attitudes towards language are the products of specific ways of looking at and talking about the world. Not only would retired English professors from Oxford or Cambridge claim that this is the place that speaks the worst English, some Mainland or Taiwan writers who have advocated the purity of the Chinese language also say that Hong Kong writers are handicapped in the Chinese language because Mandarin (Putonghua) is not the native tongue here.[20]

Articulating a space between English and Chinese, and between standard Chinese and Cantonese, Leung's poems constitute a kind of "minor literature written in a major language" that is spoken of by Gilles Deleuze and Félix Guattari.[21]

A second feature of Leung's poems is that they are full of descriptions of the material world. This is a poetry of wandering, traveling, observing, talking with people from different places and cultures. A list of some of Leung's titles suffices to show this: "The Bakery," "Sleeping on the Beach," "At the North Point Car Ferry," "At the Old Bull-Fighting Ring," "The Moon in La Jolla," "Ode to a Daoist in Del Mar," "The Visit to the Museum of Modern Art," "Tokyo Story," "Beijing Train Station," "Seagulls of Kunming," "Brecht-haus, Berlin," "Postcards from Prague." Even when he is still, the poet's eye is constantly on the move, bringing with it multiple perceptions which are constantly changing. And even in their rural images, Leung's poems attest to a material city culture with its variegated technologies of external as well as internal journeying, technologies which enable the poet not only to roam the world but also to approach, examine, and penetrate things from a variety of visual perspectives created by photography and film, from close-ups to long-takes, from microscopic detailing to distant appreciation.

At the same time, precisely because of the technical multiplication of the optical as well as other kinds of sensorial "unconscious," a host of things are admitted into writing: fruits, flowers, trees, leaves, shoes, clogs, furniture, paintings, films, music, postcards, food, drinks, and so forth. As Leung describes it, one of the conventions he follows consciously is the classical Chinese *wing mut see/yongwu shi*, the type of poetry that eulogizes things.[22]

But what exactly do things do in Leung's poetry? As "the camera looks around, gorging on imagery," the "surplus images of the city" can, in many respects, be "discarded like garbage."[23] Unwanted things can form a ridiculous environment, which sometimes expresses itself as a senseless compulsion to acquire. In the poem "Lucky Draw," acquisition becomes a form of absurdity:

> She gets a canned husband,
> and a bunch of motorized relatives.
> She gets a new set of fingernails,
> eyebrows and nose.
> She gets the title of vice-chairman
> of all associations.
> She gets four crocodiles that can sing,
> a hippopotamus that sends flowers regularly,
> a rhinoceros that waits at the corner of the street,
> a big hairy tortoise that requires talk.
> She gets a hair net.

She gets two bloody hearts.
She gets the kind of vacuum cleaner
her neighbor Asou bought just last week.
She gets identical dust to go with it.
She gets twelve certified university entrance examination approvals.
She gets as [a] bonus
small dishes offered by all the
different brands of soy sauces.[24]

The awareness of the potential absurdity of thing-culture does not mean that Leung would therefore turn away from things. Instead, his poetry indicates alternative directions. If the convention of thing-poetry allows Leung to capture the world in the form of things, the multiple material presences in his poems also tell us about basic changes in the technology of representation. The rich array of things makes us realize that the poet is not simply a poet but also a painter and a photographer. Poetry, in the sense that it allows juxtaposition of images much more effectively and literally than narrative—thereby preserving the physicality and crudity of such juxtaposition—becomes in the postmodern age a kind of verbal photography; poems are snapshots made with words. What comes across through thing-images is not the continuity of narrative prose but brokenness, the disjointed and hence stark presences of things as they impinge upon consciousness. Meanwhile, if the poet is now a painter and photographer, the "thing" in Leung's poetry is also multimediatized: it is no longer the thing in classical Chinese poetry, but an intersemiotic object that is created between classical poetry, painting, and photography; between a classical poet's eye and a modern photographer's eye; between verbal and technologized visuality. The compact thing-images are now portable, miniscule worlds we can carry with us because time has been manipulated to become a synchronized object containing different worlds.

In the busy, kaleidoscopic variety of imagistic fragments, a predominant impression of the things in Leung's poetry is that they are utterly unremarkable—a hibiscus flower, a pair of clogs, a green salad, a morning cloud, the evening fog, lights, colors. These things are unremarkable not in the sense of "uninteresting" but rather in the sense of that which is beyond remark, beyond the smooth fluency of words. Instead, words have now become a means of *bricolage*—a bricolage of sensations as well as of practices—in which things are put together in small, detailed, varied angles that produce new relations. Each phrase introduces a slightly different perspective, asking us to see a familiar thing anew, with surprising results. It is as if hundreds of images are clicked and processed in front of us in order to demonstrate their lack of heroic aspirations, their sheer material but mercurial presence. Consider, for instance, the implications of the last stanza of this poem, "The Flame Tree":

> How does something change colors?
> Does green always mean the gentleness of tolerance? Red
> the violence of revolution? No. Analogies
> are mere restrictions. I am unwilling to classify.
> As I look at you, I wish to know—
> Are you what secretly emerges from tangles of green
> to become a bright new red blossom, wide open toward
>   the white clouds?
> Or are you stamens and pistils that laugh and shake at
> the unending games of creeping branches and flirting leaves?
> This way of thinking forms with my gaze, until the bus
> turns the corner, and the scene disappears—
> and you form yet another new relation with the world.[25]

The bricolage of sensations and practices means that Leung's poetry is, ultimately, a poetry of consumption—consumption not in the sense of passive mass indoctrination but in the sense of the use of objects by those who are not the producers, in spaces that were not intended for them. In this latter sense, consumption is the representational mode of those Michel de Certeau calls "the weak," who "must continually turn to their own ends forces alien to them."[26] In Leung's poetry, consumption consists in inventing uses of the world that clearly fall outside the design and purpose of the space that is the "British colony." Watching the mist and fog on an outlying island, listening to the voice of a man selling bamboo poles for drying clothes, walking through the empty corridors of a colonial building, studying the patterns of lotus leaves: such quotidian activities consume the world around them in useless, unglamorous modes, but they also bring with them surprising illuminations. Instead of establishing permanent, fenced-off spaces, a poetry of consumption in this context specializes in a tactic of seizing opportunities as they reveal themselves momentarily *in time*.[27]

If the things in Leung's poetry are ordinary, they also become in the process of consumption agents of a democratic space, a common ground, where even the most ordinary thing can be appreciated on its own terms and shown to give unexpected delight, where the plenitude of things is not about luxury, extravagance, or passive consumerism but about accommodation, about making room and letting be. Leung always writes in dialogue, be it a dialogue between subject and object, subject and subject, or object and object. His poems offer themselves as passages which people can enter without violence and trauma, and which establish themselves as a new kind of value-making.

And yet such passages, because they intend genuine openness, are very fragile. For Leung, Hong Kong itself is such a fragile, vulnerable space, which is as easily appropriated as it is open:

> The space we have is a mixed, hybrid space, a crowded and dangerous space, carnival-like even in times of crisis, heavenly and not far from disasters. It is a field where many forces struggle together, a space we as well as everybody have to find ways to make better use of, but it will also be easily appropriated by other forces, political or economical. This space that is open to us could easily be lost to us.[28]

Leung's poems, which he writes in ways that do not "simply chime in" with Hong Kong's commodified culture,[29] nonetheless participate in that culture in a deeply committed way. While Leung does not endorse Hong Kong's "materialism," neither does he simply repudiate it with contempt or withdraw into an otherworldly metaphysics. The figure of the poet that is conjured by his work is not someone who fancies himself to be a virgin untainted by social reality; rather he involves himself in Hong Kong's materialism by making visible its abundant and over-determined forms. The immanence and centrality of the material in his poems become both an expression of the commonplace—clichéd, ordinary, unremarkable things, things which are simply there—and a common place, the place where people meet, things converge, and mutualities and reciprocities are actively reinvented. As he puts it in the preface to one of his prose collections, *Books and the City*, the topic he is most concerned with is the relation between cultures.[30]

The distinctive use of things in a poetry that does not think of itself as "representative" of Hong Kong thus tells us much more about Hong Kong than many other writers with conscious aspirations. The Hong Kong that comes across in Leung's writings is not one that is politically correct ("Down with the British imperialists! Down with mainland Chinese chauvinism!"); yet neither does it imagine itself as lacking or pleading for pity. Rather, it is a Hong Kong that reinvents its imposed fate as transporter in a new kind of production. What this Hong Kong transports is not only things; it is also the practice of things as opportunities whereby alternative values materialize in the process of allegorical juxtaposition and unconventional dialogue. In this way, postcolonial "city culture" is redefined not simply in the form of a new identity politics emanating from a specific "local" space, but also as the surprising encounters between things and human beings in common/places.

Coloniality: A Condition to Be Used

As I already indicated, the materialism of Leung's writings can be seen as a kind of tactic within the overdetermined historical situation of Hong Kong, where people are not "free" to "choose" their political system. For those who expect heroic proclamations of anticolonialism, it would be disconcerting to hear a poet from a colony describing his work primarily in terms of the pleasure of consumption: "I am more removed from poets who meditated on immortality, or those who believed their works were timeless artifacts. I would feel more comfortable with poets who wrote after dinner to tell their friends how tasty the yellow fish was."[31] What Leung's poetry makes us realize is the untenability of heroic narratives, especially as the latter continue to be mobilized with expedience by those who are in power, in the well-seasoned manner of refurnishing a home with grand old furniture—even in the aftermath of a major catastrophe. Such heroic narratives are dismantled in the ironic poem "Refurnishing," which is one of a series of poems Leung wrote after the Tiananmen Massacre of 1989. Irony here is the effect, once again, of the abundance of things:

Well, they returned with their grand old tables and chairs
the solid stuff, the elegant, classy stuff that has
symmetry, unmistakable aesthetic appeal. Nothing better.
They cleaned the floors till they shone like trackless water;
they soaped away the smells of blood and foulness, until
nothing had happened; the last heavy smoke went up the ventilators.
They hung their paintings and calligraphy where you couldn't not
  see,
honoring the good old snows, with the flowers and birds smiling
  again,
and the corner of a crimson beak changing shape with the artist's
  hand.
The master will grind ink for new poems. A circle of cultured men
will answer poem for poem sonorously in praise of their host.
He'll strut and compose, a new piece on last night's storm,
a high-sounding piece of history, fit to be framed for posterity.
It could not have been a better year, really,
what with seasonable vegetables in the markets, clear concrete
  images—
of nubby cucumbers and fresh tender green beans—that won't
  allow
indeterminate interpretations. The shortage of food is relieved.
Postmen are on their rounds and masons are mending walls.
People are going about storing up provisions
and settling accounts, to prepare for the new year.
Are the shadows of the old year still wandering in the streets?
When the cold wind blows, close the windows.
Never mind the stealthy shadows around the eaves,
or the will-o'-the-wisps in the corners;
stick up door-gods to combat all these strange sights.
There is still the great old furniture of history that we can haul

> into the parlor, so as to guard the present day,
> and unify all the words on the couplets.
> Lock the door, for a secure peace and quiet.[32]

Once heroic narratives are dismantled, how do we deal with coloniality?

The founding of Hong Kong as a city converges with an epochal change in the world's value system—from the stability of landed culture to the speeds and currencies of trade. And yet, in the evaluation of culture, we seem to remain as fixated on stability as we are on the center. Leung's writings alert us to the necessity of reversing the conventional narrative of colonialism by defixating on such stability. The relation between Hong Kong and the "landed" world is not unlike that between ripples and lotus in the poem "Ripples/Leaves." The lotus speaks:

> In the past we always praised stable things.
> Yet you appear in the pond, and keep making ripples, which
> together with the lights of dawn and shades of dusk
> transform into new image after new image.
> A series of crystalline lights appear at the margins, changing
> the glittering organization in the pond, breaking it up, then making
> a new kind of order. My roots and leaves feel being circled around—
> I seem to feel fishes kissing all over my body,
> then flowing away, in small detailed patterns.
> Amid these movements I want to hold on—yet cannot
> grab any stable center I can use for a pause.
> I cannot but let go of the safety of the soil,
> turn over the silt sediments inside me, and feel the waves
> brought by the light breeze.[33]

The implications of this defixation on stable culture are vast. Chief of all, they necessitate a rigorous revaluation of the marginal. Rather than beginning with Europe as the origin, an origin that goes out to conquer and "civilize" other lands, we might say that it is "primitive" outposts like Hong Kong and Macau, which are far away from the "motherlands" of Britain and Portugal, that provide, through their economic, materialistic, and transitory status, the "stability" of the notions of nation, people, land, and tradition that are such a crucial part of the discourse of empire-building. To use the language of territorial possession, it is the utter deprivation of land in the colony—because land has been turned into a commodity—that enables the grandiose patriotic rhetoric of "England, my England" that we find in the reflections of English national culture in modernity, as well as in the ponderous musings about the Great Wall, the Yellow River, the Central Plains, and so forth that are the symbols of Chinese national culture. To use the language of legal identity, it is the denial of secure protection to the colonized, who are reduced to "transients" and "migrants," that enables the pride and respectability of those who possess the right documents of permanent citizenship. (Most people in Hong Kong are denied an "authentic" British passport and the right of abode in Britain, and face the risk of having whatever foreign residency/citizenship they might have acquired delegitimated by the Chinese government once the latter resumes sovereignty over the colony.) Finally, to use the language of sexual crime and discipline, it is the "rape" or "violation" of Hong Kong that makes possible the pious equation, in masculinist nationalistic discourse, between sexual chastity and national integrity, between virginity and cultural purity.

In terms of the formation of modern city culture, the violence of the trading port is thus originary rather than derivative in significance. But precisely because of this, port cities such as Hong Kong often become associated with that which is of lesser and less authentic value. In their vulgar, consumerist, debased form, such port cities stand, ultimately, as the "thing" that gives colonialist imperialism its consistency: colonialist imperialism cannot thrive except with the functioning of places like Hong Kong, and yet this "thing" that gives life to the system, that makes colonialist imperialism colonialist imperialism, is at the same time what is continually treated with contempt, as feminine disease, as native degeneracy—as what is "outside" the rooted civilizations of London, Paris, Beijing.

In Leung's writings, not only are the thing qualities and associations of Hong Kong given their due place, but coloniality itself is rethought as well. Coloniality is not only the historical violence committed by the powerful of the world against the powerless; it is also a basic economic condition—for many the only condition of value—in which to live, think, and make changes. When asked what Hong Kong's colonial past means to him, Leung answers:

> I think of it in relation to the inability to tell one's past, to express one's confusion about identity, and to articulate one's feeling about this place. I think of it in relation to the education, the imbalanced cultural policies, the silence and suppression, and the actual ignorance about one's own context. *But it is not just that;* it is also very much in the background of everything we do. Ironically, Hong Kong as a colony provides an alternative space for Chinese people and culture to exist, a hybrid for one to reflect upon the problems of a "pure" and "original" state. It is very much part of my background, it is there, hindering me as well as consoling me, making me uneasy, alerting me to my lack, urging me at an early age to doubt what could be easily taken for granted.[34]

Once again a certain conventional narrative of colonialism has to be reversed. Rather than beginning with Europe, whose colonizing acts leave the colonized in a pathetic state of deprivation and make the freedom from coloniality the ultimate telos, we might say that the condition of coloniality is also the means with which the colonized must fight the violence of colonialism. In other words, coloniality, a transindividual condition of history that carries with it all the tragedies of marginalization, can nonetheless become a form of opportunity, in which the daily experience of oppression is synchronized with a self-conscious search for freedom in alternative forms.

At this point, it would be relevant to return to one of the interesting facts of Hong Kong as a colony. Hong Kong's population is made up largely of immigrants. Unlike the classic colonial situation in which European powers forced their way into lands that were already populated with indigenous peoples, most of the people who live in Hong Kong came voluntarily (many by risking their lives) in order to escape the harsher conditions in China. (The more appropriate comparisons here would be with Hispanic immigrants from Latin America in the United States, or with refugees from Eastern Europe and the former Soviet Union in Western Europe.) As Kwai-cheung Lo writes:

> The Chinese who came to Hong Kong after the colony was set up primarily aimed at gaining economic improvement or seeking refuge from political turmoil and persecution. They did not come to wage a nationalistic battle against the colonial rule, especially when the only alternative to colonial rule was the domination of the authoritarian Communist regime. Thus the "China factor" ironically buttresses colonial rule by making it invulnerable to being toppled by the colonized. . . . It renders the colonial institution more benign and attractive to immigrants. It could be said that the colonial subjects are a self-select group who voluntarily subscribe to the colonial rule.[35]

By the mid-twentieth century, not only Chinese, but a host of other peoples, from India, Pakistan, Southeast Asia, as well as England, had also established permanent residency in Hong Kong in order to have—scandalous though it may sound—a better life under colonial rule than at home. Coloniality in Hong Kong is therefore not simply the condition of deprived enlightenment that critics of colonialism usually make it; rather it is something that the colonized actively use as a way of life—it is a form of violence, yes, but a form of violence that is lived as an alternative to greater violence elsewhere. In Hong Kong, the violence of coloniality is, we might say, a practicable way of escaping the violence that comes with living as "nationals" and "citizens" of independent countries.

This is why, much as Hong Kong culture is a marginalized culture,

Leung's loyalty to the city is not an attempt to idealize the position of the marginal. ("I don't want to romanticize the marginal position."[36]) Rather, marginality is as much a personal discipline and a form of social instruction as it is the reality of living in Hong Kong. It is not marginalization alone, but the conscious effort to reflect on one's own culture by means of others, an effort which perhaps comes more "easily" with marginalization, that makes one develop a bi- or multicultural consciousness:

> I don't think the special situation of Hong Kong makes its artists automatically bi-cultural or poly-cultural. . . . It is when one reflects upon one's culture *by means of another* that one eventually develops "bi-cultural" awareness.[37]

And, precisely because marginalization alone does not necessarily prevent one from chauvinism or violence, one needs to be very careful when approaching questions of coloniality and postcoloniality:

> We should not look upon ourselves as victims, in self-pity, but should be conscious of victims turned tyrants, as in the way some Hong Kong people treat the Vietnamese boat people, Filipino maids, or new Mainland immigrants. But of course I am also skeptical towards people who shift the attention by pointing out these latter examples so as to level out all issues, to universalize colonialism and in the end successfully avoid the issue of British colonialism.[38]

Leung's work can be summarized by a line from his poem "Images of Hong Kong": "Always at the edge of things and between places."[39] In this line we find a special kind of agency, which is not that of a call for the end of coloniality, but the insistence on an openness, an insistence that comes paradoxically with the much more difficult task of *living as the continually colonized*. Leung warns that coloniality will always live in us if we are not careful:

> [O]ne has to be conscious of not just the marker on the outside, the year 1997, for example, but rather the ways people think and reflect upon themselves; otherwise one would carry the colonial mentality into another phase of colonialism.[40]

I would like to conclude with stanzas from one of Leung's poems, "An Old Colonial Building." This title refers to the Main Building of the University of Hong Kong, where Leung currently teaches. It is here, in his professional environment, that he experiences firsthand the tensions and conflicts of coloniality as it impinges upon the practices of education. In spite of the frustrations he encounters daily, Leung persists in his work, refusing to give in to the powers that be:

ETHICS AFTER IDEALISM

So much dust swirls through sunlight and shadow,
through the scaffolding and the wooden planks raised up around
the colonial edifice, as if
to dismantle it brick by brick. Perhaps
its basic shape will remain, perhaps
the bitterness deep in the soil will emerge.
The noble rotunda and the wide hollow corridors
are still facing a blocked wall. Perhaps when it's all knocked open,
there will be stairs leading to more ordinary places.

* * *

Might the pieces of ruins put together compose
a new architecture? Ridiculous are the portraits of leaders,
laughable those with power. We meet in the corridor.
Looking by chance: the surface of the lotus pond is changing.
Thinking does not evade ripples, and does not bend with the wind.
I know that you don't believe in flags or fireworks.
I will give you fragmented words rather than "realistic" portrayals,
(showing that you are) not a center surrounded by magnificent
    buildings,
but simply a (circular) pond
of ripples, where moving signs come and go.[41]

NOTES

Introduction

1. See Paul de Man, *The Resistance to Theory*, foreword by Wlad Godzich (Minneapolis: U of Minnesota P, 1986), pp. 3–20.

2. This distinction is a well-known one. See for instance the discussions in Raymond Williams, *The Sociology of Culture* (1981), with a new foreword by Bruce Robbins (Chicago: U of Chicago P, 1995). For a detailed discussion of the historical changes involved in the use of the word "culture," see Robert J. C. Young, *Colonial Desire: Hybridity in Theory, Culture and Race* (New York: Routledge, 1995), in particular chapters 2 and 3.

3. Even though, as an academic discipline, anthropology has since its inception been inscribed in problems of racism. Since I have discussed this at length elsewhere, I shall simply refer the reader to the following: the chapter "Where Have All the Natives Gone?" *Writing Diaspora: Tactics of Intervention in Contemporary Cultural Studies* (Bloomington: Indiana UP, 1993); Parts One and Three, *Primitive Passions: Visuality, Sexuality, Ethnography, and Contemporary Chinese Cinema* (New York: Columbia UP, 1995).

4. For a set of discussions on this topic, see *Culture/Contexture: Explorations in Anthropology and Literary Studies*, ed. E. Valentine Daniel and Jeffrey M. Peck (Berkeley: U of California P, 1996), in particular the editors' introduction, pp. 1–33.

5. I borrow this phrase from John Frow, *Cultural Studies and Cultural Value* (Oxford: Oxford UP, 1995).

6. For a comparable situation, see Sneja Gunew's discussion of the hierarchical difference between what is considered "poetry" and what is considered "sociology" in the multicultural politics of Australia. Gunew, "Denaturalizing Cultural Nationalisms: Multicultural Readings of 'Australia,'" in *Nation and Narration*, ed. Homi K. Bhabha (London: Routledge, 1990), pp. 99–120.

7. See Frow, *Cultural Studies and Cultural Value*, in particular chapter 3. Frow acknowledges his indebtedness, among others, to the work of Pierre Bourdieu.

8. For related interest, see Ketu H. Katrak's discussion of postcolonial studies in her essay "Decolonizing Culture: Toward a Theory for Post-colonial Women's Texts," *Modern Fiction Studies* 35 (1), 1989: 157–79. Katrak writes that "a new hegemony is being established in contemporary theory that can with

impunity ignore or exclude postcolonial writers' essays, interviews, and other cultural productions while endlessly discussing concepts of the 'Other,' of 'difference,' and so on." This quotation is taken from the excerpt of the essay in *The Post-colonial Studies Reader,* ed. Bill Ashcroft et al. (New York: Routledge, 1995), p. 256.

9. An exemplary text which theorizes otherness in this manner is Emmanuel Levinas's *Totality and Infinity: An Essay on Exteriority* (1961), trans. Alphonso Lingis (Pittsburgh: Duquesne UP, 1969).

10. This phrase is from Gayatri Chakravorty Spivak, "Can the Subaltern Speak?" originally published in *Marxism and the Interpretation of Culture,* edited and with an introduction by Cary Nelson and Lawrence Grossberg (Urbana: U of Illinois P, 1988), pp. 271–313. My quotation is taken from the excerpt of the essay in *Colonial Discourse, Postcolonial Theory: A Reader,* ed. Laura Chrisman and Patrick Williams (New York: Columbia UP, 1994), p. 72. Spivak's aim is in part to explain the importance of the negative work of thinkers such as Nietzsche and Derrida.

11. See Jacques Derrida, *Spurs: Nietzsche's Styles,* trans. Barbara Harlow (Chicago: U of Chicago P, 1979). For a recent evaluation of Derrida and Western feminism, see Jane Gallop, "'Women' in Spurs and Nineties Feminism," *diacritics,* 25.2 (Summer 1995), pp. 126–34.

12. See Gallop's essay, which dates Derrida's reading of Nietzsche's writings on women as a kind of reading from which deconstruction and feminism of the 1970s and 1980s derived their antiessentialist politics. By the 1990s, however, things have become very different. Gallop writes astutely: "In our US context, feminists have learned not only that race was intrinsic to the definition of a 'lady' in the nineteenth century but, perhaps more painfully, that it functioned likewise to define the 'woman' who was liberating herself in the 1970s. The latter is part of the recognition that seventies feminism was functioning in history, that we not only envisioned a future but also spoke in archaicisms. The critique of our 'essentializing fetishes' has led us to historicize but has not made us less anxious about our own inevitable embedding in history. *Not only is 'woman' not a timeless universal, but neither are feminists:* we cannot be endlessly up-to-date" (pp. 133–34; my emphasis). For an excellent critique of how Western feminism has tended, *methodologically,* to perpetuate the universalism and privilege that are inherent to the patriarchal thinking it wants to overcome, see Elizabeth V. Spelman, *Inessential Woman: Problems of Exclusion in Feminist Thought* (Boston: Beacon, 1988). Spelman argues that such universalism and privilege are typically the results of an exclusive, solipsistic focus on white middle-class women as the norm and of a peripheralizing of issues of racism and classism even as such issues bear inextricable relations with sexism. Playing on Nietzsche and on the logic of *Animal Farm,* she sums up the methodological inequity of prevalent feminist theories in this manner: "Just as some humans are more human than others (which Plato and Aristotle held), so . . . some women are more 'woman' than others" (p. 175).

13. A work such as Stefan Tanaka's *Japan's Orient: Rendering Pasts into History* (Berkeley: U of California P, 1993) is enormously instructive here in that it provides an informative account of how a non-Western culture, Japan, also produces its own "orient"—*tōyō*—in the discursive processes of constructing

its modern national identity. Tanaka's book not only moves beyond the East-West dichotomy of Edward Said's *Orientalism* by showing Orientalism to be an "Eastern" as well as "Western" historical phenomenon; in its careful delineation of the contradictions inherent in modern Japanese historians' attempts to create a culturally exceptionalist Japan, it also serves, methodologically, as an example of a kind of scholarship that is not culturally exceptionalist.

14. Williams, *The Sociology of Culture*, pp. 181–82; my emphasis.

15. According to Etienne Balibar, such a theoretical stance is actually racist. In his chapter "Is There a 'Neo-Racism'?" Balibar argues that what he calls a new racism is based not on biological but on cultural differentiations. This new racism takes as its starting point that "races do not constitute isolable biological units and that in reality there are no 'human races.'" However, while it abandons biological or genetic nationalism, it turns "culture" into a nature and makes it "function as a way of locking individuals and groups a priori into a genealogy, into a determination that is immutable and intangible in origin." See Balibar and Immanuel Wallerstein, *Race, Nation, Class: Ambiguous Identities*, translation of Balibar by Chris Turner (New York: Verso, 1991), pp. 21–22. Similarly, writing in critique of the habits of cultural essentialism in Japanology, Marilyn Ivy argues succinctly: "Although an initial insistence on clearly delineated cultural otherness can constitute the first step in the recognition of historical domination and Orientalism, it can hardly stand as the *final* step in a truly critical anthropology (or history, or literary analysis) . . . what are imagined as the specificities of Japan or Japanese culture can never be unilaterally deployed as unexamined critical tools to undo presumed western hegemonies." *Discourses of the Vanishing: Modernity, Phantasm, Japan* (Chicago: U of Chicago P, 1995), p. 8; emphasis in the original.

16. In her interesting study *George Sand and Idealism* (New York: Columbia UP, 1993), Naomi Schor has criticized the academic tendency to equate idealism with German idealist philosophy. See her informed and informative discussions of the term on pages 10–20 and throughout.

17. For a critique of the tendency on the part of major Western thinkers to assume achievement of idealized alterity without praxis, see Franco Rella, *The Myth of the Other: Lacan, Foucault, Deleuze, Bataille*, trans. Nelson Moe (Washington, D.C.: Maisonneuve, 1994).

18. It is also one that I have elaborated at length elsewhere. See, for instance, the preface to *Woman and Chinese Modernity: The Politics of Reading between West and East* (Minneapolis: U of Minnesota P, 1991), pp. xi–xvii.

19. In this light, see, for instance, Rella's discussion of Michel Foucault in *The Myth of the Other*, pp. 57–78. Rella criticizes Foucault's interpretation of Pierre Riviere as being complicit with the medico-legal apparatus in silencing Riviere as an absolute "other": "To repudiate translatability as the resolution of contradictions and plurality does not have to mean setting up in opposition to the languages of power the other silence of the subject that is dominated by that power. It means rather making these languages clash with one another, so that, having broken the stone of the loquacious truth of the dominant apparatus, we do not find ourselves once again before the stone of the silent truth of that which is thought and spoken *otherwise*" (*The Myth of the Other*, pp. 66–67; emphasis in the original). To the extent that I consider idealism as the central

problem of rather than a solution to identity politics, I am very skeptical about Schor's suggestion that "rethinking idealism is a way of reclaiming its utopian dimension, the ability of an ideal to empower and to mobilize the disenfranchised" (*George Sand and Idealism*, p. 14).

20. Many critics have discussed ethics and morality explicitly in relation to the question of otherness. For instance, for Emmanuel Levinas, ethics suggests the encounter with the other that lets the other remain in its otherness, an encounter which coincides thus with infinity; see, for instance, *Totality and Infinity* and *Ethics and Infinity: Conversations with Philippe Nemo*, trans. Richard A. Cohen [Pittsburgh: Duquesne UP, 1985]). For Gayatri Spivak, ethics is the experience of the impossible, of love; see her discussion in the translator's preface to *Imaginary Maps: Three Stories by Mahasweta Devi*, translated and introduced by Gayatri Chakravorty Spivak (London: Routledge, 1995), pp. xxiii–xxix. See also my discussion of Spivak's work in chapter 3. Iain Chambers connects ethics specifically to the intellectually migrant modes of discourses of cultural studies. See chapter 7 ("The Wound and the Shadow") of *Migrancy, Culture, Identity* (London: Routledge, 1994), in particular: "So cultural studies, as a conjunctural metaphor for critical encounters, can only imply a travelling voice, a disseminating criticism. As a migrant intellectual disposition, it acquires shape and pertinence in the crossings, intersections and interlacing of the lives, situations, histories, in which it dwells and becomes. Such thought and practice are neither free-floating nor timeless, but come together in that Benjaminian instance in which past and present are fused in the constellation of the now (*Jetzt*). Its language does not emerge from a single site or perspective. Its voice is therefore not merely critical; it is ultimately ethical. Comprehended in this mode, 'cultural studies' is not simply a radical additive to be stirred into the different mixes of historiography, sociology, film studies or literary criticism. It is suspended between these realms. It shadows them, questioning the nature and pertinence of their languages—existing, if you like, as a wound in the body of knowledge, exposed to the infections of the world" (p. 123). Chambers also distinguishes between morality and ethics in the following terms: morality is "the name of the law . . . , in which we are positioned and apparently held in custody," whereas ethics is "the language of becoming, in which we become responsible for what sustains our being" (p. 130).

1. Theory, Area Studies, Cultural Studies

1. This chapter continues the discussions I have given in several other chapters and essays about multiculturalism and cultural studies. Instead of repeating my own arguments, I will simply refer the reader to these other pieces at the appropriate moments.

2. Quoted in Ken Shulman, "Bloom and Doom" (an interview with Harold Bloom), *Newsweek*, October 10, 1994, p. 75.

3. This is a point made by Gabriele Schwab in her presentation in the forum "Why 'Comparative Literature'?" at the University of California, Irvine, April 1994. For those who are less familiar with the controversies of "theory" in the United States, the term has been used generally to refer to the debates about

language, signification, and discourse in literary and humanistic studies that began in the 1960s with the introduction of French poststructuralist thinkers such as Jacques Derrida, Jacques Lacan, Roland Barthes, and Michel Foucault into the English-speaking world. Over the decades, even though those who attack "theory" invariably speak from specific theoretical positions—in other words, even though there are no positions, not even anti-theory ones, that are not implicitly theoretical—the term "theory" continues to be used more or less exclusively to refer to poststructuralist theory and deconstruction.

4. See for instance the introductions in *Cultural Studies,* edited and with an introduction by Lawrence Grossberg, Cary Nelson, Paula Treichler, with Linda Baughman and assistance from John Macgregor Wise (New York: Routledge, 1992), and *The Cultural Studies Reader,* edited by Simon During (New York: Routledge, 1993). See also the historical and critical accounts in Fred Inglis, *Cultural Studies* (Oxford: Blackwell, 1993), which discusses, in addition to the British background, the significance of certain continental European thinkers for the conception of cultural studies.

5. Gayatri Chakravorty Spivak, "Can the Subaltern Speak?" in *Marxism and the Interpretations of Culture,* edited and with an introduction by Cary Nelson and Lawrence Grossberg (Urbana: U of Illinois P, 1988), pp. 271–313. See my discussion of Spivak's essay in the chapter "Where Have All the Natives Gone?" in *Writing Diaspora: Tactics of Intervention in Contemporary Cultural Studies* (Bloomington: Indiana UP, 1993), pp. 27–54.

6. Spivak, *The Post-Colonial Critic: Interviews, Strategies, Dialogues,* ed. Sarah Harasym (New York: Routledge, 1990), p. 158. See my related discussions of the problem of *naming* (the subaltern) in postcolonial cultural politics in the chapter "Against the Lures of Diaspora," in *Writing Diaspora,* pp. 99–119 and in chapter 3 ("Ethics after Idealism") of this book.

7. See Gilles Deleuze and Félix Guattari, *Kafka: Toward a Minor Literature,* translation by Dana Polan, foreword by Réda Bensmaïa (Minneapolis: U of Minnesota P, 1986); *The Nature and Context of Minority Discourse,* edited and with an introduction by David Lloyd and Abdul JanMohamed (New York: Oxford UP, 1990). The latter was originally published as *Cultural Critique* 7 and 8 (1987–88).

8. For Bhabha's most influential essays, see those collected in *The Location of Culture* (New York: Routledge, 1993). I am, as I have indicated elsewhere, skeptical of the larger implications of Bhabha's formulations of hybridity; see my discussion in "Where Have All the Natives Gone?"

9. Jacques Derrida, "Structure, Sign, and Play in the Discourse of the Human Sciences," in *The Structuralist Controversy: The Languages of Criticism and the Sciences of Man,* ed. Richard Macksey and Eugenio Donato (Baltimore: Johns Hopkins UP, 1970), pp. 247–72.

10. During, introduction to *The Cultural Studies Reader,* p. 16. Similarly, Grossberg, Nelson, and Treichler write that "cultural studies offers a bridge between theory and material culture" (introduction to *Cultural Studies,* p. 6).

11. See the essays in *The Structuralist Controversy.*

12. I should emphasize here that my argument *for* the theoretical significance of cultural studies is made from the perspective of those working in the United States. Ironically, to those who work outside the United States, American

cultural studies can appear to be—contrary to the charge that it is too empirical—already too theoretical. Stuart Hall, for instance, attributes to American cultural studies what he calls "theoretical fluency," by which he means that cultural studies tends to be so institutionalized in the United States that it runs the risk of constituting power and politics as exclusively textual and discursive matters. See Hall, "Cultural Studies and Its Theoretical Legacies," in *Cultural Studies*, ed. Grossberg et al., p. 286.

13. See Cornel West, "The New Cultural Politics of Difference," in *The Cultural Studies Reader*, pp. 203–17. This is a version of an essay that appears in *Out There: Marginalization and Contemporary Cultures*, ed. Russel Ferguson et al. (New York: New Museum of Contemporary Art; Cambridge, Massachusetts: MIT P, 1990).

14. I will cite here merely a handful of the many important works that have been done to delineate the workings of this violence: Peter Hulme, *Colonial Encounters: Europe and the Native Caribbean 1492–1797* (London: Routledge, 1986); Roberto Fernandez Retamar, *Caliban and Other Essays*, translated by Edward Baker, foreword by Fredric Jameson (Minneapolis: U of Minnesota P, 1989); Gauri Viswanathan, *Masks of Conquest: Literary Study and British Rule in India* (New York: Columbia UP, 1989); Sara Suleri, *The Rhetoric of English India* (Chicago: U of Chicago P, 1992); Mary Louise Pratt, *Imperial Eyes: Travel Writing and Transculturation* (New York: Routledge, 1992); Jenny Sharpe, *Allegories of Empire: The Figure of Woman in the Colonial Text* (Minneapolis: U of Minnesota P, 1993).

15. For a related discussion, see the chapter "The Politics and Pedagogy of Asian Literatures in American Universities," in *Writing Diaspora*.

16. See also my essay "In the Name of Comparative Literature," in *Comparative Literature in the Age of Multiculturalism*, ed. Charles Bernheimer (Baltimore: Johns Hopkins UP, 1994), pp. 107–16.

17. David Gates, "It's Naughty! Haughty! It's Anti-Multi-Culti!" *Newsweek*, October 10, 1994, p. 73.

18. For a detailed argument about the Eurocentrism of comparative literature, see, for instance, Edward W. Said's discussion of the modern novel in *Culture and Imperialism* (New York: Vintage, 1994).

19. For a set of responses from comparative literature teachers to the challenge posed by cultural studies, see the essays in *Comparative Literature in the Age of Multiculturalism*.

20. See my discussion in "In the Name of Comparative Literature."

21. This is what Charles Bernheimer means when he writes: "On the face of things, it would appear that multiculturalism, inherently pluralistic, would have a natural propensity toward comparison. But this propensity has been checked by the mimetic imperatives of an essentialist politics" ("Introduction: The Anxieties of Comparison," *Comparative Literature in the Age of Multiculturalism*, p. 9). Bernheimer's word "comparison" could easily be substituted with the word "theory."

22. Spivak, *The Post-Colonial Critic*, p. 69.

23. Fazal Rizvi, "The Arts, Education and the Politics of Multiculturalism," in *Culture, Difference and the Arts*, ed. Sneja Gunew and Fazal Rizvi (St. Leonards:

Allen and Unwin, 1994), p. 60. This essay offers a succinct argument about the contradictions inherent in multiculturalism.

24. Spivak, *Outside in the Teaching Machine* (New York: Routledge, 1993), p. 279.

25. Spivak, *Outside in the Teaching Machine*, p. 56.

26. See for instance the discussion of this point in Tony Bennett, "Putting Policy into Cultural Studies," *Cultural Studies*, ed. Grossberg et al., pp. 23–37.

27. Jean-François Lyotard, *The Postmodern Condition: A Report on Knowledge*, trans. Geoff Bennington and Brian Massumi, foreword by Fredric Jameson (Minneapolis: U of Minnesota P, 1984).

28. This is a point made by Fazal Rizvi in his presentation, "Trajectories of Racism and Australian Multiculturalism," at the conference on Multicultural Critical Theory: Between Race and Ethnicity, University of Victoria, Canada, January 1995.

29. I am indebted to Judith Butler for my formulation of the problem here. For a related discussion, see Cornel West, "The New Cultural Politics of Difference," in particular the section "The Existential Challenge" (pp. 214–16), in which he describes the options available to people of color who are interested in representation.

30. Rizvi, "The Arts, Education and the Politics of Multiculturalism," p. 63.

31. Spivak, *Outside the Teaching Machine*, p. 284. She is referring specifically to certain practices of "transnational feminism."

2. The Fascist Longings in Our Midst

1. Blaise Pascal, *Thoughts of Blaise Pascal* (London: Kegan Paul, 1888), p. 279.

2. Roland Barthes, *Leçon* (Paris: Seuil, 1977), p. 14; quoted in Jean Baudrillard, *For a Critique of the Political Economy of the Sign,* trans. Charles Levin (St. Louis: Telos, 1981), p. 26; emphasis in the original.

3. For an informative analysis of some of the well-known and/or widely adopted interpretations of fascism in Germany, see Linda Schulte-Sasse, "National Socialism in Theory and Fiction: A Sampling of German Perspectives, 1923–1980," in *Fascismo y Experiencia Literaria: Reflexiones para una Recanonización,* ed. Hernan Vidal (Edina: Society for the Study of Contemporary Hispanic and Lusophone Revolutionary Literatures, 1985), pp. 64–91. For some of the more recent discussions of fascism in Europe and European writers, see the essays in *Fascism, Aesthetics, and Culture,* ed. Richard J. Golsan (Hanover: UP of New England, 1992). This volume contains a useful "Selective Bibliography" of recent works in English on fascism.

4. Michel Foucault, "Power and Strategies," *Power/Knowledge: Selected Interviews and Other Writings 1972–1977,* ed. Colin Gordon, trans. Colin Gordon, Leo Marshall, John Mepham, Kate Soper (New York: Pantheon, 1980), p. 139.

5. For Althusser's and Barthes's versions of ideology, see "Ideology and Ideological State Apparatuses (Notes towards an Investigation)," *Lenin and Philosophy and Other Essays,* trans. Ben Brewster (New York: Monthly Review, 1971), pp. 127–86; *Mythologies,* selected and translated by Annette Lavers (Pala-

din, 1973). The argument that ideology is the history that has been "natural-ized" or "disguised" is a predominant way of understanding fascism; accord-ingly, fascism is construed as a matter of *lies*. As it will become clear in the course of this chapter, my argument differs from this major view of ideology in that I do not see fascism simply as lying.

6. It is well known that even today members of the Japanese Parliament attempt to deny their country's war atrocities. "Magee's Testament" shows one such MP, Shintaro Ishihara, declaring in an interview with *Playboy* that the atrocities did not happen and then changing his mind in a subsequent inter-view with *Time*. In the second interview, Ishihara proclaimed that merely 20,000, rather than 300,000, Chinese were killed in the Nanjing Massacre—as if a smaller number would make the massacre of less concern. This denial is so determined that the Japanese government ensured that Emperor Akihito's visit to China in 1992 would not be used as the occasion for an apology. "There was an unfortunate period in which my country inflicted great sufferings on the people of China," Akihito said, speaking in Japanese. "I feel deep sorrow about this." Meanwhile, the Japanese Education Ministry exercised its constitutional right to dictate the contents of schoolbooks by censoring descriptions of the Japanese army's germ warfare experiments on prisoners and of episodes such as the Rape of Nanjing. According to a Reuters report in March 1993, Japan's Supreme Court upheld this censorship and rejected the lawsuit by Saburo Ienaga, a retired history professor, who had waged a thirty-year battle against the whitewashing of wartime history ("Japanese Court OKs Censoring of Schoolbooks," *Los Angeles Times*, Wednesday, March 17, 1993, p. A7). Ienaga finally won his battle in May 1994 ("Scholar Wins Ruling on Nanjing Massa-cre," *New York Times*, May 13, 1994, p. A3). As Claude Lanzman writes in *Shoah: An Oral History of the Holocaust* (New York: Pantheon, 1985), for the invention of genocide no one wants "copyright." Lanzman is quoted by Michael Lestz in a review essay on holocaust literature, "Lishi de mingji" (The unforgettable memory of history), trans. Lin Zhiling and Xie Zhengguang, *Jiuzhou xuekan* (*Chinese Culture Quarterly*), vol. 1, no. 4 (Summer 1987), p. 100. For discussions of Japanese war atrocities in China published in Chinese, see for instance Xu Zhigeng, *Najing da tusha* (Hong Kong: Luzhou chuban gongsi; Beijing: Kunlun chubanshe, 1987); Gao Xingzu, *Rijun qin hua baoxing—Nanjing da tusha* (Shang-hai: Shanghai renmin chubanshe, 1985). For an account in English of the Nanjing Massacre, see the relevant pages in Ian Buruma, *The Wages of Guilt: Memories of War in Germany and Japan* (New York: Farrar Straus Giroux, 1994). Buruma compares "Hiroshima" and "Auschwitz," and indicts Japan for getting away with its war crimes without apologizing to the rest of Asia. For an overview of Sino-Japanese political and cultural relations since the Second World War, see Arif Dirlik, "'Past Experience, If Not Forgotten, Is a Guide to the Future'; or, What Is in a Text? The Politics of History in Chinese-Japanese Relations," *boundary 2*, vol. 18, no. 3 (Fall 1991), pp. 29–58. This essay was part of a special issue, "Japan in the World" (which became a book with a new introduction and additional articles, Duke UP, 1993), ed. Masao Miyoshi and H. D. Harootunian.

7. Lestz, "Lishi de mingji," p. 105.

8. Foucault, preface, in Gilles Deleuze and Félix Guattari, *Anti-Oedipus:*

Capitalism and Schizophrenia, trans. Robert Hurley, Mark Seem, and Helen R. Lane (Minneapolis: U of Minnesota P, 1983), p. xiii.

9. "The subject attributes tendencies, desires, etc., to others that he refuses to recognize in himself: the racist, for instance, projects his own faults and unacknowledged inclinations on to the group he reviles. This type of projection . . . seems to come closest to the Freudian sense of the term." J. Laplanche and J.-B. Pontalis, *The Language of Psychoanalysis,* trans. Donald Nicholson-Smith, with an introduction by Daniel Lagache (New York: Norton, 1973), p. 351. See also the entire entry under "Projection," pp. 349–56.

10. For instance, in an interesting essay on the 1932 Exhibition of the Fascist Revolution in Rome, Jeffrey T. Schnapp describes "the structural undergirding of fascist ideology" as a "taut but hollow frame over which a canvas must be stretched in order for the illusion of fullness to spring forth." Fascism "required an aesthetic *overproduction*—a surfeit of fascist signs, images, slogans, books, and buildings—to compensate for, fill in, and cover up its forever unstable ideological core." See Schnapp, "Epic Demonstrations: Fascist Modernity and the 1932 Exhibition of the Fascist Revolution," in *Fascism, Aesthetics, and Culture,* p. 3; emphasis in the original. As I go on to argue in this chapter, the twin components of lack and compensation are crucial to Freud's concept of projection.

11. Albert Memmi associates fascism with colonialism: "every colonial nation carries the seeds of fascist temptation in its bosom. . . . What is fascism, if not a regime of oppression for the benefit of a few? . . . colonialism is one variety of fascism." See Memmi, *The Colonizer and the Colonized,* expanded edition, introduction by Jean Paul Sartre, afterword by Susan Gilson Miller, translated by Howard Greenfeld (Boston: Beacon, 1991), p. 62. Wilhelm Reich associates fascism with authoritarianism and mysticism. Ernesto Laclau analyzes fascism as a kind of populism or failed socialism. Alice Yaeger Kaplan studies fascism from the point of view of the banal and the everyday. See Reich, *The Mass Psychology of Fascism,* trans. Vincent R. Carfagno (New York: Farrar, Straus & Giroux, 1970); Laclau, *Politics and Ideology in Marxist Theory: Capitalism—Fascism—Populism* (London: New Left, 1977), pp. 81–142; Kaplan, *Reproductions of Banality: Fascism, Literature, and French Intellectual Life,* foreword by Russell Berman (Minneapolis: U of Minnesota P, 1986).

12. José Ortega y Gasset, "Sobre el Fascismo," 1927, *Obras Completas,* vol. 11, Madrid, 1954; quoted in Laclau, *Politics and Ideology in Marxist Theory,* pp. 81–82.

13. See Reich, *The Mass Psychology of Fascism,* pp. 37–40.

14. Quoting from Nietzsche's *On the Genealogy of Morals,* Deleuze and Guattari write: "In the latency system of terror, what is no longer active, en-acted, or reacted to, 'this *instinct for freedom* forcibly made latent . . . pushed back and repressed, incarcerated within and finally able to discharge and vent itself only on itself,'—that very thing is now *ressenti.* . . ." *Anti-Oedipus,* p. 214; emphases in the original.

15. Laclau, *Politics and Ideology in Marxist Theory,* pp. 84–86.

16. Nicos Poulantzas, *Fascism and Dictatorship: The Third International and the Problem of Fascism* (London: New Left, 1974).

17. Hermann Rauschning, *Gespräche mit Hitler* (Zurich, 1940), p. 77; quoted in

Alexander Mitscherlich, *Society without the Father: A Contribution to Social Psychology (Auf dem Weg zur Vaterlosen Gesellschaft,* 1963), trans. Eric Mosbacher (New York: Harcourt, Brace & World, 1969), p. 288.

18. "What interests me is French fascist aesthetics at its most obvious and most banal. Because I am convinced that, like Poe's purloined letter, so visible it can't be found, the obvious is quite often the last place we look to study ideology." Kaplan, *Reproductions of Banality,* p. 46.

19. Kaplan, *Reproductions of Banality,* p. 6. By reading novels, autobiographies, and letters of the Freikorps officers, as well as illustrating his readings ironically with cartoons, posters, advertisements, and other graphic materials, Klaus Theweleit's work on fascism shares with Kaplan's a methodological focus on the obvious and everyday as the place to look for fascist aesthetics. See Theweleit, *Male Fantasies,* vols. 1 (*Women, Floods, Bodies, History*) and 2 (*Male Bodies: Psychoanalyzing the White Terror*), trans. Stephen Conway in collaboration with Erica Carter and Chris Turner, foreword by Barbara Ehrenreich (in vol. 1) (Minneapolis: U of Minnesota P, 1987, 1989).

20. Kaplan, *Reproductions of Banality,* p. 5.

21. Ibid., p. 155.

22. Thomas Elsaesser, "Primary Identification and the Historical Subject: Fassbinder and Germany," in *Narrative, Apparatus, Ideology: A Film Theory Reader,* ed. Philip Rosen (New York: Columbia UP, 1986), p. 545. Elsaesser emphasizes throughout his essay the historicity of fascism and the historicity of film theory's privileged ability to explain processes of specularization.

23. Having said this, I should add, however, that the imagistic or projectional implications of fascism go well beyond the medium of film itself.

24. Susan Sontag, "Fascinating Fascism," in *Movies and Methods,* vol. 1, ed. Bill Nichols (Berkeley: U of California P, 1976), pp. 31–43. The essay was first published in *The New York Review of Books,* vol. 22, no. 1 (February 6, 1975). The passage from which the title of the present chapter is taken is on p. 43, as follows: "Riefenstahl's current de-Nazification and vindication as indomitable priestess of the beautiful—as a film maker and now, as a photographer—do not augur well for the keenness of current abilities to detect the fascist longings in our midst. The force of her work is precisely in the continuity of its political and aesthetic ideas. What is interesting is that this was once seen so much more clearly than it seems to be now."

25. Sontag, "Fascinating Fascism," p. 43.

26. Sontag's argument here is comparable to that of George Bataille, who describes fascist authority in terms of a "double character" in which "cruel tendencies" coexist with "the need, characteristic of all domination, to realize and idealize order." See Bataille, "The Psychological Structure of Fascism," in *Visions of Excess: Selected Writings 1927–1939,* edited and with an introduction by Allan Stoekl, trans. Allan Stoekl et al. (Minneapolis: U of Minnesota P, 1985), p. 146.

27. Sontag, "Fascinating Fascism," pp. 40–41.

28. Kaplan, *Reproductions of Banality,* p. 23.

29. Ibid., p. 34. Unlike orthodox Marxism, which reduces spiritual and artistic phenomena to economics, the fascism of the 1920s and 1930s had a great appeal to artists and intellectuals because it gave the potentially creative role of be-

liefs—of mythmaking—a central place in social life. This was especially so in the case of Italian fascism, which was, unlike German fascism, aesthetically compatible with the avant-garde tenets of modernism. For an informative argument, see Reed Way Dasenbrock, "Paul de Man: The Modernist as Fascist," in *Fascism, Aesthetics, and Culture,* pp. 229–41.

30. André Bazin, "The Stalin Myth in Soviet Cinema" (with an introduction by Dudley Andrew), trans. Georgia Gurrieri, in *Movies and Methods,* vol. 2, ed. Bill Nichols (Berkeley: U of California P, 1985), pp. 29–40. The essay was first published in *L'Esprit* (July-August 1950) and then in English in *Film Criticism,* vol. 3, no. 1 (Fall 1978).

31. Bazin, "The Stalin Myth in Soviet Cinema," p. 36.

32. See Bazin, "The Stalin Myth in Soviet Cinema," p. 40.

33. Ibid., p. 37.

34. See Kaplan's very interesting discussion of the "slogan text" in chapter 3 of her book. For Kaplan, the slogan is a form of encapsulation with the performative aura of the "self-evident," luminous, transparent speech act, which appeals through the clarity of refrain rather than through thought and discourse. Both visual and auditory in effect, slogans are brief strings of words that tell and make history at the same time, and "a kind of self-fulfilling prophecy" (*Reproductions of Banality,* p. 68).

35. Paul Virilio, *War and Cinema: The Logistics of Perception,* trans. Patrick Camiller (London: Verso, 1989).

36. Ibid., p. 71; emphases in the original.

37. Quoted in Virilio, *War and Cinema,* p. 53.

38. Ibid., p. 81.

39. Joan Scott, "The Evidence of Experience," *Critical Inquiry,* no. 17 (Summer 1991), pp. 773–97.

40. Scott, "The Evidence of Experience," p. 777. For a similar critique of the positivistic manner in which some non-white feminists turn to "lived experience" as "an alternative mode of radical subjectivity," see Sara Suleri, "Woman Skin Deep: Feminism and the Postcolonial Condition," *Critical Inquiry* 18 (Summer 1992), pp. 756–69.

41. Scott, "The Evidence of Experience," p. 775.

42. Ibid., p. 776.

43. The manner in which critical judgments are suspended in the luminosity of an idealized presence can also be read in the light of Freud's *Group Psychology and the Analysis of the Ego,* translated and edited by James Strachey (New York: Norton, 1959): O functions as the hypnotist, the cathected object, with whom the masses fall in love. See especially chapter 8, "Being in Love and Hypnosis."

44. This environment can in part be described in terms of what Paul A. Bové calls "the facile professionalization of the U.S. academy." See Bové, *In the Wake of Theory* (Hanover: Wesleyan UP/UP of New England, 1992), p. xv. However, the ramifications involved go far beyond the U.S. academy.

45. I want to emphasize once again that my point is not to defend Western imperialism or Eurocentrism per se, but rather to mobilize criticism of the trends of uninformed and unanalytical claims about "cultural pluralism" that are being made in the name of anti-imperialism and anti-Eurocentrism. By

implication, it is also to criticize those who are kind and lenient whenever it comes to dealing with non-Western scholars—those, in other words, who base their judgments on the sole basis of skin color.

46. The situation here is comparable, though not identical, to Slavoj Žižek's analysis of the popular support for Kurt Waldheim in the 1986 Austrian presidential campaign. The Austrian people, to put the matter in the form of a joke of the time, wanted to have "Waldheimer's Disease," the disease of not being able to remember that one has been a Nazi, but this is precisely what Waldheim's opponents missed. As Žižek writes: "Starting from the assumption that Waldheim was attracting voters because of his great-statesman image, leftists put the emphasis of their campaign on proving to the public that not only is Waldheim a man with a dubious past (probably involved in war crimes) but also a man who is not prepared to confront his past, a man who evades crucial questions concerning it—in short, a man whose basic feature is a refusal to 'work through' the traumatic past. What they overlooked was that it was precisely this feature with which the majority of centrist voters identified. Postwar Austria is a country whose very existence is based on a refusal to 'work through' its Nazi past—proving that Waldheim was evading confrontation with his past emphasized the exact trait-of-identification of the majority of voters." The theoretical lesson to be learned from the campaign, Žižek continues, "is that the trait-of-identification can also be a certain failure, weakness, guilt of the other, so that by pointing out the failure we can unwittingly reinforce the identification." See *The Sublime Object of Ideology* (London: Verso, 1989), pp. 105–106. Žižek's book is entirely relevant to the critique of idealism in fascist and totalitarian operations. See my discussion in the following chapter.

47. Elsaesser, "Primary Identification and the Historical Subject," p. 545.

48. Gayatri Spivak refers to the current constructions of the "third world" and "marginality" in the academy as a "new Orientalism." See Spivak, "Marginality in the Teaching Machine," *Outside in the Teaching Machine* (New York: Routledge, 1993), p. 56. See also Sara Suleri's critique of what she calls "alteritism," which is characterized by an indiscriminate reliance on the centrality of otherness and tends to replicate the familiar category of the exotic in imperialist discourse: "alteritism enters the interpretive scene to insist on the conceptual centrality of an untouchable intransigence. Much like the category of the exotic in the colonial narratives of the prior century, contemporary critical theory names the other in order that it need not be further known." Suleri, *The Rhetoric of English India* (Chicago: U of Chicago P, 1992), p. 13.

49. For a discussion of this epochal change from the viewpoint of the "others," see chapter 5, "Against the Lures of Diaspora: Minority Discourse, Chinese Women, and Intellectual Hegemony," in Rey Chow, *Writing Diaspora: Tactics of Intervention in Contemporary Cultural Studies* (Bloomington: Indiana UP, 1993).

50. Nancy Armstrong and Leonard Tennenhouse, *The Imaginary Puritan: Literature, Intellectual Labor, and the Origins of Private Life* (Berkeley: U of California P, 1992). Among other things, this book is a significant contribution to the vast project of deconstructing and thus provincializing Western European culture, in particular that of England.

51. See Armstrong and Tennenhouse, *The Imaginary Puritan.*

52. At this juncture, the following related questions are especially thought-provoking: "Is the current fascination with the black or colored body—especially the female body—a contemporary version of the primitivism of the 1920s? Is multiculturalism to postmodernism what primitivism was to modernism?" See Ann duCille, "Dyes and Dolls: Multicultural Barbie and the Merchandising of Difference," *differences* 6.1 (Spring 1994), pp. 46–68; the quotation is on p. 53.

53. Many people must be acknowledged for having contributed to the final shape of this chapter. Nancy Armstrong, Chris Cullens, Prabhakara Jha, Kwai-cheung Lo, Austin Meredith, and Dorothea von Mücke were readers who responded with constructive comments to the first draft when it was completed in December 1992. Members of the Critical Theory Institute at the University of California, Irvine, devoted a session to a subsequent version of the chapter in the fall of 1993, and I thank in particular Lindon Barrett, Alexander Gelley, and John Rowe for their extended remarks. I am also grateful to Iain Chambers, Chris Connery, Hal Foster, and Kathleen Woodward for their assistance at various stages. To Livia Monnet, who gave me her indefatigable enthusiasm and support, I owe a special debt of friendship.

3. Ethics after Idealism

1. The works being reviewed include Gayatri Chakravorty Spivak, *The Post-Colonial Critic: Interviews, Strategies, Dialogues,* ed. Sarah Harasym (New York: Routledge, 1990); "Scattered Speculations on the Question of Value" (originally published in *diacritics* 1985), in *In Other Worlds: Essays in Cultural Politics* (New York: Methuen, 1987), pp. 154–75; "Speculations on Reading Marx: After Reading Derrida," in *Poststructuralism and the Question of History,* ed. Derek Attridge, Geoff Bennington, and Robert Young (New York: Cambridge UP, 1987), pp. 30–62; and Slavoj Žižek, *The Sublime Object of Ideology* (London: Verso, 1989). Hereafter these four texts will be abbreviated respectively as PCC, "SSQV," "SRM," and SOI.

2. See Jean Baudrillard, *For a Critique of the Political Economy of the Sign,* trans. and intro. Charles Levin (St. Louis: Telos, 1981); *The Mirror of Production,* trans. and intro. Mark Poster (St. Louis: Telos, 1975).

3. See Jean-Joseph Goux, *Symbolic Economies after Marx and Freud,* trans. Jennifer Curtiss Gage (Ithaca, Cornell UP, 1990).

4. Spivak, "Poststructuralism, Marginality, Postcoloniality and Value," in *Literary Theory Today,* ed. Peter Collier and Helga Geyer-Ryan (Ithaca: Cornell UP, 1990), p. 228. See pp. 241–42, note 20, for an explanation of "catachresis." I cite part of this note in the section "Naming."

5. Ibid., p. 226.

6. Alfred Sohn-Rethel, *Intellectual and Manual Labour: A Critique of Epistemology,* trans. Martin Sohn-Rethel (London: Macmillan, 1978).

7. When he needed an example to make his point about language, Saussure too would use money: "it is impossible for sound alone, a material element, to belong to language. . . . All our conventional values have the characteristic of

not being confused with the tangible element which supports them. For instance, it is not the metal in a piece of money that fixes its value. A coin nominally worth five francs may contain less than half its worth of silver. Its value will vary according to the amount stamped upon it and according to its use inside or outside a political boundary. This is even more true of the linguistic signifier, which is not phonic but incorporeal—constituted not by its material substance but by the differences that separate its sound-image from all others." Ferdinand de Saussure, *Course in General Linguistics,* intro. Jonathan Culler, ed. Charles Bally and Albert Sechehaye in collaboration with Albert Reidlinger, trans. Wade Baskin (London: Fontana/Collins, 1974), pp. 118–19.

8. "[T]he Enlightenment is defined, not so much by an adherence to a certain ideal or a doctrine, but by the choice of an ethical attitude. Foucault illustrates this with the example of what Baudelaire called 'the heroism of modern life': the choice of a certain way of life, the style of a dandy, of a *flâneur,* an 'aesthetics of existence', finding 'eternity in the passing moment' etc. What makes this attitude typical of modernity is the constant reconstruction and reinvention of the present which goes along with the reconstruction and the reinvention of the self. Both elements—the subject and the present it belongs to—have no 'objective' status; they have to be perpetually (re)constructed, and their status is purely 'ethical'. So modernity essentially results in an ethics of self-construction." See Mladen Dolar, "The Legacy of the Enlightenment: Foucault and Lacan," *New Formations* 14 (Summer 1991), p. 46. This is an essay in which Dolar traces the origins of Foucault's and Lacan's interest in the Enlightenment back to Kant. Dolar argues that whereas for Foucault, the legacy of the Enlightenment lies in Kant's new attitude toward the subject—"the ethical attitude in which he constructs himself as well as the age he belongs to" (p. 53)—for Lacan, Kant's novelty lies in his pointing to the inner impossibility of an autonomous subject and thus to an inner limit to the project of the Enlightenment (p. 54).

9. "[I]f the designing of the future and the proclamation of ready-made solutions for all time is not our affair, then we realize all the more clearly what we have to accomplish in the present—I am speaking of a *ruthless criticism of everything existing,* ruthless in two senses: The criticism must not be afraid of its own conclusions, nor of conflict with the powers that be." Karl Marx, "For a Ruthless Criticism of Everything Existing," *Marx-Engels Reader,* second edition, ed. Robert C. Tucker (New York: Norton, 1972, 1978), p. 13; emphasis in the original.

10. Ernesto Laclau and Chantal Mouffe, *Hegemony and Socialist Strategy: Towards a Radical Democratic Politics,* trans. Winston Moore and Paul Cammack (London: Verso, 1985).

11. Žižek, "Beyond Discourse-Analysis," in Ernesto Laclau, *New Reflections on the Revolution of Our Time* (London: Verso, 1990), p. 259; emphasis in the original.

12. I have already read Spivak's "Can the Subaltern Speak?" (in *Marxism and the Interpretation of Culture,* ed. Cary Nelson and Lawrence Grossberg [Urbana: U of Illinois P, 1988], pp. 271–313) in this light; see chapter 2, "Where Have All the Natives Gone?" in *Writing Diaspora: Tactics of Intervention in Contemporary Cultural Studies* (Bloomington: Indiana UP, 1993). The discussion in this section will therefore focus primarily on Žižek.

13. It is beyond the scope of the present discussion to consider the relevance of this critique to the "English tradition" as advocated by "pro-life" critics like F. R. Leavis and to English literature's complicity with England's imperialism and colonialism.

14. Žižek's reading of the Jesus-Judas teamwork has its predecessors in Robinson Jeffers's "Dear Judas" (in *Dear Judas and Other Poems* [1929, 1957], afterword by Robert J. Brophy [New York: Liveright, 1977]), Hugh Joseph Schonfield's *The Passover Plot: New Light on the History of Jesus* (New York: B. Geis Associates, 1965), Nikos Kazantzakis's *The Last Temptation* (1950–51), trans. P. A. Bien (Oxford: Oxford UP, 1961), and Martin Scorsese's film *The Last Temptation of Christ*, which was based on Kazantzakis's novel. Žižek's comment on Scorsese's film is that "its theme is simply the *hystericization of Jesus Christ himself;* it shows us an ordinary, carnal, passionate man discovering gradually, with fascination and horror, that he is the son of God, bearer of the dreadful but magnificent mission to redeem humanity through his sacrifice. The problem is that he cannot come to terms with this interpellation: the meaning of his 'temptations' lies precisely in the hysterical resistance to his mandate, in his doubts about it, in his attempts to evade it even when he is already nailed to the cross" (SOI, p. 114; emphasis in the original).

15. See also Žižek, "Act as the Limit of Distributive Justice," *New Formations* 14 (Summer 1991), in which he briefly discusses the trials of the Stalinist era as an explicit form of "cynical-utilitarian sacrificial logic": "[T]he answer to the question 'Did the prosecutors really believe in their victim's guilt?' is far more difficult and ambiguous than it may seem. A 'true' Stalinist would probably say that, even if, on the level of immediate facts, the accused are innocent, they are all the more guilty on a deeper level of historical responsibility since, by the very insistence on their abstract-legal innocence, they have given preference to their individuality over the larger historical interests of the working class expressed in the will of the Party" (p. 73). This discussion of sacrificial logic is part of a larger discussion of the relation between "repetition" and ethical "choice."

In an interesting essay on the Stalin myth in Soviet cinema, André Bazin makes a similar point by showing the sacrificial imperative of Stalinism to be "a retroactive purge of History": "According to the Soviet 'Stalinist' communist perspective, no one can 'become' a traitor. That would imply that he wasn't always a traitor. . . . It was necessary to proceed with a retroactive purge of History, proving that the accused was, since birth, a willful traitor whose every act was satanically camouflaged sabotage. . . . As confession is indispensable to divine absolution, so solemn retraction is indispensable to the reconquering of historical virginity." Bazin, "The Stalin Myth in Soviet Cinema," trans. Georgia Gurrieri, in *Movies and Methods*, vol. 2, ed. Bill Nichols (Berkeley: U of California P, 1985), p. 37; see also my related discussion in the previous chapter of the relation between the Stalinist logic of retroaction and certain uses of the image.

16. Louis Althusser, *Lenin and Philosophy and Other Essays*, trans. Ben Brewster (New York: Monthly Review, 1971), pp. 168–69; emphasis in the original.

17. Saul Kripke, *Naming and Necessity* (Cambridge: Harvard UP, 1980).

18. Spivak, "Poststructuralism, Marginality, Postcoloniality and Value," pp. 241–42, note 20.

19. This, for instance, is Derrida's reading of apartheid in South Africa: "racism always betrays the perversion of a man, the 'talking animal.'" "Racism's Last Word," trans. Peggy Kamuf, in *"Race," Writing, and Difference,* ed. Henry Louis Gates, Jr. (Chicago: U of Chicago P, 1985), p. 331.

20. "[I]n order to make any kind of ethical decision you have to assume that there is such a thing as just *the* human being. . . . If an ethical question cannot be entertained on that basis then it is not an ethical decision; then it is a decision that is in fact situational." Spivak, "Reflections on Cultural Studies in the Post-Colonial Conjuncture: An Interview with the Guest Editor," *Cultural Studies* 3.1 (1991), p. 69; emphasis in the original.

21. One is thus not surprised to find that the word "subaltern" is "already" in Derrida's formulation of the supplement: "Compensatory [*suppléant*] and vicarious, the supplement is an adjunct, a subaltern instance which *takes-(the)-place* [*tient-lieu*]." (The French original: "Suppléant et vicaire, le supplément est un adjoint, une instance subalterne qui *tient-lieu*.") Derrida, *Of Grammatology,* trans. G. C. Spivak (Baltimore: Johns Hopkins UP, 1974), p. 145; *De la grammatologie* (Paris: Minuit, 1967), p. 208; emphasis in the original.

22. Spivak, "Subaltern Studies: Deconstructing Historiography," in *In Other Worlds,* pp. 197–221.

23. Joan Scott: "Once we recognize the limits of representation, is history possible? The answer . . . is decidedly yes" ["Comment," *differences: A Journal of Feminist Cultural Studies* 3.3 (Fall 1991), p. 174]. Scott is responding to Spivak's "Feminism in Decolonization," *differences* 3.3 (Fall 1991), pp. 139–70.

24. Žižek, "Beyond Discourse-Analysis," p. 253; emphases in the original.

25. Ibid., pp. 251–52; my emphasis.

26. These events are told in the chapter "Autobiography" in *The Sutra of Hui Neng: Sutra Spoken by the 6th Patriarch on the High Seat of "The Treasure of the Law,"* trans. Wong Mou-lam, Christmas Humphreys (Hong Kong: Buddhist Book Distributor, 1982). The two stanzas are on pages 15 and 18 respectively; translation from the Chinese modified. Wong Mou-lam, the first translator of the Sutra into English, described Hui Neng's Sutra in these terms: "of all the Chinese works which have been canonized in the Tripitaka, this standard work of the Dhyana School is the only one that bears the designation of 'Sutra,' a designation which is reserved for the sermons of Lord Buddha and those of great Bodhisattvas. Hence, it is not without justification to call it, as someone does, 'the only Sutra spoken by a native of China'" (*Sutra,* p. 9).

27. See Spivak's reading of Marx's Eleventh Thesis on Feuerbach, in which she points out that Marx, in his call for the need "to change" the world, had actually written *zu verändern,* the infinitive of the German verb which literally means "to make other." "Subaltern Studies: Deconstructing Historiography," p. 208.

28. See also Spivak's translator's preface and afterword to Mahasweti Devi, *Imaginary Maps* (New York: Routledge, 1994). In discussing the difficulty of representing subaltern tribal women in postcolonial India, she uses "ethics" to refer to "the experience of the impossible"—to a "witnessing love and a supplementing collective struggle"; a "two-way road" with "the compromised other as teacher." Ethics, she writes, is not the "rationalist" notion of doing the right thing.

29. Žižek, "Beyond Discourse-Analysis," pp. 259–60; emphasis in the original.

4. The Politics of Admittance

1. Henry Louis Gates, Jr., "Critical Fanonism," *Critical Inquiry* 17 (Spring 1991), p. 458. The three epigraphs at the beginning of this essay are taken respectively from *Selected Subaltern Studies*, ed. Ranajit Guha and Gayatri Chakravorty Spivak, foreword by Edward Said (New York: Oxford UP, 1988), p. 28; "Identity and Its Discontents: Women and the Nation," in *Colonial Discourse and Post-Colonial Theory: A Reader*, ed. and intro. Patrick Williams and Laura Chrisman (New York: Columbia UP, 1994), p. 32; *Lethal Love: Feminist Literary Readings of Biblical Love Stories* (Bloomington: Indiana UP, 1987), p. 61, emphasis in the original.

2. In certain passages of *Orphée Noir*, preface to *Anthologie de la nouvelle poésie nègre et malgache* (Paris: Presses Universitaires de France, 1948), Sartre offers the view that negritude, as a subjective, existential, and ethnic idea, is insufficient as a means of asserting a future society without race discrimination, and that it must by necessity pass into the objective, positive, and exact idea of the proletariat. "Thus," he writes, "negritude is the root of its own destruction, it is a transition and not a conclusion, a means and not an ultimate end." These passages are quoted by Fanon in *Black Skin, White Masks*, trans. Charles Lam Markmann (New York: Grove Weidenfeld, 1967), pp. 132–33. (Further references to this edition will be indicated in the text by BSWM, followed by page numbers.) Fanon strongly objects to Sartre's view: "I felt that I had been robbed of my last chance. . . . In terms of consciousness, the black consciousness is held out as an absolute density, as filled with itself, a stage preceding any invasion, any abolition of the ego by desire. Jean-Paul Sartre, in this work, has destroyed black zeal" (pp. 132–34).

3. See for instance Homi Bhabha, "Remembering Fanon: Self, Psyche and the Colonial Condition," in *Colonial Discourse and Post-Colonial Theory: A Reader*, pp. 112–23 (this essay was originally published as the foreword to Frantz Fanon, *Black Skin, White Masks* [London: Pluto, 1986], pp. vii–xxvi); Mary Ann Doane, *Femmes Fatales: Feminism, Film Theory, Psychoanalysis* (New York: Routledge, 1991) pp. 215–27; Diana Fuss, "Interior Colonies: Frantz Fanon and the Politics of Identification," *diacritics* 24: 2–3 (Summer-Fall 1994), pp. 20–42 (this essay contains a useful and detailed bibliography of works on Fanon); Gwen Bergner, "Who Is That Masked Woman? or, The Role of Gender in Fanon's *Black Skin, White Masks*," *PMLA* 110: 1 (January 1995), pp. 75–88 (I share many of the observations of Bergner's essay, which was published after this present chapter was first completed and presented as a paper at the conference on Intellectuals and Communities in Sydney, Australia, in early December 1994); *The Fact of Blackness: Frantz Fanon and Visual Representation*, ed. Alan Read (Seattle: Bay, 1996) (I had access to this collection only after the final revisions of this chapter had already been completed). See also the comments on the various readings of Fanon by Edward Said, Abdul JanMohammed, Benita Parry, and Homi Bhabha among others in Gates, "Critical Fanonism." For biographical studies of Fanon,

see Peter Geismar, *Fanon* (New York: Dial, 1971) and Irene Gendzier, *Frantz Fanon: A Critical Study* (New York: Grove, 1973).

4. For an example of a detailed theoretical reflection on community, see Jean-Luc Nancy, *The Inoperative Community,* edited by Peter Connor, trans. Peter Connor et al., foreword by Christopher Fynsk (Minneapolis: U of Minnesota P, 1991). Nancy deconstructs—de-works—the notion of "community" and argues for "mortal truth" and "limit" as the basis of a community's sharing.

5. I am using the word "race" here not only to signify "racial difference" or "racial identity" in a neutral sense. More importantly, "race" signifies the major historical legacy of colonialism—namely, the injustices and atrocities committed against so-called "peoples of color" in the name of their racial inferiority. "Race" as such is thus implicated in the history of racism. To that extent I find the following analytic formulation of "race" useful: "Race is not part of an unproblematic continuum alongside discursive categories such as linguistic rupture, syncretism, hybridity and so on. In all kinds of oppositional post-colonialism (within settler countries themselves and without) race was part of a larger struggle for self-respect. The post-colonial is the single most important phenomenon in which it played such a decisive role." Vijay Mishra and Bob Hodge, "What is Post(-)colonialism?" in *Colonial Discourse and Post-colonial Theory: A Reader,* p. 285. This essay was originally published in *Textual Practice* 5:3 (1991), pp. 399–414.

6. Both Bhabha and Doane, for instance, cite Fanon's line "I know nothing about her" as "proof" of how he actually deals with the woman of color. Bhabha uses the strategy of deferral: "Of the woman of colour he has very little to say. 'I know nothing about her,' he writes in *Black Skin, White Masks.* This crucial issue requires an order of psychoanalytic argument that goes well beyond the scope of my foreword. I have therefore chosen to note the importance of the problem rather than to elide it in a facile charge of 'sexism'" ("Remembering Fanon," p. 123). For more detailed criticisms of Bhabha, see Bergner, "Who Is That Masked Woman?" pp. 84–85. Doane, focusing on the white woman as the pivotal point of a racist representational economy, asserts time and again the "disappearance" of the woman of color from Fanon's analytic schema (see pp. 220–21, 222, 225 of her book). By interpreting Fanon's claim of lack of knowledge at its face value, Bhabha and Doane avoid having to deal with its most important aspect—its self-contradiction—which is a clear indication of Fanon's troubled views about colored female sexuality. By the same gesture, they also avoid having to examine closely the disturbing manner in which Fanon does, in fact, give the woman of color agency.

7. See also Fuss's discussion of what she calls "Fanon's retrieval of an essentialist discourse of black femininity" (Fuss, p. 28) in his reading of the Algerian Revolution in *A Dying Colonialism* (1959), trans. Haakon Chevalier (New York: Grove Weidenfeld, 1965). Fuss is referring to Fanon's notion that the act of mimesis—mimicry and/or masquerade—is *natural* to women.

8. Sigmund Freud, *Totem and Taboo: Some Points of Agreement between the Mental Lives of Savages and Neurotics,* trans. James Strachey (New York: Norton), pp. 146: "Thus psycho-analysis, in contradiction to the more recent views of the totemic system but in agreement with the earlier ones, requires us to assume

that totemism and exogamy were intimately connected and had a simulta-
neous origin."

9. Ibid., p. 144.

10. Ibid., pp. 33–34.

11. See Claude Lévi-Strauss, *Elementary Structures of Kinship* (1949) (English
translation, London, 1969); Marcel Mauss, *The Gift: The Form and Reason for
Exchange in Archaic Societies* (1950), trans. W. D. Halls, foreword by Mary
Douglas (New York: Norton, 1990).

12. Gayle Rubin, "The Traffic in Women: Notes on the 'Political Economy' of
Sex," in *Toward an Anthropology of Women*, ed. Rayna Reiter (New York: Monthly
Review, 1975), p. 174.

13. See for instance René Girard, *Violence and the Sacred*, trans. Patrick Gregory
(Baltimore: Johns Hopkins UP, 1977), in particular chapters 8 and 9. For a
feminist analysis of the Freudian framework of community formation, see
Juliet Mitchell's discussions in *Feminism and Psychoanalysis: Freud, Reich, Laing
and Women* (New York: Vintage, 1975), in particular the conclusion.

14. Freud, "Some Psychological Consequences of the Anatomical Distinction
between the Sexes" (1925), in *Sexuality and the Psychology of Love*, edited and
introduced by Philip Rieff (New York: Collier, 1963), pp. 187–88.

15. See Gayatri Spivak's explication of these two senses of representation in
"Can the Subaltern Speak?" in *Colonial Discourse and Post-Colonial Theory: A
Reader*, pp. 66–111. This essay was originally published in *Marxism and the
Interpretation of Culture*, ed. Cary Nelson and Larry Grossberg (Basingstoke:
Macmillan Education, 1988), pp. 271–313.

16. Doane: "Fanon's analysis situates rape only as the white woman's fantasy
and neglects its status as the historical relation between the white male and the
black female both in the colonial context and in that of slavery" (p. 222).

17. Whether or not skin color is simply an accident in a more universal scheme
of oppressive experience is a point on which Fanon remains ambivalent. For
instance, in the chapter "The Man of Color and the White Woman" in *Black Skin,
White Masks*, Fanon argues that blackness is, for the black man, but a coincidence that compounds his neurotic condition: "Jean Veneuse, alias René Maran,
is neither more nor less a black abandonment-neurotic. And he is put back into
his place, his proper place. He is a neurotic who needs to be emancipated from
his infantile fantasies. And I contend that Jean Veneuse represents not an
example of black-white relations, but a certain mode of behavior in a neurotic
who by coincidence is black" (p. 79). And yet, if this passage clearly suggests
that the black man has psychic problems *just like any other man*, Fanon is much
more emphatic elsewhere about the absolutely determining power of skin
color. See, for instance, p. 163 of *Black Skin, White Masks:* "It is in his corporeality
that the Negro is attacked." See also the chapter "The Fact of Blackness"
(BSWM, pp. 109–40) in which Fanon is primarily concerned with race as the
determining factor for individual identity.

18. "Fanon does not ignore sexual difference altogether, but he explores
sexuality's role in constructing race only through rigid categories of gender. In
Black Skin, White Masks, women are considered as subjects almost exclusively in
terms of their sexual relationships with men; feminine desire is thus defined as

an overly literal and limited (hetero)sexuality." Bergner, "Who Is That Masked Woman?" p. 77. See also the discussion in Lola Young, "Missing Persons: Fantasising Black Women in *Black Skin, White Masks,*" in *The Fact of Blackness,* pp. 86–101.

19. The black woman's predicament is succinctly summarized in the title of the anthology *All the Women Are White, All the Blacks Are Men, but Some of Us Are Brave* (Old Harbury, NY: Feminist P, 1982), ed. Gloria Hull, Patricia Bell Scott, and Barbara Smith.

20. See the very different analyses of black female agency in, for instance, Hazel V. Carby, *Reconstructing Womanhood: The Emergence of the Afro-American Woman Novelist* (New York: Oxford UP, 1987). Carby alerts us to how the consideration of black womanhood must take into account the sexism of black men. She also offers very different ways of reading the mulatto figure, who stands as a mediator between the races rather than simply as the offspring of black women's desire for upward social mobility (as Fanon describes it).

21. In this regard the biographical details about Fanon—that his mother was of Alsatian descent, that he grew up in Martinique thinking of himself as white and French, that he "became" a black West Indian only when he arrived in Paris, and that, however, he never afterward returned to Negritude and to the West Indies—become an interesting and thought-provoking intertext. See the brief account by Gates in "Critical Fanonism," p. 468. Gates's major source of information is Albert Memmi, review of *Fanon,* by Peter Geismar, and *Frantz Fanon,* by David Caute, *New York Times Book Review,* 14 March, 1971, p. 5.

22. Deniz Kandiyoti, "Identity and Its Discontents: Women and the Nation," p. 378; emphases in the original.

23. Rubin, "The Traffic in Women," p. 178.

24. See for instance the chapter "Concerning Violence" in *The Wretched of the Earth,* preface by Jean-Paul Sartre, trans. Constance Farrington (New York: Grove P, 1968), pp. 35–106. Fanon argues that for the colonized people, the violence of destroying the colonizer "invests their characters with positive and creative qualities. The practice of violence binds them together as a whole" and mobilizes their consciousness toward "a common cause," "a national identity," and "a collective history" (p. 93).

25. See descriptions in Fanon, *The Wretched of the Earth,* pp. 52–53, 60–61, and throughout.

26. This last possibility is the one taken up, for instance, by Homi Bhabha, who emphasizes the "ambivalence" of the imperialist's speech as a way to subvert imperialist discourse. See Bhabha, "Remembering Fanon," p. 116; "Signs Taken for Wonders: Questions of Ambivalence and Authority under a Tree Outside Delhi, May 1817," in *"Race," Writing, and Difference,* ed. Henry Louis Gates, Jr. (Chicago: U of Chicago P, 1986), pp. 163–84. I have elsewhere critiqued Bhabha's reading of "ambivalence" as a critical gesture that makes it ultimately unnecessary to pay attention to anything other than the imperialist's speech. See the chapter "Where Have All the Natives Gone?" in *Writing Diaspora: Tactics of Intervention in Contemporary Cultural Studies* (Bloomington: Indiana UP, 1993).

27. It is important to note that Fanon conceives of the moment of decolonization as a kind of *tabula rasa:* "we have precisely chosen to speak of that kind

of *tabula rasa* which characterizes at the outset all decolonization." *The Wretched of the Earth*, p. 35. Among male revolutionary thinkers, Mao Zedong's attitudes toward "the people" come readily to mind in resonance with Fanon's. For comparison, see Maurice Meisner's incisive analysis of the manner in which Mao Zedong imagined "the people" for his political purposes: "Mao Tse-tung, by declaring the Chinese people 'blank,' was driven by a utopian impulse to escape history and by an iconoclastic desire to wipe the historical-cultural slate clean. Having rejected the traditional Chinese cultural heritage, Mao attempted to fill the emotional void by an even more iconoclastic proclamation of the non-existence of the past in the present. A new culture, Mao seemed to believe, could be fashioned *ex nihilo* on a fresh canvas, on a 'clean sheet of paper unmarred by historical blemishes.'" Meisner, *Mao's China and After: A History of the People's Republic* (a revised and expanded edition of *Mao's China*, 1977) (New York: Free P, 1986), pp. 316–17. Immanuel Wallerstein has analyzed how, be-cause "peoplehood" is fundamentally ambiguous, it is "an instrument of flex-ibility" into which political movements—those based on class, for instance—always collapse. See the chapter "The Construction of Peoplehood: Racism, Nationalism, Ethnicity," in Etienne Balibar and Immanuel Wallerstein, *Race, Nation, Class: Ambiguous Identities* (London: Verso, 1991), especially pp. 84–85.

28. See also Bergner's account of what she calls black women's "double oppression or exclusion," p. 78.

29. Fuss: "Fanon's disquieting discussions of not only femininity but homo-sexuality—inextricably linked in Fanon as they are in Freud—have received little if any attention from his critical commentators. Passages in Fanon's cor-pus articulating ardent disidentifications from black and white women and from white gay men (for Fanon homosexuality is culturally white) are rou-tinely passed over, dismissed as embarrassing, baffling, unimportant, unen-lightened, or perhaps simply politically risky" (p. 30). Kobena Mercer has also pointed out that Fanon's misogyny is linked to his homophobia in a defensive masculinity revolving around castration. Mercer, "Thinking through Homo-phobia in Frantz Fanon," a talk delivered at the conference entitled "Blackness and the Mind/Body Split: Discourses, Social Practices, Genders, Sexualities," October 1995, University of California, Irvine. See as well Mercer's related arguments in "Decolonisation and Disappointment: Reading Fanon's Sexual Politics," in *The Fact of Blackness*, pp. 114–25.

30. For a critique of how the study of Fanon has become a fashionable event in postcolonial criticism, see Gates, "Critical Fanonism." Gates describes Fanon as "both totem and text" (p. 457), "a composite figure, indeed, an ethnographic construct" (p. 459) that has been put together by postcolonial critics' collective desire for a global theorist. It would be interesting to juxtapose the worship of Fanon as a theoretical *leader* with the analyses of coercive group psychology as laid out in Freud's *Group Psychology and the Analysis of the Ego*, translated and edited by James Strachey (New York: Norton, 1959); see in particular chapters 7, "Identification"; 9, "The Herd Instinct"; and 10, "The Group and the Primal Horde." As Freud points out, it is precisely the father's excesses and neuroses which "forced them [the horde], so to speak, into group psychology" (p. 56). In the process, the father becomes the group ideal, which governs the ego in the place of the ego ideal.

31. Mieke Bal, *Lethal Love,* p. 36, emphasis in the original. Even though it deals with an entirely different topic, Bal's book offers many useful insights into the formation of intellectual/interpretive as well as mythic and tribal communities, a formation that often takes place at the expense of women. See in particular her chapter on the story of Samson and Delilah, a story which is, among other things, about the conflict between kinship (which is signified by loyalty to the community that is one's tribe) and sexuality (which is signified by relations with the foreigner, the "unfaithful" woman).

32. For a discussion of the problems inherent in the facile indictment of postcolonial intellectuals "selling out" or being worked over by the language of the "first world," see Sangeeta Ray and Henry Schwarz, "Postcolonial Discourse: The Raw and the Cooked," *Ariel: A Review of International English Literature* 26.1 (January 1995): 147–66. See also Victor Li, "Towards Articulation: Postcolonial Theory and Demotic Resistance," for a critique of the pitfalls of polarizing "postcolonial theory" and "demotic resistance" (same issue of *Ariel,* pp. 167–89). For a related discussion of the impasses created by moralistic dismissals of "Westernized" native intellectuals, see my reading of the debates around Zhang Yimou's films in Part II, chapter 4 of *Primitive Passions: Visuality, Sexuality, Ethnography, and Contemporary Chinese Cinema* (New York: Columbia UP, 1995).

33. In her response to the version of this chapter that was first published in *The UTS Review,* 1.1 (July 1995): 5–29, Susan Schwartz points out that Fanon did in fact attribute a revolutionary capacity to women (in the Algerian Revolution, for instance) and acknowledge women's agency in the formation of a utopian new community. (See her article "Fanon's Revolutionary Woman," *The UTS Review* 1.2 [October 1995]: 197–201.) However, insofar as "revolution" was a cause to which the Algerian women revolutionaries had, in Fanon's eyes, submitted themselves *loyally,* their "agency" was strictly confined within that cause (and the community it engendered) and therefore did not constitute a disruptive issue. Just as the father did not ask what his bomb-bearing daughter had done (Fanon, *A Dying Colonialism*), so neither did the fatherly male theorist need to interrogate such revolutionary women: from the perspective of the revolution, their "female agency" remained a gift to patriarchy (in the terms discussed in this chapter) and posed no threat. For a critique of the problematic nature of (white intellectuals' fondness for) attributing "revolutionariness" to "third world" intellectuals, men or women, see chapter 2 of this book.

5. The Dream of a Butterfly

1. I am very grateful to David Cronenberg for providing me with a copy of the shooting script of the film *M. Butterfly.* For related interest, see David Henry Hwang, *M. Butterfly,* with an afterword by the playwright (New York: Plume, 1989). For a discussion of the play in terms of the politics of transvestism, see Marjorie Garber, *Vested Interests: Cross-Dressing and Cultural Anxiety* (New York: Routledge, 1992), pp. 234–51. For a discussion of the play in terms of its criticism of essentialist identity formed through Orientalism and heterosexism, see Dorinne Kondo, "*M. Butterfly:* Orientalism, Gender, and a Critique of

Essentialist Identity," *Cultural Critique*, no. 16 (Fall 1990), pp. 5–29. For a discussion of the misogynist implications of Puccini's opera, see Catherine Clément, *Opera, or the Undoing of Women*, trans. Betsy Wing, foreword by Susan McClary (Minneapolis: U of Minnesota P, 1988), pp. 43–47. For a biography of Bernard Boursicot, the Frenchman whose love affair with the Chinese opera singer Shi Peipu gave rise to the *M. Butterfly* story, see Joyce Wadler, *Liaison* (New York: Bantam, 1993). The epigraphs at the beginning of this chapter are taken respectively from Martin Heidegger, *Poetry, Language, Thought*, trans. Albert Hofstadter (New York: Harper Colophon, 1971), p. 176; Roland Barthes, *Camera Lucida: Reflections on Photography*, trans. Richard Howard (New York: Hill and Wang, 1981), p. 117; Jacques Lacan, *Feminine Sexuality: Jacques Lacan and the école freudienne*, ed. Juliet Mitchell and Jacqueline Rose, trans. Jacqueline Rose (New York: Norton, 1985), pp. 146–47.

2. Hwang, *M. Butterfly*, p. 94.

3. Ibid., p. 100.

4. See Kondo's essay for summaries of the vexed reactions to Hwang's play from some members of the Asian American communities.

5. See, for instance, Freud's well-known discussion in "Creative Writers and Day-Dreaming," *The Standard Edition of the Complete Psychological Works of Sigmund Freud*, vol. ix, trans. James Strachey (London: Hogarth, 1959), pp. 141–53. For an authoritative, intensive reading of Freud's works on fantasy, see Jean Laplanche and Jean-Bertrand Pontalis, "Fantasy and the Origins of Sexuality" (first published in the *International Journal of Psychoanalysis*, vol. 49, part 1, pp. 1–17; 1968), in *Formations of Fantasy*, edited by Victor Burgin, James Donald, and Cora Kaplan (London: Methuen, 1986), pp. 5–34. Because I am, in this chapter, primarily interested in exploring the social and cross-cultural implications of fantasy, I am not fine-tuning the various modes of conscious and unconscious fantasies as would be necessary in a more strictly clinical analysis. For the same reasons I am also using terms such as "fantasy" and "dream" interchangeably.

6. See Laplanche and Pontalis, "Fantasy and the Origins of Sexuality." Two discussions of fantasy that I have found very helpful are Cora Kaplan, "The Thorn Birds: Fiction, Fantasy, Femininity," *Formations of Fantasy*, pp. 142–66, and Elizabeth Cowie, "Fantasia," *The Woman in Question*, edited by Parveen Adams and Elizabeth Cowie (Cambridge, MA: MIT P, 1990), pp. 149–96.

7. Examples of these uncomprehendingly dismissive reviews: "Hwang also wrote the misguided movie version of 'M. Butterfly' for director David Cronenberg, in which Jeremy Irons and an oddly sullen John Lone act out a straightforward love story devoid of heat or plausibility. The problem is not simply that Lone's drag wouldn't fool a baby. In the magnified intimacy of the camera's eye, it's clear Hwang doesn't really know who these unlikely lovers are." David Ansen, "Much Stranger than Fiction," *Newsweek*, October 18, 1993, p. 84. "The problem with 'M. Butterfly,' both play and movie, is that the audience gets the point right away—it's too crude and too facile to miss—and has nothing to do for the rest of the evening except listen to tiresome restatements of it. . . . Cronenberg's treatment of Hwang's material has the effect of exposing it for what it really is: not a pure, incandescent work of art but an extremely ordinary piece of agitprop drama." Terrence Rafferty, "The Current Cinema:

Blind Faith," *The New Yorker* 69: 33 (October 11, 1993), p. 123. If one were indeed to judge the film on the basis of verisimilitude, the obvious thing to criticize, from the perspective of those who know Chinese, is the improbability of a Cantonese-speaking servant in Song's house, while every other Chinese character, including Song, speaks in Mandarin, the language most commonly used in Beijing.

8. "Fantasy involves, is characterized by, not the achievement of desired objects, but the arranging of, a setting out of, desire; a veritable *mise-en-scène* of desire. . . . The fantasy depends not on particular objects, but on their setting out; and the pleasure of fantasy lies in the setting out, not in the having of the objects. . . . It can be seen, then, that fantasy is not the object of desire, but its setting." Cowie, "Fantasia," p. 159.

9. In the early scenes of the film, Gallimard's fascination with "Butterfly" extends even to fly swatting and dragonfly gazing. In terms of the genealogy of Cronenberg's films, *M. Butterfly* is similar to its predecessors in that it stages the manner in which a man's imagination infects him like a disease, which gradually consumes and finally destroys him. For extended discussions of this—his favorite—theme, see the director's *Cronenberg on Cronenberg*, ed. Chris Rodley (London: Faber and Faber, 1992). However, two factors make *M. Butterfly* different from the earlier films. First, the restrained, minimalist design of the film is a major departure from the elaborate special effects and shocking images that are the Cronenberg trademark. Second, the biological and science-fiction modes of Cronenberg's usual film language are here complicated by the story of a cross-cultural encounter with all its sexual, racial, and political implications. Because of these factors, I am reading *M. Butterfly* as a unique work in Cronenberg's corpus, even though the conceptual affinities with the other films are definitely present. In particular, as I will go on to argue, the significations of visuality in this film are unprecedentedly mind-boggling.

10. Even though Hwang too has referred to the notion of deconstruction, what he aims at deconstructing is the fantasy, the stereotype, and the cliché, rather than the human per se: "The idea of doing a deconstructivist *Madame Butterfly* immediately appealed to me. This despite the fact that I didn't even know the plot of the opera! I knew Butterfly only as a cultural stereotype; speaking of an Asian woman, we would sometimes say, 'She's pulling a Butterfly,' which meant playing the submissive Oriental number. Yet, I felt convinced that the libretto would include yet another lotus blossom pining away for a cruel Caucasian man, and dying for her love. Such a story has become too much of a cliché not to be included in the archtypal [*sic*] East-West romance that started it all. Sure enough, when I purchased the record, I discovered it contained a wealth of sexist and racist clichés, reaffirming my faith in Western culture." Hwang, *M. Butterfly*, p. 95.

11. Lacan, "The Line and Light," *The Four Fundamental Concepts of Psycho-Analysis*, edited by Jacques-Alain Miller, trans. Alan Sheridan (New York: Norton, 1981), pp. 102–103; emphases in the original.

12. See Jean Baudrillard, *Seduction*, trans. Brian Singer (New York: St. Martin's, 1990).

13. Ibid., p. 83.

14. On this point—namely, that *M. Butterfly* is not about the conflict of homo-

sexuality and heterosexuality—Hwang is absolutely clear: "To me, this is not a 'gay' subject because the very labels heterosexual or homosexual become meaningless in the context of this story. Yes, of course this was literally a homosexual affair. Yet because Gallimard perceived it or chose to perceive it as a heterosexual liaison, in his mind it was essentially so. Since I am telling the story from the Frenchman's point of view, it is more specifically about 'a man who loved a woman created by a man.' To me, this characterization is infinitely more useful than the clumsy labels 'gay' or 'straight.'" Hwang, personal communication, 30 April 1989, quoted in Kondo, "*M. Butterfly*," p. 21.

15. This is one of the many significant differences between the film and the play. In the play, Gallimard is familiar with the Madame Butterfly story, which he claims to like, but complains that he has only seen it "played by huge women in so much bad makeup" (Hwang, *M. Butterfly*, p. 16).

16. Lacan, "The Meaning of the Phallus," edited by Juliet Mitchell and Jacqueline Rose, trans. Jacqueline Rose (New York: Norton, 1985), p. 82.

17. See Lacan's discussion in "Feminine Sexuality in Psychoanalytic Doctrine." Responding to Freud's questions in the investigation of feminine sexuality, "What does the little girl want from her mother?" and "what does she demand of her?" Lacan writes:

> "What does the little girl demand of her mother?" But it's easy! She has no shortage of words for telling us: to dress her, to make her hurt go away, to take her for a walk, to belong to her, or to her alone, in short all sorts of demands, including at times the demand to leave her alone, that is, the demand to take a rest from all demand. If, therefore, Freud's question has any meaning, it must signify something else, that is, not so much "What is she demanding *of her?*" as "What is she *demanding*, what is she really demanding, by demanding of her mother all that?"
>
> In other words, Freud's question implies the separating out of demand onto two planes: that of the demands effectively spoken, or enounced, and that of Demand (with a capital D) which subsists within and beyond these very demands, and which, because it remains resistant to articulation, incites the little girl to make those demands at the same time as rendering them futile, both the demands and any reply they might receive. (*Feminine Sexuality*, pp. 130–31; emphases in the original)

18. Hwang, *M. Butterfly*, pp. 95–96.

19. I am following Burton Watson's English translation of Zhuang Zi's text, which appears in *Qiwulun* [a treatise on equalizing (with) all things]. See *The Basic Writings of Chuang Tzu*, trans. and ed. Burton Watson (New York: Columbia UP, 1964), p. 45.

20. Lacan, "The Eye and the Gaze," *Four Fundamental Concepts*, p. 76; emphasis in the original.

21. "When dreaming of being the butterfly, . . . he is a captive butterfly, but captured by nothing, for, in the dream, he is a butterfly for nobody." Ibid., p. 76.

22. "The butterfly may . . . inspire in him the phobic terror of recognizing that

the beating of little wings is not so very far from the beating of causation, of the primal stripe marking his being for the first time with the grid of desire." Ibid., p. 76.

23. Lacan, "The Line and Light," p. 100–101; emphases in the original.

24. See Garber for an interesting discussion of "passing" in her reading of the play *M. Butterfly:* "'What passes for a woman.' And what passes for a man. Passing is what acting is, and what treason is. Recall that the French diplomat Boursicot was accused of passing information to his Chinese contacts. In espionage, in theater, in 'modern China,' in contemporary culture, embedded in the very phrase 'gender roles,' there is, this play suggests, only passing. Trespassing. Border-crossing and border raids. Gender, here, exists only in representation—or performance." *Vested Interests,* p. 250. As my reading throughout this chapter indicates, my reading of passing—and hence of crossing, role-playing, representation, and performance—is quite different from Garber's.

25. See Cowie's discussion in "Fantasia," p. 154.

26. Lacan, "What Is a Picture?" *Four Fundamental Concepts,* p. 114.

27. The passage indicated by the previous footnote continues with these lines: "What it amounts to is the first act in the laying down of the gaze. A sovereign act, no doubt, since it passes into something that is materialized and which, from this sovereignty, will render obsolete, excluded, inoperant, whatever, coming from elsewhere, will be presented before this product." Ibid., p. 114.

28. "In our relations to things, in so far as this relation is constituted by the way of vision, and ordered in the figures of representation, something slips, passes, is transmitted, from stage to stage, and is always to some degree eluded in it—that is what we call the gaze." Lacan, "The Eye and the Gaze," p. 73.

29. This ending could also be read along the lines of Cronenberg's fascination with the resemblance of fantasy to disease. For instance, even though the vocabulary he uses is predominantly biological rather than visual, the following lines from the director could well serve as a reading of the ending of *M. Butterfly* once we substitute the word "fantasy" for the words "virus" and "disease": "To understand physical process on earth requires a revision of the theory that we're all God's creatures. . . . It should certainly be extended to encompass disease, viruses and bacteria. Why not? A virus is only doing its job. It's trying to live its life. The fact that it's destroying you by doing so is not its fault. It's about trying to understand interrelationships among organisms, even those we perceive as disease. To understand it from the disease's point of view, it's just a matter of life. It has nothing to do with disease. I think most diseases would be very shocked to be considered diseases at all. It's a very negative connotation. For them, it's very positive when they take over your body and destroy you. It's a triumph. It's all part of trying to reverse the normal understanding of what goes on physically, psychologically and biologically to [*sic*] us. . . . I identify with [the characters in *Shivers*] after they're infected. I identify with the parasites, basically. . . ." *Cronenberg on Cronenberg,* p. 82.

30. In terms of a man "painting" his fantasy, a comparison could also be made between Cronenberg's film and Hitchcock's *Vertigo,* in which the male character, Scotty, attempts to rejuvenate his fantasy world by artificially remaking—by painting—Judy, his new girlfriend, into Madeleine, his supposedly dead one. Once again, in *Vertigo* it is the female body that serves as the canvas for

male enlightenment and that is ultimately sacrificed; while in *M. Butterfly* it is the male body that bears the consequences of this cruel and crude act of painting.

31. Lacan, "God and the *Jouissance* of the Woman," *Feminine Sexuality*, p. 144.

6. Women in the Holocene

1. In the novel, An-mei's story appears in the second chapter, which is entitled "Scar." See Amy Tan, *The Joy Luck Club* (New York: Vintage, 1989). In this chapter, I am primarily following the order of events as they appear in the film.

2. For an example of how multiculturalism has become a mainstream media issue, see the special issue of *Time*, Fall 1993: "The New Face of America."

3. Examples of this fundamental perceptual difference abound in our everyday contexts. Let me cite two briefly.

At a conference on feminism and film theory held in Spain, a white feminist from a U.S. university told the audience that she wished there were black feminists present to tell them about the experiences of "women of color." I was ready to overlook her oblivion to my presence as a "woman of color," but the larger assumption behind her stated wish was alarming—namely, that "white" experiences like her own were somehow in a different category, that "white" was not "colored" and not "ethnic."

The second example is a mirror opposite of the first one. In Minneapolis, Minnesota, a black woman, Sharon Sayles Belton, became mayor a few years ago. Minneapolis police chief Tony Bouza is reported to have said about her: "She doesn't think in terms of race. Sharon is the least black person I know." See Steve Perry, "Our Ronnie: Notes on Sharon Sayles Belton and Her Unlikely Soulmate," *City Pages*, Minneapolis, November 17, 1993, p. 8. As Perry comments succinctly: "It practically goes without saying that to elect a black woman mayor flatters all our egalitarian primping and posturing; her half of the bargain is that she never, never calls us on our betrayals. . . . For her the cost of admission to the halls of power (whether it was paid consciously or not) has been to embody a fantasy of black life as seen through the eyes of middle-class white people: starting from humble origins, rising through luck and determination and the goodwill of white mentors, and finally *becoming like us*" (emphasis in the original).

4. Michel Foucault, *The History of Sexuality*, vol. 1, trans. Robert Hurley (New York: Vintage, 1989). Hereafter page references are indicated in the text.

5. E. San Juan, Jr., *Racial Formations/Critical Transformations: Articulations of Power in Ethnic and Racial Studies in the United States* (London: Humanities, 1992), p. 15. This book contains incisive criticisms of the ways "ethnicity" has been enlisted to serve the interests of mainstream cultural pluralism; see especially chapter 2, "The Cult of Ethnicity and the Fetish of Pluralism."

6. See Michel Foucault, *Discipline and Punish: The Birth of the Prison*, trans. Alan Sheridan (New York: Vintage, 1979). Hereafter page references are indicated in the text.

7. William V. Spanos, *The End of Education: Toward Posthumanism* (Minneapo-

lis: U of Minnesota P, 1993), p. 43. Spanos's argument (in chapter 2, "Humanistic Inquiry and the Politics of the Gaze") is that Bentham's Panopticon as theorized by Foucault was an instance of the post-Enlightenment culmination of a disciplinary supervisory schema that actually began much earlier in the West—among writers of the humanist Renaissance and philosophers of classical antiquity: "Bentham's Panopticon brings to fulfillment the coercive potential latent in metaphysical 'oversight' *and*, by way of this excess, makes explicit the disciplinary genealogy of the idea and practice of the modern synoptic humanist university that the metaphysical tradition authorized and elaborated. A careless reader of Foucault might object that Bentham's model applies essentially to a historically specific and appropriate architectural instance within modern Western society: the reformatory prison. But such an interpretation is what Foucault's genealogical scholarship insistently denies" (p. 40; emphasis in the original).

8. See Louis Althusser, "Ideology and Ideological State Apparatuses (Notes towards an Investigation)," in *Lenin and Philosophy and Other Essays*, trans. Ben Brewster (London: New Left, 1971), pp. 127–86.

9. See Joan Scott, "The Evidence of Experience," *Critical Inquiry*, Summer 1991. A shorter version of this essay is reprinted as "Experience," in *Feminists Theorize the Political*, edited Judith Butler and Joan Scott (New York: Routledge, 1992), pp. 22–40.

10. See Althusser, "Ideology and Ideology State Apparatuses"; Edward Said, *Orientalism* (New York: Vintage, 1978).

11. For a discussion of Orientalist representations of Chinese people in America, see James S. Moy, *Marginal Sights: Staging the Chinese in America* (Iowa City: U of Iowa P, 1993). However, if *The Joy Luck Club* were indeed to be read in the light of Orientalism, the kind of binary logic on which Moy's arguments depend—Western artists and viewers on the one hand, Chinese spectacles on the other—would break down since the writer and director in this case are themselves Chinese American.

12. This is a problem of cross-cultural reading that demands a detailed discussion. Since I have dealt with it at length elsewhere, I will not repeat myself and will ask interested readers to see my book *Primitive Passions: Visuality, Sexuality, Ethnography, and Contemporary Chinese Cinema* (Columbia UP, 1995), in particular part II, chapter 4, "The Force of Surfaces: Defiance in Zhang Yimou's Films."

13. See Michel de Certeau, "Walking in the City," in *The Practice of Everyday Life*, trans. Steven Rendall (Berkeley: U of California P, 1984); excerpted in *The Cultural Studies Reader*, ed. Simon During (London: Routledge, 1993), pp. 151–60.

14. See for instance Peter Brooks, *The Melodramatic Imagination: Balzac, Henry James, Melodrama, and the Mode of Excess* (New York: Columbia UP, 1985).

15. Walter Benjamin first used the term "optical unconscious" in the essay "A Small History of Photography" (1931), in *One-Way Street*, trans. Edmund Jephcott and Kingsley Shorter (London: New Left, 1979), pp. 240–57; he again refers to "unconscious optics" in "The Work of Art in the Age of Mechanical Reproduction," in *Illuminations*, trans. Harry Zohn (New York: Schocken, 1969), 217–51.

16. Cf. note 15 above: I can merely point here to the vast implications of the linkages between the "optical unconscious," filmic melodrama, and excessive emotions associated with cultural stereotypes. For a related argument about excessive emotions and technologized visuality, see my "Postmodern Automatons," in *Feminists Theorize the Political*, edited by Judith Butler and Joan Scott (New York: Routledge, 1992), pp. 101–17.

17. Jean Baudrillard, *Simulations*, trans. Paul Foss, Paul Patton, and Philip Beitchman (New York: Semiotext(e), 1983), p. 3.

18. Jean-François Lyotard, *The Postmodern Condition: A Report on Knowledge*, trans. Geoff Bennington and Brian Massumi (Minneapolis: U of Minnesota P, 1984); see especially pp. 31–41.

19. Max Frisch, *Man in the Holocene*, 1979; translation by Max Frisch and Geoffrey Skelton (New York: Harcourt Brace Jovanovich, 1980). The novella describes an old man who is losing his reason and who is aware of it. He approaches his doom by projecting his gradual insanity onto his natural surroundings. In the process he becomes obsessed with paleontology: as his mind disintegrates, he reintegrates into the history of the earth, into the Holocene, the geological period when human beings are caught in the act of evolving from their Neolithic stage. The paradox is, of course, that the Holocene is not only the geologically recent past but also the geological present; it is the period of our world as well. Frisch's imaginative juxtaposition of vastly different time frames (the life of a human being and the duration of a geological period) foregrounds their incommensurability and disorientates the reader on the whole question of "origins."

20. For an interesting discussion along these lines, see Michael Fischer, "Ethnicity and the Postmodern Arts of Memory," in *Writing Culture: The Poetics and Politics of Ethnography*, edited by James Clifford and George Marcus (Berkeley: U of California P, 1986), pp. 194–233.

7. We Endure, Therefore We Are

1. John Guillory has offered a thorough critique of the assumptions and consequences of the use, currently in vogue in the U.S. academy, of identity politics in debates about literary canon formation. Guillory argues that, in assuming a certain transparency between "identities" and "works," those who reduce problems of the canon to excluded social identities tend to neglect the issues of access to literacy, the means of production of what he calls "cultural capital"; see his *Cultural Capital: The Problem of Literary Canon Formation* (Chicago: U of Chicago P, 1993). On the problematic of resistance and literature, see the interesting alternatives to "resistance"-thinking discussed in Ross Chambers, *Room for Maneuver: Reading (the) Oppositional (in) Narrative* (Chicago: U of Chicago P, 1991). Instead of "resistance," Chambers proposes the notion of "oppositionality," which he defines as a tactic that works within power but that seeks to make changes in the desires involved in power. The medium that Chambers adopts for an oppositional practice is narrative reading.

2. On the affinities between events in modern China and events in the contemporary Western academy, see the first chapter of Rey Chow, *Writing*

Diaspora: Tactics of Intervention in Contemporary Cultural Studies (Bloomington: Indiana UP, 1993), pp. 1–26. For an astute analysis of the ambiguities of "people-hood," see Immanuel Wallerstein, "The Construction of Peoplehood: Racism, Nationalism, Ethnicity," in Wallerstein and Etienne Balibar, *Race, Nation, Class: Ambiguous Identities,* trans. of Balibar's portions by Chris Turner (London: Verso, 1991), pp. 71–85.

3. For a thoughtful and informative historical discussion of events in Communist China, see Maurice Meisner, *Mao's China and After: A History of the People's Republic* (a revised and expanded edition of *Mao's China,* 1977) (New York: Free P, 1986). Readers unacquainted with contemporary Chinese history are referred to James M. Ethridge's summary account of the Cultural Revolution in *China's Unfinished Revolution: Problems and Prospects since Mao* (San Francisco: China Books and Periodicals, 1990), pp. 247–52:

> Most people believed that the need for class struggle . . . had essentially passed with the completion of land reform and socialist transformation of private enterprise in the fifties. However, Mao continued to see (as he had for years) a constant need for permanent, unrelenting, widespread—and sometimes violent—class struggle to combat the rise of a new bourgeoisie. . . . He encouraged such class struggle in the Socialist Education Movement . . . , which began in 1962 and was merged with the Cultural Revolution in 1966. During the same period, Mao's status as a demi-god was enhanced by the compilation of the "Little Red Book" containing hundreds of quotations from his speeches and writings. The book was an immediate sensation and strengthened the personality cult that was to make Mao even more formidable in days to come. "The Great Proletarian Cultural Revolution," as the movement was called officially, was launched in a speech by Zhou Enlai at a huge May Day celebration in Beijing in 1966. (p. 248)

4. Works by some of these authors in English translation include Bai Hua, *The Remote Country of Women,* trans. Qingyun Wu and Thomas O. Beebee (Honolulu: U of Hawaii P, 1994); Mo Yan, *Red Sorghum,* trans. Howard Goldblatt (New York: Penguin, 1993); *Explosions and Other Stories,* edited by Janice Wickeri (Hong Kong: Renditions, 1991); Ah Cheng, *Three Kings: Three Stories from Today's China,* trans. and with an introduction by Bonnie S. McDougall (London: Collins Harvill, 1990); and Han Shaogong, *Homecoming? and Other Stories,* trans. Martha Cheung (Hong Kong: Renditions, 1992). See also the short stories by some of the same authors in the following relatively recent anthologies: *Spring Bamboo: A Collection of Contemporary Chinese Short Stories,* comp. and trans. Jeanne Tai, with a foreword by Bette Bao Lord and an introduction by Leo Ou-fan Lee (New York: Random House, 1989); *Worlds of Modern Chinese Fiction: Short Stories and Novellas from the People's Republic, Taiwan and Hong Kong,* ed. Michael S. Duke (Armonk: M. E. Sharpe, 1991); *Running Wild: New Chinese Writers,* ed. David Der-wei Wang with Jeanne Tai (New York: Columbia UP, 1994); and *The Columbia Anthology of Modern Chinese Literature,* ed. Joseph S. M.

Lau and Howard Goldblatt (New York: Columbia UP, 1995). Chinese films known to Western audiences include Wu Tianming's *Old Well;* Chen Kaige's *Yellow Earth* and *Farewell My Concubine;* Tian Zhuangzhuang's *Horse Thief* and *The Blue Kite;* Zhang Nuanxin's *Sacrifice Youth;* Xie Jin's *Hibiscus Town;* and Xie Fei's *A Girl from Hunan.*

5. See, for instance, Nick Browne's discussion of Xie Jin's *Hibiscus Town* in "Society and Subjectivity: On the Political Economy of Chinese Melodrama," in *New Chinese Cinemas: Forms, Identities, Politics,* ed. Nick Browne, Paul G. Pickowicz, Vivian Sobchack, Esther Yau (Cambridge: Cambridge UP, 1994), pp. 40–56: "Suffering is linked ultimately to the injustices of the political adminis-tration of social power. In this sense, subjectivity is part of a new political language of the post–Cultural Revolution period. It indicates an aspect of the person beyond that of the citizen" (p. 53).

6. Wallerstein, "The Construction of Peoplehood," p. 78; my emphasis.

7. In "The Nation Form: History and Ideology," (in *Race, Nation, Class,* pp. 86–106), Etienne Balibar argues that the imagining of a people as a national unity is an ideological form based on a specific handling of *difference* or *the foreign:* "That ideological form must become an a priori condition of communi-cation between individuals (the 'citizens') and between social groups—not by suppressing all differences, but by relativizing them and subordinating them to itself in such a way that it is the symbolic difference between 'ourselves' and 'foreigners' which wins out and which is lived as irreducible. In other words, to use the terminology proposed by Fichte in his *Reden an die deutsche Nation* of 1808, the 'external frontiers' of the state have to become 'internal frontiers' . . ." (p. 94).

8. For a summary account of the chief events of the Great Leap Forward, see Ethridge, *China's Unfinished Revolution,* pp. 259–60:

> By mid-1957, shortly before the Great Leap Forward began, land reform and socialist transformation of most private enterprises had been accomplished. The First Five-Year Plan had been completed with satisfactory success. Continued steady, if not spectacular, progress seemed entirely possible.
>
> For some reason not entirely clear, however, the government (and apparently Mao in particular) felt some compulsion to achieve a dra-matic advance in economic development at that time. Specialists in Chinese affairs themselves differ in their perspectives on the forces behind the Great Leap Forward. . . .
>
> For whatever reason, the Party, beginning early in 1958, launched the heady, radical, inspiring, and catastrophic Great Leap Forward, a movement calculated, to cite one slogan of the time, to "Overtake and surpass Britain within fifteen years in the output of steel and other important products!" Other slogans were more memorable and emo-tional, such as "Dare to storm the heavens!" . . .
>
> But, just as there was great progress there was also great waste, great expense, and near exhaustion. Crops failed . . . problems in the countryside multiplied. . . . The steel that was made in hundreds of

thousands of makeshift furnaces was useless, and much new construction was of poor quality. . . . By the end of 1959, what Frank K. M. Su has called "a romantic period in China's socialist construction" was over. Its wisdom and consequences are still debated.

9. Yu Hua, *Huozhe* (Hong Kong: Publications [Holdings] Limited, 1994). (I am grateful to Shan Qiang He for my copy of the novella.) The novella originally appeared in the mainland Chinese literary journal *Shouhuo* (Harvest), no. 6 (1992). Yu Hua also co-authored the screenplay with Lu Wei. For a discussion in English of other works by Yu Hua, see Lu Tonglin, *Misogyny, Cultural Nihilism, and Oppositional Politics: Contemporary Chinese Experimental Fiction* (Stanford: Stanford UP, 1995), pp. 155–79. Lu argues that Yu Hua's writings replicate the structures of patriarchal violence they seek to transgress.

10. In Yu Hua's novella, Fugui is the only survivor.

11. See the chapter "Pedagogy, Trust, Chinese Intellectuals in the 1990s— Fragments of a Post-Catastrophic Discourse," in *Writing Diaspora*, pp. 73–98, especially my discussion of Ah Cheng's novella *King of the Children*.

12. There are actually two first-person narrators in Yu Hua's story—the character Fugui and the narrator who records Fugui's tale, which constitutes the bulk of the narrative.

13. For a more detailed discussion of Zhang's tactics as a popular artist, see Rey Chow, *Primitive Passions: Visuality, Sexuality, Ethnography, and Contemporary Chinese Cinema* (New York: Columbia UP, 1995), pp. 142–72. Zhang is reported to have said, in relation to the making of his 1995 film *Yao ah yao! yao dao waipo qiao* (*Shanghai Triad*): "In the past, our Fifth Generation directors were fascinated with such [intellectual] things, introducing history, culture, and philosophy into films. . . . These are precisely the things I want to avoid now"; see Wang Bin, "Feature," *Dianying shuangzhoukan* (*City Entertainment*), no. 421 (1 June 1995), p. 37.

14. See especially chapter 4 in Yu Hua, *Huozhe*, pp. 164–82.

15. Browne, "Subjectivity and Society," p. 46. See Ethridge, *China's Unfinished Revolution*, pp. 268–72, for a summary account of China's legal system. Among other things, Ethridge notes that the Chinese legal system differs from those of many Western countries in that "there is no presumption of innocence at a trial (just the opposite, in fact, because preliminary investigation is supposed to have already established the need for having a trial); there are no rules of evidence; there is no independent judiciary; and there is no expectation that a judicial decision will necessarily be made according to precedents offered by similar cases" (p. 269). He also quotes from "a surprisingly frank article" that appeared in the *Beijing Review* "after the conservatives took over" (that is, after June 4, 1989): "'Not many people say outright that power is bigger than the law. But actually nowhere in the country has a mechanism yet been established capable of restricting power abuse in the true sense of the word. There are no hard and fast rules which can subject power-holders to legal restrictions or bring power-abusers to justice. Some power-wielders, who think themselves superior, always take it for granted that laws are something designed for other people, the rank-and-filers, while they themselves stand high above the law, far out of its reach, and do not need to be limited by it'" (p. 271).

16. See my discussions in *Writing Diaspora,* pp. 73–98. Zhang's 1992 film, *The Story of Qiuju,* depicts a peasant woman's stubborn fight for justice through the many levels of bureaucracy. Although it has a more or less happy ending, the film is nevertheless a direct comment on the difficulty of telling the truth in public in China.

17. Lest I give the impression that I am simply applauding the Western conception of the space of the public, let me add that, living in the United States, I am fully aware of the problems at the other end of the spectrum from China—the problems that result from the systemic legislation of every aspect of life, including the most private and personal. This "public space of litigation," however, is not my focus here.

18. For a related discussion, see my opening arguments in the chapter "Media, Matter, Migrants," in *Writing Diaspora,* pp. 165–80.

19. Wei Jingsheng and Fang Lizhi are two of the People's Republic's most outspoken dissidents. Both have been punished for demanding democracy: Wei, a worker, had been imprisoned since 1979 before being briefly released in September 1993; he was detained again in April 1994, formally charged with attempting to overthrow the Chinese government in November 1995, and sentenced to another fourteen years in prison in December 1995. Fang, an astrophysicist, was held in house arrest at the U.S. Consulate in Beijing before he was allowed to leave the country in June 1990 after signing an affidavit saying that he would not criticize the Chinese government; he now teaches in Arizona. Martin Lee, Szeto Wah, Christine Loh, and Emily Lau are among the most outspoken politicians fighting for the continuation of democratic rule in Hong Kong after China's resumption of sovereignty in 1997; among the most contentious issues over which they have opposed and criticized the Chinese authorities are those having to do with *rule by law,* such as China's murky handling of the Basic Law Agreement (concerning the future administration of Hong Kong) and the question of whether a Court of Final Appeal will be established in Hong Kong before 1997. Harry Wu is a human rights activist who had spent nineteen years in a labor camp before he left China. Now a U.S. citizen, Wu has been disseminating information in the West about China's abuse of political prisoners. Arrested in the summer of 1995 on one of his clandestine trips into the country to collect more information, he was sentenced to fifteen years in prison but then was expelled by the Chinese authorities.

20. "Outcasting" is, of course, simply the other side of a coercive "unifying" of all people, territories, and things "Chinese," so that any public demonstration of departing from this Chinese "oneness" must be penalized. This is why the U.S. visit of Li Denghui, Taiwan's president, in the early summer of 1995, for instance, provoked such heated debates in Chinese newspapers. As part of an attempt to counter and contain this public challenge to the idea of "one China," the People's Republic has been threatening, since Li's visit, to invade Taiwan—such as by ostensibly practicing missile launches across the Taiwan Straits during the summer of 1995 and in the early part of 1996 (prior to Taiwan's presidential election).

21. In Yu Hua's story, Long'er offers Fugui a few acres of land.

22. When Fugui mentioned this series of fantastical transformations to You-

qing during the period of the Great Leap Forward, it culminated in the coming of the Communists. With Mantou, at a time after the peak of the Cultural Revolution, Fugui makes the series culminate instead in "trains and airplanes."

23. My reading of the relationship between ideology and representation (literary or otherwise) follows Pierre Macherey's in *A Theory of Literary Production*, trans. Geoffrey Wall (London: Routledge and Kegan Paul, 1978).

24. I should clarify at this point that my reading of Zhang's critique of the will "to live" as an ideology is not intended as a demand for living at a "higher" level, for attaining something more "noble" and "dignified" than mere survival. In other words, my reading is not based on a kind of humanist imperative to distinguish human beings from "lower" life forms, but rather on the assumption that it is, indeed, a human condition to be preoccupied with survival, and that *that* is the ideological problem. Unlike nonhuman animals, which, in their complete absorption in life, are not concerned with "survival" as such, humans, in their struggles "to live," are always fantasizing a "better" future for which absolute sacrifice and absolute accommodation are required. My criticism of the imperative "to live," then, proceeds from the premise that preoccupation with survival is not honorably animalistic but pejoratively humanistic because such a preoccupation can be and has been exploited by totalitarian regimes for purposes of massive organized violence, violence that is, moreover, legitimized as sacrifices for a "better" human life to come.

25. For a discussion of how ethics and ethos coalesce and merge in the question of "dwelling," in particular human dwelling in language (understood as the site of human "being"), see Martin Heidegger, "Building Dwelling Thinking," in *Poetry, Language, Thought,* trans. Albert Hofstadter (New York: Harper Colophon, 1971), pp. 145–61.

26. See Louis Althusser, "Ideology and Ideological State Apparatuses (Notes towards an Investigation)," in *Lenin and Philosophy and Other Essays,* trans. Ben Brewster (London: Monthly Review, 1971), pp. 127–86: "What is represented in ideology is . . . not the system of the real relations which govern the existence of individuals, but the imaginary relation of those individuals to the real relations in which they live" (p. 165).

27. For instance, Zhang's films have been censored more than once in China. When *To Live* was entered in the 1994 Cannes Film Festival without the permission of the Chinese government, Zhang was penalized by being forbidden to collaborate with foreign investors for the next two years.

8. A Souvenir of Love

1. Many of the Chinese words and names quoted in this chapter were originally meant to be read in Cantonese. When citing such words and names, I will give both Cantonese and standard *pinyin* transliterations, and thereafter repeat in *pinyin*. In cases which do not necessarily involve Cantonese, only *pinyin* transliterations will be given. Even though *Yinji kau/Yanzhi kou* is the title for both the novella and the film in Chinese, I will use it to refer only to the novella by (Lilian) Lee Bik-wa/Li Bihua (Hong Kong: Cosmos, 1986), in order to distinguish it from the film, which was scripted by the Chengho Chuangzuo

Zu (Chengho Writing Team) and entitled *Rouge* in English. The opening quotation is from p. 49 of the novella.

2. Chan Bing-chiu/Chen Bingzhao, "Ying ding guo hui sik dik mei gum/ Ningding guoqushi de meigan" [Beauty in the condensed past tense], *Xin Bao* (*Hong Kong Economic Journal*, Overseas Edition), August 16, 1992, p. 6.

3. In her study of the relations between music and Hollywood films, for instance, Caryl Flinn writes: "The point is, [nostalgia] is still going strong today. Contemporary art music audiences get more opportunities to hear Beethoven performed than they do Steve Reich; commercials promote everything from regional health centers to champagne using the tired-and-true war-horses of Western art music. Pop culture in the United States takes us back through retro dressing, contemporary television shows like *China Beach* and *The Wonder Years* (not to mention reruns), and the golden oldie programs that saturate radio airwaves on weekends." Flinn, *Strains of Utopia: Gender, Nostalgia, and Hollywood Film Music* (Princeton: Princeton UP, 1992), p. 151.

4. Ibid., p. 152.

5. According to one account, the term *jau ga/jiujia*, which literally means "wine house," originated with the famous Gum ling jau ga/Jinling Jiujia in Hong Kong's Shek Tong Tsui/Shitangzui area in the early part of the twentieth century. Most Chinese restaurants at that time used the term *jau lau/jiulou*. See Ng Ho/Wu Hao, *Fung yuet tong sai/Fengyue tangxi* [Snippets from the Shitangzui era] (Hong Kong: Publications [Holdings], 1989), p. 13.

6. Gilles Deleuze, *Cinema 2: The Time-Image*, trans. Hugh Tomlinson and Robert Galeta (Minneapolis: U of Minnesota P, 1989), p. 49.

7. Pier Paolo Pasolini, "The Cinema of Poetry" (from the French translation by Marianne de Vettimo and Jacques Bontemps in *Cahiers du Cinema* 171, October 1965), in *Movies and Methods*, ed. Bill Nichols (Berkeley: U of California P, 1976), pp. 542–58.

8. Ibid., p. 545.

9. Ibid., p. 547.

10. Mikhail Bakhtin, *Problems of Dostoyevsky's Poetics*, ed. and trans. Caryl Emerson, intro. Wayne C. Booth (Minneapolis: U of Minnesota P, 1984).

11. Pasolini, "The Cinema of Poetry," p. 551.

12. Ibid., p. 544.

13. See "Minutes from the Seminar on Two Hong Kong Films: *Days of Being Wild* and *Rouge Button*," *Jintian* (*Today*) 2 (1992): pp. 2–11; the point referred to is on p. 8. One critic mentioned that the story of *Rouge* is a reproduction of classical *chuanqi* and popular folklore stories.

14. It is clear from the contexts of both the novella and the film that Ruhua no longer "slept with" her clients at this point. Instead, as a few scenes with a rich patron show, she let him touch certain parts of her body, such as an ear and a lower leg, at deliberately inflated prices. When this patron tried to mock her loyalty to Shier Shao by lying down in the brass bed the latter had bought to indicate his own possession of Ruhua, she responded subtly but defiantly to the rich man: "*I* did not lie down (with you)."

15. There are some minor alterations between the film and the novella. In the novella, the time of the suicide is 7 past 7 on March 8, and the secret signal between the lovers is 3877.

16. Li Bihua, *Yanzhi kou*, p. 28.

17. In the novella, we read descriptions of extras walking about in the movie studio but are given no clear indication that Shier Shao is among them. Ruhua simply disappears at this point, leaving behind the locket, which Yongding afterward finds in his pocket. The next day, Yongding reads in the newspaper that someone by the name Chen Zhenbang was prosecuted for smoking opium and fined $50. In the film, Ruhua identifies her lover among the movie extras, follows him to a dark corner, and finally approaches him as he falls asleep. Bending down near Shier Shao, she hums the lines she was singing when they first met. As the old man awakens in shock, Ruhua speaks to him briefly and returns the locket to him before disappearing.

18. In the novella, Ruhua first lets Shier Shao drink the wine with the sleeping pills in it, then takes the opium herself, waiting to see if he would follow suit; her last memory is of him raising the spoon to his lips. In the film, the lovers drink the wine together before Ruhua takes some opium herself and offers some to Shier Shao. Seeing that he is hesitant, she gives him more wine and then spoons the opium into his mouth. The two then get dressed, walk into the next room, and embrace each other at the approach of death.

19. In the novella, they are struck by the possibility of finding Shier Shao through the beeper when they hear someone else's beeper go off.

20. Well known to Cantonese audiences in Guangdong, Hong Kong, and overseas, "Ke tu qiu hen" was originally sung in the 1910s and 1920s by Bak kui-wing/Bai Qürong (1892–1974), one of the most highly acclaimed male Cantonese opera singers in the first few decades of the twentieth century.

21. See, for instance, Lee Cheuk-hung/Li Zhuoxiong, "Mingzi de gushi: Li Bihua *Yanzhi kou* wen ben fenxi" [The story of names: a textual analysis of Li Bihua's *Yanzhi kou*], parts 1 and 2, *Su ye wenxue* 30 (November 1991), pp. 22–29; 33 (February 1992), pp. 38–47. (I am very grateful to William Tay for providing me with copies of this essay). A slightly shorter version of the essay is also available in *Xianggang wenxue tanxiang* [An investigation and appreciation of Hong Kong literature], ed. Chan Bing-leung/Chen Bingliang (Hong Kong: Sanlian shudian, 1991), pp. 285–330. In a discussion of the relation between popular literature and Hong Kong's current political and economic situation, Li Zhuoxiong analyzes Li Bihua's writings in terms of the latter's fondness for words and names. This fondness, argues critic Li, leads Li Bihua sometimes to base her narratives entirely on fascinating words and to include information that is often out of place in the story line. Li compares such love of words to the love of opium, since both enable one to see only the world one needs to see. Li's meticulous attention to Li Bihua's use of words could have led to a reading in which words themselves become signs that open up areas usually neglected by the conscious mind, so that "unconscious" meanings return to interrupt the surface of rational thinking. But this is not the reading he produces. Instead, in a manner characteristic of the historiographic tendencies of traditional Chinese literary criticism, Li ultimately charges Li Bihua for sacrificing a broad "histori- cal vision" to an indulgence in words (that is, we might say, an indulgence in the literary). Li Bihua's fondness for "words and names" thus becomes, for Li, a limitation and a dangerous, self-destructive kind of pleasure. The anti-fiction

moralism of this criticism is obvious, but I find it especially disturbing in an account that is supposedly about popular/mass culture and literature.

22. Especially since the lifting of martial law in 1987, Taiwanese people from different walks of life have been demanding full knowledge of the controversial events surrounding the bloody origins of Chinese Nationalist rule, events that are commonly abbreviated as the "February 28 Taiwan Incident" of 1947. Hou Hsiao-hsien's *Beiqing chengshi* (*A City of Sadness*) is exemplary of this popular passion for (the truth of) the past.

23. Slavoj Žižek, *Looking Awry: An Introduction to Jacques Lacan through Popular Culture* (Cambridge: MIT P, 1991), p. 114.

24. Ibid., p. 112.

25. Ibid., p. 114.

26. See remarks by Leung Ping-kwan/Liang Bingjun in "Minutes from the Seminar on Two Hong Kong Films," p. 6.

27. For an English translation of the last title, see Lilian Lee, *The Last Princess of Manchuria*, trans. Andrea Kelly (New York: William Morrow, 1992).

28. This chapter is for my sister Pearl Chow, in appreciation of her assistance with locating some of the materials mentioned in my discussion, her opinions about *Rouge* and other films, and her delightful companionship during a month of intensive film- and video-watching in the summer of 1992.

9. Between Colonizers

1. Ranajit Guha's work is exemplary in this regard. "There was one Indian battle that Britain never won. It was a battle for appropriation of the Indian past," writes Guha ("Dominance Without Hegemony and Its Historiography," in *Subaltern Studies VI: Writings on South Asian History and Society*, ed. Ranajit Guha [Delhi: Oxford UP, 1989], p. 210). See also his *An Indian Historiography of India: A Nineteenth-Century Agenda and Its Implications* (Calcutta: K. P. Bagchi, 1988). For a more recent discussion of the same issues, see Dipesh Chakrabarty, "Postcoloniality and the Artifice of History: Who Speaks for 'Indian' Pasts?" *Representations* 37 (Winter 1992), pp. 1–26. Chakrabarty charges that Europe and European history remain the dominant conceptual paradigms even in writings on non-European histories. This has to do with "what European imperialism and third-world nationalisms have achieved together: the universalization of the nation state as the most desirable form of political community" (p. 19).

2. For instance, to Patrick Williams and Laura Chrisman, editors of the anthology *Colonial Discourse, Postcolonial Theory: A Reader* (New York: Columbia UP, 1994), "the era of formal colonial control is over, apart from aberrations such as the Falklands/Malvinas" (pp. 3–4 of the introduction). The fact that such omission of Hong Kong and Macau comes from politically correct intellectuals working in Britain in the 1990s, when the issue of Hong Kong's "decolonized" future vis-à-vis both Britain and China is regularly being debated, is doubly ironic. It should also be added that many in the West are confused about or simply unaware of the colonial status of Hong Kong and

Macau to begin with. Many people from Hong Kong have the experience of being told by Americans and Europeans that they are from "China." A newspaper report some years ago told of a Macau-born tourist being arrested in France because he was suspected of having forged his travel documents. On a train from Switzerland to France, this tourist was inspected by French customs officials, who, after scrutinizing him, asked: "How is it that you, a Chinese person, hold a Portuguese passport?" The tourist was released only after the officials obtained a certified copy of his birth certificate from the Macau government. Even then, his passport continued to be withheld in France and he had to collect it from the Portuguese Consulate in Paris. See Yin Mishi, "Zai faguo juliusuo de sishiba xiaoshi" [Forty-eight hours in the French detention house], *Xinbao* (*Hong Kong Economic Journal*, Overseas Edition), July 11, 1992, p. 6.

3. A discussion of the meaning of "postcolonial" is found in Anthony Kwame Appiah, "Is the Post- in Postmodernism the Post- in Postcolonial?" *Critical Inquiry* 17 (Winter 1991), pp. 336–57. While I share some of Appiah's views, I disagree with his premises, which I find idealist. I understand Appiah's argument in these terms: First, Appiah follows Jean-François Lyotard and defines the "post" in "postmodernism" as a "space-clearing," the distinction-making gesture of going beyond the exclusivist claims of the metanarratives of modernism. Ideally, for Appiah, the "post" in "postcolonial" should be the same as that of "postmodern" defined in this sense. Without stating it explicitly, therefore, Appiah distinguishes within the category of "postcolonial" *the good and the bad*. The good or what he calls the "relevant sense of postcolonial," he argues, should mean "going beyond" or "transcending" colonialism (p. 348). However, "postcoloniality" is also the condition of what he calls the "comprador" intelligentsia, whose cultural activity consists in producing genres such as the "neotraditional" for Western readers' consumption. For Appiah, this intelligentsia's postcoloniality is bad because it remains *colonial*. Second, even though, throughout the essay, Appiah applauds postmodernism as defined by Lyotard, he is ambivalent on the point of postmodernism's relation to nationalism. This is why the African writers who challenge the legitimating narratives of the nation (in a postmodern manner Appiah otherwise seems to approve of) are criticized by him for having turned postcoloniality into "a condition of pessimism" (p. 353). In other words, by rejecting nationalism, these writers too have produced a bad postcoloniality that departs from the proper sense Appiah wants the term to have. See also Appiah's discussions of the postcolonial and the postmodern in his *In My Father's House: Africa in the Philosophy of Culture* (London: Methuen, 1992).

4. The music and lyrics of "Long de chuan ren" were composed by Hou Dejian. "Xieran de fengcai" was first sung by Dong Wenhua during China's war with Vietnam in the 1970s. The version that has been popularized since June 1989 is sung by Wang Hong.

5. It is important to note that such music is produced and consumed in Hong Kong and Taiwan as much as it is in mainland China. In other words, I am not trying to argue for alternative modes of cultural production based purely on geographical locations. For a discussion of the nostalgia more specific to contemporary Hong Kong culture, see my reading of the film *Rouge* in the previous chapter.

6. "What is . . . remarkable is that this identity has been internalized by the citizens of the state so that it seems to stem from within, to be an expression of their own inner being. This is precisely the *beauty* of national culture. It compels identification with the homeland paradoxically without compulsion because it becomes part of people's lives." Gregory Jusdanis, *Belated Modernity and Aesthetic Culture: Inventing National Literature* (Minneapolis: U of Minnesota P, 1991), pp. 81–82; emphasis in the original. Jusdanis is describing Greek nationalism in modern times, but his description is equally appropriate for Chinese nationalism. Similarly, Chinese nationalism can be understood as the construction of what Etienne Balibar calls a "fictive ethnicity," by which individuals are made to think they have a common origin, a common culture, and a unified community in terms of their "ethnicity," even though it is usually "a particular representation of ethnicity" which "should be dominant." See "The Nation Form: History and Ideology," in Immanuel Wallerstein and Etienne Balibar, *Race, Nation, Class: Ambiguous Identities,* trans. of Balibar by Chris Turner (London: Verso, 1991), pp. 96, 104.

7. Leung Ping-kwan, "Doushi wenhua yu xianggang wenxue" [City culture and Hong Kong literature], *Dangdai (Con-Temporary)* 38 (June 1, 1989), pp. 16–17; translation mine.

8. Guha's analyses are based largely on Bengali materials. See his *A Rule of Property for Bengal: An Essay on the Idea of Permanent Settlement* (Paris: Mouton, 1963) as well as *An Indian Historiography of India.* We should note also that the British were not the only foreign colonizers in the history of India. The Moghul dynasty that ruled much of India from the 1520s to the 1850s was also ethnically and religiously alien (Turko-Persian-Afghan in ethnicity and Muslim in religion).

9. Chakrabarty, "Postcoloniality and the Artifice of History," p. 21; my emphasis.

10. Partha Chatterjee, *The Nation and Its Fragments: Colonial and Postcolonial Histories* (Princeton: Princeton UP, 1993), p. 115.

11. For an elaborate discussion of the historical discourse around the notion of a folk in an East Asian context, see H. D. Harootunian, *Things Seen and Unseen: Discourse and Ideology in Tokugawa Nativism* (Chicago: U of Chicago P, 1988).

12. "The experience of being colonized . . . signified a great deal to regions and peoples of the world whose experience as dependents, subalterns, and subjects of the West did not end—to paraphrase from Fanon—when the last white policeman left and the last European flag came down. To have been colonized was a fate with lasting, indeed grotesquely unfair results, especially after national independence had been achieved. Poverty, dependency, underdevelopment, various pathologies of power and corruption, plus of course notable achievements in war, literacy, economic development: this mix of characteristics designated the colonized people who had freed themselves on one level but who remained victims of their past on another." Edward Said, "Representing the Colonized: Anthropology's Interlocutors," *Critical Inquiry* 15 (Winter 1989), p. 207.

13. For a related critique—of how the histories of postcolonized *ethnicities* can become conflated with and hence falsified by the fashionable formalisms of postmodernism such as irony, duplicity, language-games, and so forth—see

E. San Juan, Jr., *Racial Formations/Critical Transformations: Articulations of Power in Ethnic and Racial Studies in the United States* (London: Humanities International, 1992), especially chapters 2 and 4. San Juan's context is the contemporary United States, but his arguments against postmodern pluralism are relevant to similar issues elsewhere in the postcolonized world such as Hong Kong.

14. Luo Dayou, Production Notes to the Disc Collection "Huanghou da dao dong" [Queen's Road East], catalog no. MFCR91012 (Hong Kong: Music Factory, 1991). All translations of Luo's works in this chapter are mine.

15. This is Kwai-cheung Lo's argument; see his "Crossing Boundaries: A Study of Modern Hong Kong Fiction from the Fifties to the Eighties," M. Phil. dissertation, U of Hong Kong, 1990.

16. See "Minutes from the Seminar on Two Hong Kong Films: *Days of Being Wild* and *Rouge Button*," compiled by Yu Gang, *Jintian (Today)* 2 (1992), p. 10.

17. In general, I would argue that even within mainland China, the state has not really retreated as many observers optimistically assert. The areas which are experiencing apparent liberalization in the 1990s tend to be those that are not, from the state's point of view, threatening to its authoritarian status—such as financial and economic development, consumer culture, and public discourses about previously tabooed subjects such as sex. When it comes to political matters such as questions of human rights, the Chinese state remains as repressive as ever.

18. See also my "Listening Otherwise, Music Miniaturized: A Different Type of Question about Revolution," *Discourse* 13.1 (Fall-Winter 1990–91), pp. 129–48. This essay has been revised and expanded in Chow, *Writing Diaspora: Tactics of Intervention in Contemporary Cultural Studies* (Bloomington: Indiana UP, 1993). Since I have already dealt with the musical effects and the environment of reception of Luo's compositions in this earlier piece, I will not repeat myself and will focus mainly on the verbal aspects of his work here.

19. Some of the lyrics in Luo's songs have been written by authors other than himself. One author with whom Luo regularly collaborates is Lin Xi.

20. Raymond Williams, *Marxism and Literature* (Oxford: Oxford UP, 1977), pp. 122, 126.

21. The titles of many of Luo's works are borrowed from classical Chinese poetry (*shi* and *ci*) or popular fiction, as for instance "Tan chang ci, bie hou," "Jiang jiu jin," and "Hai shang hua," the theme song of a film of the same name.

22. See the lyrics of Luo's "Qingchun wu qü" and "Qingchun wu qü 2000."

23. Williams, *Marxism and Literature,* p. 126; emphasis in the original.

24. Gayatri Chakravorty Spivak, *The Post-Colonial Critic: Interviews, Strategies, Dialogues,* ed. Sarah Harasym (London: Routledge, 1990), p. 93.

25. "Gaobie de niandai" [The era of saying goodbye], catalog no. RD-1059 (Hong Kong: Praiseplan, 1989).

26. See, for instance, the film *To Liv(e)*, directed by Evans Chan (Chan Yiu-sing), 1991. The film tells of a love story between a young man and an older, divorced woman, but the action is interestingly framed by another narrative, the youth's sister's letters to the actress Liv Ullmann. On a visit to Hong Kong, Ullmann criticized Hong Kong's treatment of Vietnamese refugees as "inhumane." The film demonstrates that, in a way typical of the hypocrisy of liberal Western humanitarianism, Ullmann's pronouncement was informed neither

by the predicament of Hong Kong caught between the refugees and the indifferent international community at large nor by any understanding of the chronic social problems facing Hong Kong people themselves.

27. "I feel I am a broker conducting the biggest deal between history and the future. Among those who live in Hong Kong at this time, who doesn't?" (Luo, Production Notes to the Disc Collection "Huanghou da dao dong").

28. A very busy and crowded business and residential district on the Kowloon Peninsula, "Mongkok" is the English name for "Wongkok," which literally means "prosperity corner."

29. This is evident in films made by Taiwan directors such as Hou Hsiao-hsien and Edward Yang (Yang Te-ch'ang), which explore the brutality of the mainland Chinese takeover of Taiwan in the period after Japan's surrender in 1945. See, for instance, Hou's *A City of Sadness* (1989) and Yang's *A Brighter Summer Day* (1991). Taiwan's "postcoloniality" will have to be the topic of a separate essay or book.

30. Williams, *Marxism and Literature*, pp. 128–35.

10. Things, Common/Places, Passages of the Port City

1. Chinese names in this chapter are transcribed first in Cantonese and then in Mandarin/Putonghua pronunciations. Even though such transcriptions are cumbersome, they serve as markers of resistance against mainland Chinese imperialism in the present context.

2. Richard Hughes, *Borrowed Place, Borrowed Time: Hong Kong and Its Many Faces* (London: Andre Deutsch, 1976). For detailed discussions of the history of Hong Kong leading up to 1997, see, for instance, Jan Morris, *Hong Kong: Epilogue to an Empire* (London: Penguin, 1988, 1989) and Robert Cottrell, *The End of Hong Kong: The Secret Diplomacy of Imperial Retreat* (London: Murray, 1993).

3. This chapter is a continuation of a series of discussions about Hong Kong I have offered elsewhere. Interested readers are asked to see Chow, *Writing Diaspora: Tactics of Intervention in Contemporary Cultural Studies* (Bloomington: Indiana UP, 1993), chapters 1 and 7, as well as the two chapters preceding this one in this book.

4. This is the English title of the film *Lung mun/Long min,* directed by Cheung Ji-leung/Chang Zhiliang, Wan-ying (Filmigica) Co., Hong Kong, 1992.

5. "Capital" (music by Law Dai-yau/Luo Dayou, lyrics by Lam Jik/Lin Xi) is both the leading song and title of this disc collection.

6. In the early 1990s, many of the Hong Kong professionals who emigrated to Canada, the United States, and Australia in the previous decade began returning to Hong Kong for more highly paid jobs and more satisfying careers.

7. Lau Siu-kai, *Society and Politics in Hong Kong* (Hong Kong: Heung Gong, 1985), p. 173.

8. Ackbar Abbas, "Introduction: The Last Emporium: Verse and Cultural Space," in Leung Ping-kwan, *City at the End of Time,* trans. Gordon T. Osing (Hong Kong: Twilight Books in association with the Department of Comparative Literature, U of Hong Kong, 1992), p. 5; emphasis in the original. Notably,

instead of criticizing the "very efficient colonial administration" he mentions, Abbas goes on to mock Hong Kong people for their "false consciousness"—for being motivated by economic self-interest even in their political demonstrations. With determination, his passage continues as follows: "By the same logic, the only form of political idealism that has a chance is that which can go together with economic self-interest, when 'freedom' for example could be made synonymous with the 'free market'. This, I believe, is how one can understand the unprecedented mass demonstrations over the Tiananmen Massacre by the hundreds of thousands of the middle-class who have never before marched in the streets. June 1989 in Hong Kong was a rare moment when economic self-interest could so easily misrecognise itself as political idealism. There was genuine emotion and outrage to be sure, which does not preclude the possibility that many of the marchers were moved by how much they were moved. In any event, the patriotic fervor in most cases was short-lived and without political outcome" (p. 5). Such a display of derision and sarcasm is unfortunate in an essay which otherwise contains interesting insights into Hong Kong culture. Aside from their questionable puritanical assumption that political idealism should not be tainted with economic self-interest, Abbas's remarks are also contradicted by the fact that political demonstrations commemorating the June 4th Massacre have been held and attended by thousands in Hong Kong every year since 1989.

9. See Sigmund Freud, "Femininity," *New Introductory Lectures on Psychoanalysis,* trans. and ed. James Strachey (New York: Norton, 1964, 1965), p. 117.

10. Ai Wu, "One Night in Hong Kong," trans. Zhu Zhiyu, *Renditions: A Chinese-English Translation Magazine* 29–30 (Special Issue: Hong Kong) (1988), p. 62.

11. Wen Yiduo, "Two Poems," trans. Zhu Zhiyu, *Renditions* 29–30, p. 65. Wen also has a poem called "Kowloon":

> While big brother Hong Kong tells of his suffering
> Mother, have you forgotten your little daughter Kowloon?
> Since I married that Demon King who ruled the sea,
> I've been tossed upon endless waves of tears
> Mother, I count the days until our joyous reunion
> Yet fear my hope is only a dream.
> Mother! I want to come back, Mother! ("Two Poems," p. 66)

12. Ha Gong, "The Legalization of Rape," trans. Don J. Cohn, *Renditions* 29–30, p. 326.

13. Wang Tingzhi, "Support the Construction of Daya Bay Power Plant," trans. John Steinhardt, *Renditions* 29–30, p. 170.

14. Eva Hung, "Preface," *Renditions* 29–30, p. 7.

15. With the exception of Spanish America, colonial cities are almost always ports. See *Colonial Cities: Essays on Urbanism in a Colonial Context,* ed. Robert Ross and Gerard T. Telkamp (Dordrecht: Martinus Nijhoff Publishers, 1985), p. 6.

16. G. B. Endacott, *Government and People in Hong Kong 1841–1962* (Hong

Kong: Hong Kong UP, 1964), pp. vii–viii; quoted in Lau, *Society and Politics in Hong Kong*, p. 41.

17. See, for instance, Jacques Derrida, "Structure, Sign, and Play in the Discourse of the Human Sciences," in *The Structuralist Controversy: The Languages of Criticism and the Sciences of Man*, ed. Richard Macksey and Eugenio Donato (Baltimore: Johns Hopkins UP, 1970), pp. 247–72. Even though I am not reading "economic" texts here, my understanding of "value" and the mutual implications between "economics" and "writing" owes much to Gayatri Chakravorty Spivak's work on Marx and Derrida. See my discussions in chapter 3.

18. "It has always been difficult to find ways to publish poems in Hong Kong. Without good literary journals, poems are published in newspapers, variety magazines or short-lived poetry journals. . . . I am . . . the one in town with the greatest number of unpublished poems and novels. My experiences of finding accommodation for my homeless poems were frustrating. Some of my poems ended up in non-literary magazines like *Film Biweekly*, *In*, the woman magazine with feminist overtones, or *Crossover*, a small magazine for performances and the arts. Before, I had published in magazines like *Music and You*, *Youth Weekly*, or other less respectable places. One of my recent achievement is to get a long story published in a photography magazine, *NuNaHeDuo*. . . .

"In order to make this place a home, we have taken up other roles, as teachers, critics, columnists, script-writers and so on. I have tried all these roles. An evening post which had just cancelled the literary pages asked me to write a column on food. So I had a better chance to survive as a food critic than as a poet. I finally settled on the role of a film critic, and as long as I do not print my poems in my column, my editor is flexible enough to let me say whatever I want to say." Leung, "The Homeless Poems and Photographs," *NuNaHeDuo* (*Dislocation*) 2.2 ("Public vs. Images" Issue), p. 1.

19. My readings are based on the poems collected in *Leung Ping-kwan guen/ Liang Bingjun juan*, ed. Jap See/Ji Si (Hong Kong: Sanlian shudian, 1989). In some cases, I use the English translations provided by Osing in Leung's *City at the End of Time* (often with significant modifications); in other cases, when no translations exist in English, I provide my own. In each case I try as much as possible to stay close to the tone and syntax of Leung's originals, which means that my translations tend to be literal and may not always read smoothly in English.

20. *City at the End of Time*, p. 165. On the use of English in Hong Kong, Leung has more extended comments: "I think growing up in Hong Kong has put a particular psychological block on us in the use of English. It has become in this society *a means of evaluation*, a measure of one's social or economic status, a source of snobbery or mockery and so on, rather than a means of communication" (ibid., pp. 180–81; my emphasis).

21. Kwai-cheung Lo has used Deleuze and Guattari's notion of "minor literature" (in *Kafka: Toward a Minor Literature*, trans. Dana Polan, foreword by Reda Bensmaïa [Minneapolis: U of Minnesota P, 1986]) to discuss Hong Kong literature; see his "Crossing Boundaries: A Study of Hong Kong Modern Fiction from the Fifties to the Eighties," M. Phil. thesis, U of Hong Kong, 1990.

22. For a brief discussion of "thing-poetry" in both China and the West, see

Leung Ping-kwan guen, pp. 171–72. It should be mentioned that thing-poetry has been viewed with suspicion in Chinese communist literary criticism because of its "fetishizing" tendencies. Poets who indulge in this genre are often regarded as limited because they spend too much time on things rather than on the "important" events of nation, people, revolution, and so forth.

23. Leung, "Ap-liu Street," *City at the End of Time*, pp. 36–37.

24. Leung, "Lucky Draw," *City at the End of Time*, p. 83.

25. Leung, "The Flame Tree," *City at the End of Time*, p. 101; translation significantly modified.

26. Michel de Certeau, *The Practice of Everyday Life*, trans. Steven Rendall (Berkeley: U of California P, 1984), p. xix.

27. See de Certeau, *The Practice of Everyday Life*; see also Mark Poster's discussion of de Certeau's work in "The Question of Agency: Michel de Certeau and the History of Consumerism," *diacritics* 22.2 (1992), pp. 94–107.

28. Leung, "The Homeless Poems and Photographs," p. 2.

29. "When I returned to Hong Kong [after being in the United States for several years], I naturally realized the great popularity of commodified culture, the shrinking territory of literary culture, and the mutual relations and implications between the two phenomena. . . . Poetry cannot depart from this image-dominated world, but it cannot simply chime in either." Leung, Preface to *Leung Ping-kwan guen*, p. 3.

30. Leung, *Sue wo sing see/Shu he chengshi* [Books and the City] (Hong Kong: Heung Gong, 1985).

31. Leung, *City at the End of Time*, p. 168.

32. Leung, "Refurnishing," *City at the End of Time*, p. 75; translation significantly modified.

33. "Ripples/Leaves," *Leung Ping-kwan guen*, p. 147; my translation. This is one of a series of ten poems on lotus leaves; see *Leung Ping-kwan guen*, pp. 143–50. Translations of other poems in the series can be found in *City at the End of Time* and in "Lotus Leaves: Seven Poems," trans. Kwok Kwan Mun and Lo Kwai Cheung with John Minford, *Renditions* 29–30, pp. 210–21.

34. Leung, *City at the End of Time*, p. 182; my emphasis.

35. Lo, "Crossing Boundaries," p. 163. See also Lau, *Society and Politics in Hong Kong*, pp. 174–76: "As most of the immigrants came to Hong Kong in pursuit of economic opportunities, they largely constituted a self-selected group whose intention is not to question or attack the political system in Hong Kong, which existed prior to their decisions to emigrate. The memories of political disorder in their homeland would make them receptive to a political system whose avowed purpose is to maintain political stability and which has demonstrated a capability of doing so" (p. 174).

36. Leung, *City at the End of Time*, p. 175.

37. Ibid., pp. 161–62; my emphasis.

38. Ibid., p. 185.

39. Ibid., p. 35.

40. Ibid., p. 185.

41. Ibid., p. 31; translation significantly modified. Leung left the University of Hong Kong as this book was in its final stages of production.

INDEX OF NAMES AND TITLES

Index of Names and Titles